STEPHEN SONDHEIM

CASEBOOKS ON MODERN DRAMATISTS
VOLUME 23
GARLAND REFERENCE LIBRARY OF THE HUMANITIES
VOLUME 1916

Casebooks on Modern Dramatists

Kimball King, *General Editor*

Sam Shepard
A Casebook
edited by Kimball King

Christopher Hampton
A Casebook
edited by Robert Gross

Howard Brenton
A Casebook
edited by Ann Wilson

David Storey
A Casebook
edited by William Hutchings

Peter Shaffer
A Casebook
edited by C.J. Gianakaras

David Mamet
A Casebook
edited by Leslie Kane

Simon Gray
A Casebook
edited by Katherine H. Burkman

John Arden and
Margaretta D'Arcy
A Casebook
edited by Jonathan Wike

August Wilson
A Casebook
edited by Marilyn Elkins

John Osborne
A Casebook
edited by Patricia D. Denison

David Hare
A Casebook
edited by Hersh Zeifman

Marsha Norman
A Casebook
edited by Linda Ginter Brown

Brian Friel
A Casebook
edited by William Kerwin

Neil Simon
A Casebook
edited by Gary Konas

Terrence McNally
A Casebook
edited by Toby Silverman Zinman

Stephen Sondheim
A Casebook
edited by Joanne Gordon

Horton Foote
A Casebook
edited by Gerald C. Wood

STEPHEN SONDHEIM
A CASEBOOK

EDITED BY
JOANNE GORDON

GARLAND PUBLISHING, INC.
NEW YORK AND LONDON
1997

Library of Congress Cataloging-in-Publication Data

Stephen Sondheim : a casebook / edited by Joanne Gordon.
      p.   cm. — (Garland reference library of the humanities ;
vol. 1916. Casebooks on modern dramatists ; vol. 23)
    Includes bibliographical references and index.
    ISBN 0-8153-2054-X (alk. paper)
    1. Sondheim, Stephen—Criticism and interpretation.   I. Gordon,
Joanne Lesley, 1947–   . II. Series: Garland reference library of the
humanities ; vol. 1916. III. Series: Garland reference library of the
humanities. Casebooks on modern dramatists ; vol. 23.
ML410.S6872S74 1997
782.1'4'092—dc21   97-25563
                                                    CIP
                                                    MN

Cover photograph of Stephen Sondheim by Michael Le Poer Trench.

Printed on acid-free, 250-year-life paper
Manufactured in the United States of America

A VAST AND GRACIOUS TIDE

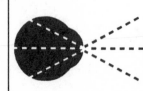

This Large Print Book carries the
Seal of Approval of N.A.V.H.

A Vast and Gracious Tide

Lisa Carter

THORNDIKE PRESS
A part of Gale, a Cengage Company

Farmington Hills, Mich • San Francisco • New York • Waterville, Maine
Meriden, Conn • Mason, Ohio • Chicago

LIBRARY OF CONGRESS CIP DATA ON FILE.
CATALOGUING IN PUBLICATION FOR THIS BOOK
IS AVAILABLE FROM THE LIBRARY OF CONGRESS

ISBN-13: 978-1-4328-5475-1 (hardcover)

Published in 2018 by arrangement with Gilead Publishing

Printed in the United States of America
1 2 3 4 5 6 7 22 21 20 19 18

Everything comes with a price, freedom most especially.

To the members of the United States military and for my Uncle Bill — who never quite managed to make it all the way home from Vietnam.

I am humbled by the incalculable price our armed forces have willingly paid so that the rest of us wouldn't have to. There is something of the sacred in your sacrifice. A love of country. A love for home.

I believe the longing for home is at the core of what it means to be human. And it is my prayer that you will all one day truly find the Home you've been made for.

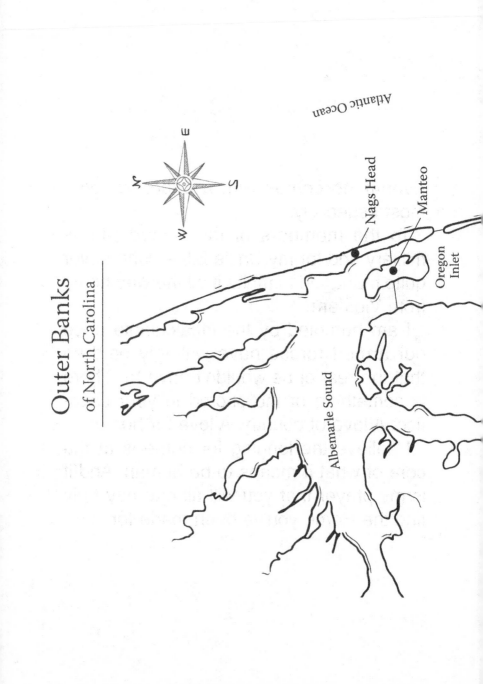

Outer Banks
of North Carolina

Atlantic Ocean

Nags Head

Manteo

Oregon
Inlet

Albemarle Sound

Cape Hatteras National Seashore

Rodanthe
Waves
Salvo

Hatteras Island

Avon

Buxton/Cape Hatteras
Lighthouse

Frisco

Yaupon Island
(Fictional)

Tuckahoe
(Fictional)

Pamlico Sound

Hatteras Village

Ferry to Ocracoke

Ocracoke

Ferry to Swan Quarter

Ferry to Cedar Island

Design by dc Graphics

You see, at just the right time, when we were still powerless, Christ died for the ungodly. Very rarely will anyone die for a righteous person, though for a good person someone might possibly dare to die. But God demonstrates his own love for us in this: While we were still sinners, Christ died for us.

ROMANS 5:6-8 NIV

HERE IS LOVE
(Love Song of the Welsh Revival)
WILLIAM REES

Here is love, vast as the ocean,
Loving-kindness as the flood,
When the Prince of Life, our Ransom,
Shed for us His precious blood.
Who His love will not remember?
Who can cease to sing His praise?
He can never be forgotten,
Throughout heav'n's eternal days.

On the mount of crucifixion,
Fountains opened deep and wide;
Through the floodgates of God's mercy
Flowed a vast and gracious tide.
Grace and love, like mighty rivers,
Poured incessant from above,
And heav'n's peace and perfect justice
Kissed a guilty world in love.

Let me, all Thy love accepting,
Love Thee, ever all my days;
Let me seek Thy kingdom only,
And my life be to Thy praise;
Thou alone shalt be my glory,
Nothing in the world I see;
Thou hast cleansed and sanctified me,
Thou Thyself hast set me free.

In Thy truth Thou dost direct me
By Thy Spirit through Thy Word;
And Thy grace my need is meeting,
As I trust in Thee, my Lord.
Of Thy fullness Thou art pouring
Thy great love and pow'r on me,
Without measure, full and boundless,
Drawing out my heart to Thee.

PROLOGUE

Sergeant First Class Caden Wallis grinned as his CO whistled — perhaps the fifteenth time today — that same tune again. On the floor of the Humvee, the six-year-old Belgian Malinois' ears perked. And Caden's canine friend, K9 Sergeant First Class Friday, barked.

Caden laughed. "Even Friday's sick of that song."

His team leader, Master Sergeant Joe Nelson, was the closest he'd ever come to a best friend, and to the younger guys Joe was a father figure. They'd all — Caden and Friday included — follow him without hesitation into a death trap if so ordered.

From the front passenger seat, Joe angled. His eyebrows arched, vanishing underneath his combat helmet. "Not just any tune. A hymn, but also a love song. 'Here is love,'"

13

he warbled in his terrible off-key baritone. " 'Vast —' "

The vehicle rattled over the bomb-pitted road, jostling them. Bracing, Caden grabbed hold of the side to keep from lurching forward.

Sanchez, team medic, cut his eyes at Caden and nudged Pulaski at the wheel. They took up where Joe left off, but in a shrill falsetto.

" 'Vast as an ocean, loving kindness as the flood . . .' "

Joe rolled his eyes as they hammed it up.

" 'Who his love will not remember? Who can cease to sing His praise?' "

Biting the inside of his cheek, Joe tolerated the impromptu concert. Anything to lessen pre-mission tension.

" 'Through the floodgates of God's mercy flowed a vast and gracious tide . . .' "

Friday howled.

Sanchez and Pulaski broke into laughter, as did Joe.

Caden smiled. Joe was the best man he'd ever known. A godly man, the real deal. Caden wasn't into religion, but he'd come to believe that Joe's faith had somehow buffered them, protected them by proxy, throughout their long deployment thus far.

The only thing on Caden's radar was getting home to his girlfriend in one piece. Thinking of Nikki, his stomach cramped. She hadn't answered his calls in over a month. Sensing her handler's disquiet, Friday insinuated her head underneath her hand and licked his fingers.

Had Nikki, as threatened, grown tired of waiting for him?

The armored personnel vehicle jerked to a standstill. And the dust — always the dust — swirled through the open windows. In terms of mileage, the village wasn't far from base camp, but lately anywhere outside the wire had become a killing zone. Out of the other Humvees in the convoy, the rest of their team emptied onto the deserted street. Including the Afghan military officer.

Caden had taken a dislike to him during their extensive pre-mission planning. Maybe he was hyperparanoid, or maybe on his third tour he didn't trust any of the locals. The officer was a necessary evil in his opinion, considered essential in brokering the agreement between coalition forces and the tribal leader.

"Keep your head on a swivel for unfriendlies." Joe made eye contact with each member of their twelve-man Alpha team. "We're on foot from here."

Yazz — Navajo Hosteen Yazzie, their communications specialist — grunted. Caden seconded the feeling.

The dirt street disappeared into a maze of mud-brick dwellings three stories high. Row after row of potential sweet spots for a sniper. Or an entire terrorist faction. Silence reigned as the men assumed a defensive posture, clutching their M-4 rifles.

Joe adjusted the black-checkered shemagh around his neck. "I don't need to tell you how kinetic this area has been. The headman's support will pave the way to peace in this province."

Weapons Specialist Tavon Miller's dark face tightened. "So where is everyone?"

Scruggs — the newest and youngest team member — snickered. "Maybe the spooks didn't hand out enough chocolate when they set up this meet and greet."

Pulaski's mouth thinned. "Or we're walking into an ambush."

"What they pay us the big bucks for," Scruggs smirked.

Yazz sighed. "Not."

One look from Joe silenced the chatter. Their nerves were frayed. Too many back-to-back encounters of a deadly kind. But the quiet was unnerving. Caden grasped a tighter hold on Friday's leash.

"Glad you go first, Sergeant Friday," joked

Table of Contents

General Editor's Note

While many contemporary playwrights have been influenced by musical composers, have included musical interludes in their plays or have even collaborated on musical shows, the Garland Casebooks on Modern Dramatists series has not previously concentrated on a playwright who has written exclusively for musical theater. The American musical is deservedly famous and the country's indigenous theatrical art form. It is fitting that Stephen Sondheim should be the focus of an essay collection, for he is arguably the world's leading practitioner of the musical form. An heir to the genius of Oscar Hammerstein and Richard Rodgers, Sondheim has created musical theater which has all the depth and range of so-called "legitimate" theater.

The editor of this volume of essays, Joanne Gordon, holds her doctorate from the University of California at Los Angeles and is currently a professor of theatre arts at California State University, Long Beach. Her earlier book, *Art Isn't Easy: The Theatre of Stephen Sondheim*, is the first serious text analyzing the intellectual depth of Sondheim's work. A professional director and teacher for more than seventeen years, Gordon, born in South Africa, was chosen to direct Sondheim's *Sweeney Todd* for her first production in the United States, one which was presented ultimately at the Kennedy Center in Washington, D.C., and which won the American College Theater Festival. Her editorial work in this particular volume combines both her scholarly and directorial skills in an enlightening exploration of Sondheim's achievement.

Kimball King

Acknowledgments

I would like to thank the following publishers for their permission to use extended quotations from copyrighted works:

A Funny Thing Happened on the Way to the Forum
Music and Lyrics by Stephen Sondheim
©1962 (Renewed 1990) by Stephen Sondheim
Burthen Music Co., Inc., owner of publication and allied rights for the World
Chappell & Co., sole selling agent
Used by Permission

A Little Night Music
Music and Lyrics by Stephen Sondheim
©1973 Rilting Music, Inc.
All rights administered by WB Music Corp.
Used by Permission

Anyone Can Whistle
Music and Lyrics by Stephen Sondheim
©1964 (Renewed 1992) by Stephen Sondheim
Burthen Music Company, Inc., owner of publication and allied rights for the World
Chappell & Co., sole selling agent
Used by Permission

Assassins
Music and Lyrics by Stephen Sondheim
©1988 Rilting Music, Inc.
All rights administered by WB Music Corp.
Used by Permission

Company
Music and Lyrics by Stephen Sondheim
©1970 Rilting Music, Inc. and Herald Square Music
All rights on behalf of Rilting Music, Inc. administered by WB Music Corp.
Used by Permission

Follies
Music and Lyrics by Stephen Sondheim
©1971 Rilting Music, Inc., Burthen Music Company, Inc. and Herald Square Music

All rights on behalf of Rilting Music, Inc. administered by WB Music Corp.
Used by Permission

Into the Woods
Music and Lyrics by Stephen Sondheim
©1987 Rilting Music, Inc.
All rights administered by WB Music Corp.
Used by Permission

Merrily We Roll Along
Music and Lyrics by Stephen Sondheim
©1981 Rilting Music, Inc.
All rights administered by WB Music Corp.
Used by Permission

Pacific Overtures
Music and Lyrics by Stephen Sondheim
©1981 Rilting Music, Inc.
All rights administered by WB Music Corp.
Used by Permission

Passion
Music and Lyrics by Stephen Sondheim
©1994 Rilting Music, Inc.
All rights administered by WB Music Corp.
Used by Permission

Sunday in the Park with George
Music and Lyrics by Stephen Sondheim
©1984, 1985 Rilting Music, Inc.
All rights administered by WB Music Corp.
Used by Permission

Sweeney Todd
Music and Lyrics by Stephen Sondheim
©1979 Rilting Music, Inc.
All rights administered by WB Music Corp.
Used by Permission

Introduction
Joanne Gordon

In trying to define Stephen Sondheim's significance one finds oneself constantly bumping up against seemingly incompatible categories: an avant-garde ártist working in *the* populist art form; an apparently dry and acerbic cynic capturing all the ambivalent pain of passion; a brilliant intellectual whose work contains some of the funniest bawdy lines in dramatic literature. How does one characterize this artist?

In attempting to strike the appropriate tone for this introduction, I kept returning to an anecdote related to me by one of my contributors. Len Fleischer was recommended to me as a potential source. I approached him and asked whether or not he would be interested in writing an article for this collection. Len readily agreed, but warned me that his work might be delayed as he was not well. I did not wish to pry, but then Len shared his story and in many ways this experience encapsulates all the intensity and ignorance that surrounds the Sondheim phenomenon.

Len had been told that he had a brain tumor and would have to have radiation therapy. At one of the major hospitals in New York City, they placed a elaborate contraption on his head and prepared him for treatment. A nurse then kindly asked him to choose what kind of music he would like to listen to as they zapped his brain. To say the least, Len was a trifle taken aback. He had not expected musical accompaniment to the procedure. He was assured that it was standard practice, as music soothed and relaxed the patient. Being a typical Sondheim fanatic, Len immediately requested anything by Sondheim. Here he was in this huge hospital, near to Broadway and all its brightly lit marquees, surrounded by every gadget that medical science could devise, and no one could find anything by Sondheim. He ended up having to endure his first treatment listening to Frank Sinatra sing "My Way." He came prepared to all subsequent treatments, and the nurses and doctors are now all familiar with *Company*,

Follies, and *Pacific Overtures*.

Why is this story an apposite introduction to Sondheim? It reveals clearly the profound commitment of those of us who are awed and enthralled by his work. It also illustrates the neglect that his work still suffers from in the milieu of popular music. Sondheim's work is gradually seeping into the national consciousness, but he is still a cult figure. His genius is acknowledged and reinforced with each new musical, but because his constant attempts to create something innovative and different result in work that is unique and challenging, it takes the public decades to appreciate, comprehend and embrace his art.

The basic facts about Sondheim's life are well known. He was born on March 22, 1930 in New York City into a comfortable upper-middle-class family. A precocious child, his destiny was determined when his parents divorced and he moved with his mother to Doylestown, Pennsylvania. Living nearby was the world-renowned lyricist, Oscar Hammerstein. The almost fairy tale coincidence of this relationship was to define Sondheim's life.

Sondheim graduated from Williams College and proceeded to use the Hutchinson Prize, a two-year fellowship, to study with avant-garde composer, Milton Babbitt. After a brief career as a writer for the television series *Topper*, Sondheim returned to New York, and was commissioned by set designer/producer Lemuel Ayers to write a musical. The result, *Saturday Night*, never reached the stage owing to Ayers's untimely death. Sondheim's next commission was to launch him into Broadway history. Although he longed to be both composer and lyricist, he was persuaded by Hammerstein to become the lyricist for a new project by Leonard Bernstein and Arthur Laurents, *West Side Story* (1957). The success of this work established his reputation as America's foremost lyricist, but Sondheim was not content. Although he was to work as lyricist with two of the theater's most distinguished composers, Jule Styne and Richard Rodgers, in *Gypsy* (1959*)* and *Do I Hear a Waltz?* (1965) respectively, he was frustrated.

It was finally in 1962 that Sondheim's first work as both composer and lyricist opened on Broadway. Although *A Funny Thing Happened on the Way to the Forum* was a critical success, winning a number of Tony Awards, including Best Musical, Sondheim's work was largely ignored. His next musical, *Anyone Can Whistle* (1964) was panned and closed after nine performances. In 1970, however, with the opening of *Company*, Sondheim was finally recognized as the innovative voice in the American musical theater.

Prior to Sondheim, musicals were almost exclusively viewed as escapist entertainment for the middle classes. Even exceptions like *Show Boat* and *Johnny Johnson* evoked a larger-than-life world in which emotion was expressed in melody and ultimate happiness was guaranteed. During the so-called Golden Age of the musical the optimism of America under Eisenhower was reflected in this quintessentially popular form of entertainment. Bourgeois values predominated and the audience believed in the romantic idealism that was depicted.

This naïveté did not last. After the social and artistic upheavals of the sixties, Sondheim and his primary collaborator, director Harold Prince, could not simply churn out this kind of escapist entertainment. They chose instead to confront their audience with the very issues it had fled to the theater to avoid. This was an audacious course to follow. Sondheim was flouting convention and this alienated many. He and his many collaborators have remained undeterred, however, blazing a trail of creativity on Broadway. They have chosen *the* populist form of theater and invested it with a truth and seriousness of purpose rarely associated with the musical. This choice has robbed Sondheim of the kind of commercial success gained by other contemporary composers, but has endowed his work with a theatrical exhilaration and intellectual veracity.

Sondheim's musicals are each unique and their subject matter ranges from such diverse topics as the invasion of Japan by Western Imperialists to the history of assassination in America. His innovation is not limited to his choice of subject matter, however. The form of his dramatic pieces is equally novel, for his musicals are not plot driven. Time and space are often fragmented. The basic structure which informs a Sondheim musical is the *idea*. Music, lyric, dance, dialogue, design and direction fuse to support a focal thought. A central metaphor shapes the entire production. Content and form cannot be separated for the one dictates and is dependent on the other. Sondheim's music and lyrics grow out of the dramatic idea inherent in the show's concept. They become part of the drama that previous theatre songs would only reflect.

Since *Company*, Sondheim has managed to produce a new musical almost every three years. His major work includes: *Follies* (1971); *A Little Night Music* (1973); *Pacific Overtures* (1976); *Sweeney Todd*

(1979); *Merrily We Roll Along* (1981); *Sunday in the Park with George* (1984);*Into the Woods* (1987); *Assassins* (1991) and *Passion* (1994). With each new work Sondheim redefines the parameters of musical theater. Despite numerous Tony Awards, accolades and a Pulitzer Prize, Sondheim's work remains controversial because it is not easy, and audiences of the musical theater still do not expect to be challenged or provoked. Yet, Sondheim's prolific output continues unabated. His work now provides the defining standard by which all other musicals are assessed.

In this very eclectic collection of essays something of the scope of Sondheim's work can be comprehended. The authors' approach to his work is as varied as the subject matter they tackle. The essays are organized according to the chronology of the shows, as this seemed the clearest order. Each writer was encouraged to find in Sondheim something that excited them. The essays reflect the enormous range and appeal of his work. This collection is far from exhaustive and there are many aspects of Sondheim's work that are not covered. Some of the musicals are analyzed in detail, while others are mentioned only in passing. His work as a lyricist to other composers and as a composer of incidental music for film is not studied. However, these essays do provide an insight into the complex genius of Stephen Sondheim.

Musicals have traditionally been associated with a happily-ever-after realm in which a sweet young ingenue marries a gallant young man as the chorus sings a final reprise. Laura Hanson places Sondheim's work within this context and examines the very different kind of woman that inhabits Sondheim's world. Taking us from the idealized romance of earlier musical heroines, Hanson traces the evolution of the complex, adult women in Sondheim's major musicals. This essay serves as an ideal introduction to this volume as it spans Sondheim's career and touches upon all his major work. Hanson applauds Sondheim's efforts to shatter the female stereotype and present in his musicals the interrelationship of men and women in all its complex-ity. Sondheim's depiction of women is not based on some mythic idealized vision , but throughout his work he presents all the difficulties of surviving in our contemporary world. His characters are not simple and their relationships are fraught with tension. His women are not submissive helpmates, but strong and opinionated protagonists who, like their male counterparts, are urged to seek a fulfillment of self and authentic identity through tough choices. This is a theme that is to resonate through other essays as the authors examine individual shows.

In her essay, Lois Kivesto explores the Roman antecedents of *A Funny Thing Happened on the Way to the Forum*. By investigating the Plautine conventions that Sondheim, Shevelove and Gelbart employ to structure this great farce, Kivesto exposes the comic richness of the work. Basing her research on the work of Plautus and scholars of Roman farce, she examines how Sondheim departs from the integrated song/scene structure and character model developed by Rodgers and Hammerstein. Her essay clarifies and reinforces the timeless appeal of this early work.

John Olson also examines the issue of timelessness in his analysis of *Company*. Focusing on the issue of what constitutes "the present" in the revival of this definitive work, Olson disputes the claims that the musical is dated. Utilizing sociological data to substantiate his point of view, Olson deduces that *Company*'s themes of loneliness, alienation and the need for commitment are as relevant and pertinent today as they were twenty-five years ago.

In his analysis of *Follies*, James Fisher takes a contrasting position, arguing for the specific relevance of the piece as a searing commentary of America under Nixon. The socio-political depth and complexity of the musical is the focus of his article. By placing *Follies* firmly within a specific context, Fisher proves that this musical expresses a similar insight and political depth to the plays of Miller, Albee and Mamet.

Sondheim's love of puzzles is legendary. Although this brain-teasing complexity is to be found in all his work, it is in his film *The Last of Sheila*, Douglas Braverman suggests, that we have his clearest example of his love of games. Without revealing the plot's secret, Braverman delights in the twists and turns of Sondheim's screenplay. He is able to relate some of its themes and techniques to those employed by Sondheim in his musicals. It may be interesting to compare this work with Sondheim's latest play, *Getting Away with Murder*, which transferred from San Diego to Broadway in March 1996.

In contrast with the more literary approach of the preceding essays, David Craig brings to Sondheim the perspective of the theatre practitioner. As one of America's most respected teachers of musical theatre, Craig has contributed his unique talents to the creation of many Broadway hits. His personal account of the evolution of the musical staging during the 1990 Los Angeles production of *A Little Night Music* brings a veracity and immediacy to our understanding of Sondheim's work. Through his account one gains an increased respect for the detailed precision of Sondheim's sense of theatre.

Pacific Overtures is often seen as the most obscure of Sondheim's scores. By examining the connections between this musical and Sondheim's other work, Len Fleischer reveals the continuity of thematic focus in Sondheim's oeuvre. The general structuring idea of growing from self-protective illusion to mature acceptance of reality is shown to be the core belief in all Sondheim's major works. Consequently, Fleischer's study is clearly related to Hanson's essay about Sondheim's women and points forward to Mari Cronin's examination of Sondheim's idealism.

Judith Schlesinger is a therapist and brings her own skills and understanding to her investigation of *Sweeney Todd*. Analyzing the different connotations of madness within the text and in the relationship between the musical, its audience and the society it represents, Schlesinger examines contemporary moral boundaries. Using *Sweeney Todd* as her paradigm, she is able to elucidate some of our most troubling social issues. The differences between inherent evil and justifiable rage has a distinctly relevant appeal for those of us bewildered by the seeming inconsistencies of our system of justice.

In her analysis of the final Sondheim/Prince collaboration to date, Mari Cronin posits the argument that despite many claims to the contrary, Sondheim is an unambiguous idealist. *Merrily We Roll Along* does not offer greeting card platitudes but exemplifies Sondheim's code of personal responsibility and loyalty. By presenting his audience with the undeniable pain and difficulty of contemporary life, Cronin argues, Sondheim is asking them to confront their problems and choose a more humane path. There are no simplistic solutions, but Cronin finds in all Sondheim's work the call to act in a more honest and aware manner.

The legendary relationship between Oscar Hammerstein and Sondheim is detailed in Andrew Milner's contribution. Concentrating on the comparison between *Allegro* (a show on which the seventeen-year-old Sondheim had been a gofer) and *Merrily We Roll Along*, Milner contrasts the work of these two theatrical giants. Both musicals dramatize the cost of personal and professional compromise, but each expresses the unique voice of its creator.

Sondheim's work has consistently been described as "radical," "revolutionary" and "avant-garde." As a student of contemporary literary theory Ed Bonahue takes exception to these categorizations. In his analysis of *Sunday in the Park with George*, Bonahue argues that in his philosophy of art Sondheim and his work are essentially conservative and traditional. However, by providing this theorist with such complex material for analysis, it is clear that no matter how one labels this work, *Sunday in the Park with George* is unquestionably one of the great works of twentieth-century dramatic literature.

The notion of "concept" musical is the central focus of Scott Miller's analysis of *Assassins*. By delineating *Assassins'* place in the evolution of the concept musical, Miller reveals the intricate sophistication of the work. His analysis explains why the piece did not transfer to a large commercial New York house, but has found an avid audience elsewhere. His rather pessimistic evaluation of Broadway theatre is balanced by his faith that Sondheim's work will continue to flourish in the less commercial, more adventurous environment of regional theatre.

Gary Konas' erudite analysis of *Passion* reveals how this profound musical differs from the obvious romantic myths of *Beauty and the Beast* and *Phantom of the Opera*. Focusing on the intricate musical structure, Konas provides a detailed, intelligent exploration of this exciting theatrical piece. Further, he utilizes Jungian archetypes and symbols to explore the emotional and intellectual depths of the work. The dark dreamlike structure of *Passion* is clarified in Konas's careful evocation of subconscious patterns in this moving "tone poem."

In the final essay in the collection Barbara Fraser examines the resemblances between Sondheim's use of the chorus and the chorus of classical Greek and traditional musical theatre. Fraser briefly describes the culture that gave rise to the Greek chorus and shows how the sense of a dominant cultural community contrasts with the contemporary American celebration of the individual. For the Greeks, the chorus was the voice of the state, speaking to and for the audience's sensibility. In traditional American musical theatre, the chorus is relegated to a supportive role. It creates an environment to reflect the struggles of the individual hero or heroine. Fraser reveals how Sondheim incorporates elements of these two contrasting worldviews and perhaps more significantly evolves a chorus that is unique to his own work.

Nothing can replace the exhilaration of seeing a Sondheim musical live on stage. The analytic pleasure of these essays cannot hope to
duplicate that visceral experience. I trust, however, that the insights
provided by these essays will give the reader a more profound respect,
understanding and love of Sondheim's work and will result in an even
greater appreciation and joy when the curtain rises on another
Sondheim show.

ℰℐ

Chronology

1930   22 March, Stephen Sondheim born to Herbert and Janet Sondheim, New York City

1946   Enters Williams College, Williamstown, MA; graduates in 1950

1948   *Phinney's Rainbow* produced, Williams College

1949   *All That Glitters* produced, Williams College

1956   *Girls of Summer** opens on Broadway, Longacre Theatre

1957   *West Side Story*** opens on Broadway, Winter Garden Theatre

1959   *Gypsy*** opens on Broadway, Broadway Theatre

1960   *Invitation to March** opens on Broadway, Music Box Theatre

1962   *A Funny Thing Happened on the Way to the Forum* opens on Broadway, Alvin Theatre; film of *West Side Story* released

1963   *Hot Spot** opens on Broadway, Majestic Theatre; film of *Gypsy* released

1964   *Anyone Can Whistle* opens on Broadway, Majestic Theatre

1965   *Do I Hear a Waltz?*** opens on Broadway, 46th Street Theatre

1966   *The Mad Show**** opens off-Broadway, New Theatre

1967   *Evening Primrose* telecast on ABC; film of *Forum* released

1970   *Company* opens on Broadway, Alvin Theatre (Tony Award, Best Music and Lyrics; New York Drama Critics' Circle Award, Best Musical)

1971   *Follies* opens on Broadway, Winter Garden Theatre (Tony Award, Best Music and Lyrics; New York Drama Critics' Circle Award, Best Musical)

1973   *A Little Night Music* opens on Broadway, Shubert Theatre (Tony Award, Best Music and Lyrics; New York Drama Critics' Circle Award, Best Musical); *The Last of Sheila* (film) released

1974   *Candide* (Second Version)*** opens on Broadway, Broadway Theatre; *The Frogs* produced, Yale University

1976   *Pacific Overtures* opens on Broadway, Winter Garden Theatre (New York Drama Critics' Circle Award, Best Musical); *Side By Side By Sondheim* (revue) opens, Mermaid Theatre, London

1977   *Side By Side By Sondheim* opens on Broadway, Music Box Theatre

1978   Film of *A Little Night Music* released

1979   *Sweeney Todd, The Demon Barber of Fleet Street* opens on Broadway, Uris Theatre (Tony Award, Best Score; New York Drama Critics' Circle Award, Best Musical)

1981   *Marry Me A Little* opens off-Broadway, Actors Playhouse; *Merrily We Roll Along* opens on Broadway, Alvin Theatre

1984   *Sunday in the Park with George* opens on Broadway, Booth Theatre (New York Drama Critics' Circle Award, Best Musical; 1985 Pulitzer Prize for Drama)

1987   *Into the Woods* opens on Broadway, Martin Beck Theatre (Tony Award, Best Score); revised version of *Follies* opens in London

1991   *Assassins* opens off-Broadway, Playwrights Horizons

1994   *Passion* opens on Broadway, Plymouth Theatre; revised *Merrily We Roll Along* opens off-Broadway, York Theatre

1996   *Getting Away With Murder* opens on Broadway, Broadhurst Theatre

*composed incidental music only
**wrote lyrics only
***assisted with lyrics and/or music

Broadway Babies

Images of Women in the Musicals of Stephen Sondheim
Laura Hanson

> First you're another
> Sloe-eyed vamp,
> Then someone's mother,
> Then you're camp.
> Then you career
> From career to career.
> I'm almost through my memoirs,
> And I'm here. (Sondheim, *Follies* 59–60)

The images of female characters in musical theatre have traditionally, as the Stephen Sondheim lyric suggests, been limited by certain categorizations. There is, of course, the virginal ingenue, the wise-cracking and slightly naughty secondary female lead, the wise older woman, or the suffering woman in love with the wrong kind of guy. From the early days of the musical theatre, young love was emphasized; physical beauty and a soprano singing voice were the staples of the heroine as she set out on the path to love, marriage, and family. Complications with members of the opposite sex usually resulted from simple misunderstandings or superficial differences in social or economic class.[1] "The ultimate reconciliation was usually achieved a few seconds before the final curtain…and the hero and heroine lived happily-ever-after" (Coward 8). As in straight romantic comedy, the act of marriage in musicals, with its promise of children, brings the characters in line with the civilizing morés of society and promises to perpetuate those values. Musical theatre, as an idealization of life in America and celebration of its abundance, tended to idealize women's roles as well. Hope and optimism for the future surged after the end of World War II, the beginning of the musical theatre's "Golden Age." The soldiers returned from war, women came home from the factories and took up their traditional duties of wife and homemaker. These

values are reflected in the musical theatre of the post-war years, particularly in the musicals of Rodgers and Hammerstein. In his article,
"'I Enjoy Being a Girl': Women in the Plays of Rodgers and
Hammerstein," Richard M. Goldstein discusses the traditional roles
assigned to the heroines in some of America's best-known and best-
loved musicals. In those works, the "heroine is an idealist, holding an
extremely romantic view of male-female relationships." She is "not
concerned with the dull, dark reality of the everyday world" (2).

By the time Stephen Sondheim's work emerged on Broadway,
however, society and the role of women within that society were changing. A nation that had been through the Kennedy assassinations, the
Vietnam War, and the women's movement no longer believed in love
at first sight and the happily-ever-after endings of traditional musical
theatre. In the words of critic John Lahr, "Sondheim's tough glibness
echoed the mood of the unromantic era" (73). Musical heroines were
no longer the young, sweet, virginal girls of earlier works from the
twenties and beyond, but battle weary from the war between the sexes.
In his musicals, Sondheim explores the increasingly complicated and
ambiguous relationships between men and women, as well as the
doubts and ambivalence that arise as his women try to sort out, through
song, their conflicting feelings towards love, marriage, men, their own
self-images, and the pursuit of their dreams. While the characters in a
Rodgers and Hammerstein musical "kiss in the shadows" or fall in
love suddenly "across a crowded room," a Sondheim lover is often
dragged unwillingly, kicking and screaming into a relationship. This
desire *not* to carry the torch of love is expressed eloquently by
Sondheim's women in songs such as "Losing My Mind" and "Not a
Day Goes By." These contrast sharply with the straightforward declaration of emotion in more traditional love songs or those in which
the characters are so eager for love to come along that they express
their longing for it before it has really had time to take root, as in "If
I Loved You" from *Carousel* or "People Will Say We're in Love" from
Oklahoma! As Lahr points out, "Instead of celebrating the ease and
spontaneity of emotion that was the stock-in-trade of the traditional
musical responding to a world it insisted was benign, Sondheim's songs
report the difficulty of feeling in a world where, as his song says, there's
'so little to be sure of'" (74).

Sondheim's heroines no longer enjoy the self-assured ebullience
of a Nellie Forbush proclaiming to all the world, "I'm in love with a

wonderful guy!" (Hammerstein 194). For *Passion*'s Clara, her idea of love is not something to be celebrated, but hidden: "I thought where there was love/ There was shame" (5). Nurse Fay in *Anyone Can Whistle* is so emotionally inhibited, she begs to be taught "How to let go,/ ...Learn to be free" (109), and can only express herself emotionally by taking on another woman's persona. This "disguise" is kept under her bed as a constant reminder to the rational, self-controlled, professional woman that there was once a moment when spontaneous feeling prevailed. Perhaps there is hope that it could happen again; yet when Hapgood leads her to the bed, she freezes and cannot go through with consummating the relationship. The simplest human skills and emotion are beyond her ability.

In spite of Fay's logical and scientific mentality, she betrays a more emotional side of herself buried deep within by secretly wanting to believe in the town miracle. Ironically, when she is chased by the mayoress' henchmen, she sings her belief in the proverbial "knight in shining armor" who will rescue her: "There are heroes in the world,/ Princes and heroes in the world,/ And one of them will save me" (38). This is a belief that Cinderella, one of her later sisters in the Sondheim canon, will come to question. True to Fay's rationality, however, her hero won't arrive in the typical musical comedy manner; she may secretly believe in Prince Charming, but eschews the usual emotional trappings:

> There won't be trumpets or bolts of fire
> To say he's coming.
> No Roman candles, no angels' choir,
> No sound of distant drumming. (38)

Throughout the musical, Fay does develop a higher level of self-awareness and independence which can be traced through her songs. She progresses from the dichotomy of "There Won't Be Trumpets," in which she looks for a hero, but claims not to believe in the typical romantic accompaniments to his arrival, through her admission of emotional inhibition in "Anyone Can Whistle" to the realization that self-revelation has its price:

> Give yourself,
> If somebody lets you—
> See what it gets you,
> See what it gets you!

> Give yourself
> And somebody lets you
> Down. (161)

The hero she expected cannot save her, and Fay realizes, "And when you want things done, you have to do them yourself alone!" (161).

Toward the end of the play, Fay says good-bye to Hapgood, acknowledging that they would make an unlikely pair—her competent practicality juxtaposed against his crazy zest for life. In her song of farewell, in which she admits her need, but acknowledges the man's need to be his own person, Fay foreshadows a later Sondheim heroine, Dot, who (in *Sunday in the Park with George*) cannot allow her love for a man to overshadow her own need for self-respect. When Dot comes to the realization that her needs and desires will always take second place to George's work, she accepts what she cannot change: "It's because I understand that I left,/ That I am leaving" (74). She is not content to live with a man who withholds himself emotionally, who relates more easily to the still images of her that he creates than to the real woman, and who tells her, "You know exactly how I feel./ Why do you insist/ You must hear the words,/ When you know I cannot give you words?" (74). Refusing his explanation that she should be content because she is a part of his work, a silent image refracted through a man's gaze, Dot sings an assertion of her right to be her own person as well:

> No one is you, George,
> There we agree,
> But others will do, George.
> No one is you and
> No one can be,
> But no one is me, George,
> No one is me.
> We do not belong together.
> ... ˜
> I have to move on. (76)

It is interesting to compare Dot to some of her musical ancestors, such as Eliza Doolittle, who rejects the man who has negated her feelings in the tirade of "Without You," walks out on him, but inevitably returns to fetch his slippers. As Goldstein points out, at various points in the Rodgers and Hammerstein canon, "Laurey (*Oklahoma!*),

Nellie (*South Pacific*), Anna (*The King and I*), Mei Li (*Flower Drum Song*), and Maria (*The Sound of Music*) all contemplate leaving the men in their lives, but for one reason or another they all change their minds" (5).

In contrast, Dot takes the initiative, assuming responsibility for her own self-respect. Even as she prepares to leave the man she cares for, the beautiful torment of "We Do Not Belong Together" expresses more feeling and passion than most traditional love songs. Along with songs such as "Not a Day Goes By," "Losing My Mind," and "Loving You," Sondheim's female characters express the angst and agony of loving another person with chilling insight.

Before coming to her self-realization, Dot had put up with her distant lover, blaming herself for his emotional coldness: "George is very special. Maybe I'm just not special enough for him" (35). Compare her insecurity with the self-assurance of Linda Low in *Flower Drum Song* who enjoys being a girl in the traditional sense:

> I'm strictly a female female,
> And my future, I hope, will be
> In the home of a brave and free male
> Who'll enjoy being a guy,
> Having a girl like me! (Hammerstein 251)

The confident exaltation of femininity that she engages in as she gazes at herself in the mirror stands in marked contrast to Dot, who expresses self-doubt in her own mirror song:

> If my legs were longer.
> If my bust was smaller.
> If my hands were graceful.
> If my waist was thinner.
> If my hips were flatter.
> If my voice was warm.
> If I could concentrate—[2] (35)

From Fay to Fosca, this idea of woman's self-image is explored in painful detail. In another "mirror song," the former chorines of *Follies* face their own aging selves and life's disappointments. The promises of beauty and youth, when love was fresh and all things seemed possible, have turned into the breathlessness and disillusion of middle age. Self-deception is one weapon which Sally wields against the brutal realities of life. In her haunting "In Buddy's Eyes," she presents the image of herself that she wants her former love to see—that she is content with her life and is in a happy marriage. The context of the play, the emotion of the actress, and the musical accompaniment belie her words, however. As she sings, Sally is trying as much to convince herself as she is trying to convince Ben that her life without him all these years has been a happy one. Having longed for this reunion for the past thirty years, Sally is so unsure of her own image that her first words to Ben are, "No, don't look at me—" (19), a phrase echoed later by the unattractive Fosca in *Passion*. In his book, *Sondheim's Broadway Musicals*, Stephen Banfield discusses the change in vocal register required for the song "In Buddy's Eyes" and the image of the woman that each evokes. When Sally sings the chorus, her idyll of a happy marital relationship, she sings in the sweet, innocent soprano of the traditional musical theatre heroine. Yet, the rest of the song is in the lower register, more akin to the blues with its "woman as sufferer" characteristic (183).

Ben, too, is guilty of self-delusion in the image he has created for himself of his love for Sally. He expresses his feelings for her in "Too Many Mornings," yet it is not the reality of Sally as she is now that he loves, but his memory of her as a young, beautiful woman. Ben ironically sings his heart-wrenching song of unfulfilled love to the image of Young Sally, not the middle-aged woman she has become. In a similar way, *A Little Night Music's* Fredrik tries to recapture his own younger days by marrying his ideal of womanly youth and beauty. His dream marriage backfires on him, however, when his ideal woman cannot bring herself to sleep with her new husband. It is not that she is so chaste and pure, but that the relationship, as are most of the others in the play, is inappropriate. Anne is more like a daughter than a wife to Fredrik. He even admits this, obliquely, in references to her childish prattle and her habit of ruffling his ties, describing her as "So unlike a wife" (51). Anne, too, is hardly conscious of the imbalance at the beginning of the play, but her body tells her what her head refuses to admit: "When you're close and we touch,/ And you're kissing my brow,/ I don't mind it too much" (22). Anne's own insecurity manifests itself in her excuse for withholding from Fredrik for fear of losing his interest: "If I were perfect for you,/ Wouldn't you tire of me..." (23).

Ironically, even though Anne cannot bring herself to sleep with her husband, she cannot bear the thought of his sleeping with another woman and schemes to get him back when it becomes apparent that he has fallen into the arms of his former love, Desirée. What she will do with him once she has him back, however, is doubtful. She and Charlotte commiserate with each other on the agonies of love in the poignant "Every Day a Little Death." Love is described as disgusting and insane, "A humiliating business!" for the woman in love with an unfaithful man (82). Again, themes of ambivalence and the agony of loving are evident. The irony is that Charlotte truly loves her louse of a husband, while Anne only thinks that she does because he is the type of man that young girls have been taught that they should fall in love with and marry—the prosperous, established kind who will provide them with dresses, maids, and spoil them shamelessly. In the end, Anne comes to her own moment of self-awareness, that she has never loved Fredrik and is in love with his son Henrik, a man closer to her own age. Desirée has her own moment of self-realization when she sings "Send in the Clowns." Coming up empty after a life of shoddy tours and casual lovers, she yearns for a second chance at happiness, "…a chance to turn back, to find some sort of coherent existence after so many years of muddle" (157). Her self-realization is not matched by the man in her life, however, who is still seduced by the image of Anne's youth and beauty. The inequity of the different effects of age on the image of men and women is reiterated later by Charlotte, who resents Fredrik's acquiring a young, pretty wife at an age "…when a woman is lucky if a drunken alderman pinches her derrière at a village fete!" (167). In the end, however, harmony is achieved, when all the women have found their proper partners, the ones most suited to them in age and temperament.

The emphasis on youth and beauty has traditionally been a staple of musical theatre heroines, but Sondheim and his collaborators have turned it into ironic comment in shows such as *Into the Woods, A Little Night Music, Passion,* and *Follies,* where the song "Beautiful Girls" introduces a line of middle-aged, former Follies Girls. Sally, Phyllis and Desirée have left their youth behind, but instead of growing wiser with the years as Aunt Eller in *Oklahoma!,* Nettie in *Carousel,* or Anna Leonowens in *The King and I* have, they are more confused than ever about life and love. The witch in *Into the Woods* must trade the one thing that makes her unique—her magical powers—in order to acquire the physical beauty that she thinks will make her more acceptable in the eyes of her child. The idea of a woman as a beautiful, but empty-headed, ornament is lampooned in *Forum*'s "I'm Lovely," where Philia, a recent graduate from courtesan school, proclaims, "All I am is lovely,/ Lovely is the one thing I can do" (45). However, this paean to the most superficial of womanly virtues is satirized later in the play when the song is reprised by Hysterium dressed in women's clothing; it mocks the notion that all it takes are the external trappings to give one the sought-after loveliness.

Sondheim and James Lapine explored the issue of beauty and a woman's worth in the eyes of the world in their most recent collaboration, *Passion*. In this work, the musical theatre has come full-circle, from the lovely and lovable heroines who inevitably end up happily married to the man they love, to the "irredeemably ugly" Fosca, who, in the words of Sondheim, himself, "has not one redeeming quality.... If she had one ordinary, not passionate, moment, one moment that wasn't about herself, the character would not only be hateful, but unbelievable" (qtd. in Buck 278). Fosca's lack of the one thing that gives a woman her worth has denied her a normal life of domesticity and turned her into a bitter, self-pitying creature, seemingly incapable of taking other people's feelings into account. As a woman, her role in society has already been limited; her looks further constrict her choices in a way that is not felt by men:

> An unattractive man—...
> —Can still have opportunities...
> Whereas, if you're a woman,
> You either are a daughter or a wife...
> You marry—...
> —Or you're a daughter all your life. (76–77)

In a society where "Beauty is power..." and where "A woman's like a flower.../ A flower's only purpose is to please..." (84), Fosca lacks the one quality that society values.

Ironically, it is not Fosca's appearance, but the sheer force of her passion that shakes Giorgio to his very core, shattering all his traditional notions of love as something pretty, tidy and self-controlled. In the same way, *Passion,* itself, shatters an audience's expectations of what a love story in a musical should be. There is no typical boy meets girl story here. The man is attractive; the woman is not only unattractive, but unpleasant as well. The traditional roles are reversed. The woman pursues the man and praises his beauty with the same phrase that Giorgio used to praise his ideal woman, the blonde and beautiful Clara: "God, you are so beautiful" (57). In a twist on the usual musical outcomes, the ugly woman triumphs over the beautiful one, thereby gaining through the sheer force of her emotion the power that was denied her by her looks. There is no happy ending, however, when the lovers are finally united at the end of the story.

Fosca is unusual in that she is able to admit the force of her own darker impulses. Her attraction to her husband, Count Ludovic, was based in part on an element of danger she sensed in him: "Deception,/ Even violence./ I must admit to some degree/ That it excited me" (81). Traditional heroines of the musical theatre are nice girls, generally devoid of the darker impulses and conflicting passions that plague so many of Sondheim's women. In *Oklahoma!*, Laurey is only able to confront her darker desires in a dream. And there is never any real doubt in the audience's mind as to which way she is going to choose. Her predecessor, Liza Elliott, a *Lady in the Dark*, also explored her romantic desires through dream sequences. Yet, Sondheim's women confront their desires, passions, and conflicting emotions head on in the light of day.

Traditional musical heroines are usually virginal or, perhaps, chaste in their remembrance of a past love. Even those who do end up with a number of children manage to acquire them asexually either through marriage (Nellie Forbush, Maria Von Trapp), adoption (Mame), or simply by becoming a maternal figure for someone else's children (Anna in *The King and I*). But Sondheim's women deal openly, though perhaps somewhat confusedly, with the issue of their own sexuality. In *Company*, Amy expresses her fears about curtailing it with "fidelity forever" (64). From *Anyone Can Whistle* through *Passion*, Sondheim's women wrestle with their own needs and desires. For some like Fay, emotional inhibition and self-doubt prevent her from consummating a relationship. For Fosca, the compulsion to love is beyond her control and results in her own death and the destruction of the one she loves. The others in between struggle to choose between what they want, or think they want, and what they think is right. Infidelities sometimes occur as Sondheim's women explore, through song, their conflicting emotions and desires, or try to make up for a past choice they felt has gone awry.

For some, sexuality has a more practical application. It is used for business purposes by the elder Madame Armfeldt in *A Little Night*

Music: "It's but a pleasurable means/ To a measurable end" (60). She has elevated a woman's sexual allure to a high art in the game of negotiation between men and women, using youth and beauty as weapons in order to achieve the wealth and social position a woman may have been born without. She abhors the lack of discretion younger women (her daughter included) display in their amorous adventures. This practical approach to male-female relationships is echoed by the maid Petra in her song, "The Miller's Son." She, too, knows that a woman has to take care of herself, think of her own future and vows to "Pin my hat on a nice piece of property" (162). In the meantime, however, "…a girl ought to celebrate what passes by" (163). Obviously, Petra feels that she, as a woman, will have to forego sexual fulfillment within marriage in favor of economic security. Before being locked into the role that society has dictated for her, Petra will make the most of her freedom and enjoy the sampling of life's pleasures: "It's a very short day/ Till you're stuck with just one/ Or it has to be done on the sly" (164). Ironically, it is Petra, the lower-class servant girl, who has a healthier and more realistic view of her sexuality than the upper-class women, Desirée, Anne, and Charlotte, who manage to make a muddle of their relationships.

In "The Story of Lucy and Jessie," from *Follies,* Phyllis expresses the ambivalence and frustration of a woman who longs to combine the innocence, vitality, and sexual freedom she enjoyed in her youth with the maturity and financial security of her older self. Apparently, a woman cannot have it both ways. Anne, in *A Little Night Music,* has denied her own feelings for the security of marriage to an older, prosperous man; as a result, she is unable to express her sexuality at all. A similar sentiment is echoed by the Baker's Wife in *Into the Woods* after her brief extramarital affair with the Prince: "Have a child for warmth,/ And a baker for bread,/ And a Prince for whatever—" (112). She, too, takes it for granted that a woman's role as wife and mother is distinct from her own sexual fulfillment, and she must choose between the comfort and security of life with her Baker husband and a fling with the handsome Prince. Having had the brief moment enjoying that which every woman dreams of, her practical side pulls her back to reality and her duties. Yet, she relishes the moment for what it was and questions the limitations of life and society, where once one chooses one's path, there is no going back:

> Must it all be either less or more,
> Either plain or grand?
> Is it always "or"?
> Is it never "and"?[3] (112)

While marriage and the raising of children are the main purpose in the life of the traditional heroine, Sondheim's women do not seem to view this as their primary goal. While children abound in musicals such as *The King and I, The Sound of Music,* and *The Music Man,* they appear sparingly in the Sondheim canon. In *Company,* although it is known that Bobby is "Seven times a godfather" (81), the children are never seen and are only mentioned in passing, as in "Children you destroy together" (31). As can be seen in the case of the Baker's Wife in *Into the Woods,* motherhood—supposedly the goal of every heroine—does not cause her life to turn suddenly into that long-awaited happily-ever-after. With the child come problems which she never had to confront before, as well as the awesome responsibility for someone other than herself. And the perverse reward of motherhood is the eventual loss of one's child: "Children can only grow/ From something you love/ To something you lose..." (106). Jack, Cinderella, Little Red Ridinghood, and Rapunzel all grow up and come to maturity only by separating from their mothers and making their own decisions. Cinderella sings as much to herself as to the distraught Little Red Ridinghood:

> Mother cannot guide you.
> Now you're on your own... (128)
>   ...
> Mother isn't here now...
> Who knows what she'd say? (130)

In contrast, the character of the witch represents "An archetypal possessive mother" (Holden 7), perhaps harking back to the similar character of Rose in one of Sondheim's earliest musicals as a lyricist, *Gypsy.* Instead of encouraging her child's independence, she keeps her locked up, fearful and dependent, smothering her ability to cope with life:

> Don't you know what's out there in the world?
> Someone has to shield you from the world.
> Stay with me...

Who out there could love you more than I?
What out there that I cannot supply?...

Stay with me,
The world is dark and wild.
Stay a child while you can be a child.
With me. (60)

Other glimpses of women in the maternal role are not particularly rosy either. Desirée does not seem to have much of the mother-
ing instinct in *A Little Night Music*. She leaves her daughter with her
own mother while she pursues her acting career. Her staccato letter to
Fredrika is not especially communicative, focusing more on her own
activities than those of her daughter. Apparently, Desirée's relationship with her own mother is not the best. There are hints of little
barbs in the lyrics. When Desirée reports that she's performing in
some little town, she says wearily, as though she has heard the question many times before, "And don't ask where is it, please." She then
moves on to, "And are you corrupting the child?/ ...I'll come for a
visit/ And argue" (29). The elder Madame Armfeldt seems to
disapprove of the lifestyle her daughter leads. "Ordinary daughters
ameliorate their lot," she sings, "Mine tours" (28). She disapproves
especially of the mess Desirée makes of her love life, not using the art
of love skillfully for financial security:

Liaisons! What's happened to them?
Liaisons today.
Untidy—take my daughter, I
Taught her, I
Tried my best to point the way.
I even named her Desirée. (61)

Ironically, while most mothers in the musical theatre would be trying
to protect their daughters from the world of sex, Madame Armfeldt
feels she has failed because she has not been able to teach her daughter how to turn sex into a financially rewarding career.

Even the evil Mrs. Lovett in *Sweeney Todd* cannot resist assuming
the maternal role in her relationship with the slow-witted orphan
Tobias. However, her good feelings soon give way to murderous
thoughts when Tobias' suspicions of Todd are aroused. Reprising the
boy's naive and heartfelt "Not While I'm Around," Mrs. Lovett sings
her version of the song to an eerie and sinister accompaniment, which

belies the sincerity of the words. Nothing may harm Tobias while Mrs. Lovett is around except, perhaps, Mrs. Lovett, herself.

In *Passion*, Clara has to choose between her own sexual fulfillment and her identity as a mother. The fear of losing her child is the reason she initially gives for refusing to run away with lover Giorgio, though in her responses to his pleas, it seems that she may simply be using that as an excuse to maintain a convenient, uncommitted relationship with him. She has second thoughts, however, and tells Giorgio this when the child is old enough to go off to school, then she will run away with him. The child is merely one of her "obligations at home" (114), but she loves Giorgio, though not in the unconditional way he has come to expect. It is interesting that this second chance for the lovers came about in a later revision of *Passion*. In early previews, Clara put a permanent end to the affair,[4] giving her lover no choice but to fall into the arms of Fosca. By having Clara dangle the possibility of future happiness in front of Giorgio, the show's creators have actually strengthened his character, allowing Giorgio to make the choice, rather than having it imposed on him.

Not all images of woman as mother are fraught with ambivalence and anxiety, however. While *Sunday in the Park with George* may offer one character's unflattering view in "The Day Off" —

> Still, Sunday with someone's dotty mother
> Is better than Sunday with your own.
> Mothers may drone, mothers may whine—
> Tending to his, though, is perfectly fine.
> It pays for the nurse that is tending to mine
> On Sunday,
> My day off. (52)

—it is only through the women, first Marie and then Dot, that George is able to trace his lineage and find the nurturing link with his artistic heritage.

Throughout Sondheim's body of work, it is obvious that marriage is not the blissful, "happily-ever-after" of traditional musicals, but a "ferocious pillow-fight battle of the sexes.... It simply is not the placid old heaven-ordained, till-death-do-us-part, for-better-for-worse institution it used to be" (Kalem 62). Contrast the upbeat dream world of love and marriage in "You're Gonna Love Tomorrow/ Love Will See Us Through" from *Follies* with the reality of how those mar-

riages turned out. While Young Sally claims she'll bolster Young
Buddy's ego as a wife should (90), it comes out later in "Buddy's
Blues" that the middle-aged Sally thinks her husband is a washout
(98). Young Phyllis bids "...fare-thee-well, ennui" (89), yet later in
life is so bored with her marriage to Ben that the couple resorts to
hurting each other just to keep the relationship alive. The women,
who traditionally are the ones who cannot wait to step down the
aisle, are as suspicious of the old institution as the men.

The archetypal musical heroines wanted nothing more than to
fall in love, get married and live happily ever after. Yet, this myth is
exploded by Cinderella in *Into the Woods*. Pursued by the vision that
is every girl's dream, as the Baker's wife tells her, Cinderella is not sure
that a rich, handsome Prince is what she really wants. In fact, she is
not at all sure what she should want. The standard choice does not
look so appealing. "Like Robert (and more significantly from a feminist point of view), she sees commitment as limiting since any definite
decision destroys all other possibilities" (McLaughlin 36). Decision is
risky, and again the issue of self-image comes into play. Cinderella has
put on a different persona, and that is what the Prince has come to
love. She is afraid that once he discovers her true self, he will no longer
be interested. Even Cinderella is not sure which of the two versions of
herself is the one to choose:

And then what if you are

> What a Prince would envision?
> Although how can you know
> Who you are till you know
> What you want, which you don't?
> So then which do you pick:
> Where you're safe, out of sight,
> And yourself, but where everything's wrong?
> Or where everything's right
> And you know that you'll never belong? (63)

More pragmatic than her musical predecessors, Cinderella has, by the
end of the play, come to doubt the dream and to realize that the
reality of life is not painted in either black or white, but lies somewhere in the middle. Her father's house was a nightmare; the Prince's
was a dream: "Now I want something in-between" (128).

As a counterpoint to Robert's desire, but inability to commit, in
Company, Amy is afraid to get married to someone she has been

living with for a number of years; there is hesitation and ambivalence as she senses that allying herself to another person for life somehow diminishes the self. The traditionally accepted attitudes are turned upside down when she says to Bobby, "I'm afraid to get married, and you're afraid not to" (73). As a group, the female characters in *Company* represent the various levels of commitment in a woman's relationship with a man, which Bobby is able to witness first-hand: living together and then newlywed, married with children, divorced, middle-aged and much-married.

Feelings of ambivalence and self-doubt are evident in many of Sondheim's songs concerning love and the uneasy relationship between men and women. In more traditional musical theatre, love's final goal was a happy marriage where the stereotypical roles for husband and wife were well defined. The choices for a woman were clear-cut between the "nice" men (for example, a Curly) or the slightly roguish ones a woman hoped to redeem with her love (Billy Bigelow, or Gaylord Ravenal), but no matter what, a woman stood by her man. "What's the use of wond'rin'/ If he's good or if he's bad," Julie asks in *Carousel*, "He's your feller and you love him—/ That's all there is to that" (Hammerstein 156). Similar views are expressed by Lady Thiang in "Something Wonderful" from *The King and I* and in the song "A Fellow Needs a Girl" from *Allegro*:

> A fellow needs a girl
> To sit by his side
> At the end of a weary day,
> To sit by his side
> And listen to him talk
> And agree with the things he'll say. (Hammerstein 172)

But once in a relationship, the traditional male and female roles do not necessarily apply for Sondheim's characters. The Baker in *Into the Woods* discovers that he cannot achieve his goal without forming an equal partnership with his wife in "It Takes Two"; indeed, she is usually the impetus for his actions. Like the couples in *Company,* both the Baker and his wife come to realize that forging a bond with another person enables one to get through the terrors of life a little more easily, even if it means giving up a bit of one's independence. In other partnerships, Sweeney Todd's dream of revenge is only set in motion by the enterprising and amoral woman in his life, Mrs. Lovett.

Company's Sarah can best her husband at karate and takes great pleasure in doing so. She does not feel, like the heroine of *Annie Get Your
Gun,* that she has to allow the man to win in order to gain his love,[5]
or, like Julie in *Carousel,* endure his abuse for the sake of allowing him
his self-respect. Sondheim's women hit back. No longer is the woman
the submissive helpmate, and the confusion and ambivalence about
her modern role is suggested in the following lyrics from *Anyone Can
Whistle.* As Hapgood tries to separate the pilgrims from the inmates
of the sanatorium for the socially pressured, a gender-bending couple
sings of their own confusion:

> A woman's place is in the home,
> A woman's place is on the shelf.
> And home is where he hangs her hat,
> And that is where she hangs himself. (63)

The cynical Joanne in *Company* caustically comments on those
women who have bought into the traditional female stereotypes and
have been disillusioned by their false promises:

> Here's to the girls who play wife—
> Aren't they too much?
> Keeping house but clutching a copy of *Life*
> Just to keep in touch.
> The ones who follow the rules,
> And meet themselves at the schools,
> Too busy to know that they're fools—
> Aren't they a gem? (106–7)

She goes on to skewer the various types of upper-middle-class women
who, not having any kind of career of their own, fill up their days
with pastimes. She comes to the painful realization during the song
that she, herself, can be counted among their number. To shield herself from this harsh view, she anesthetizes herself with alcohol and
caustic wit.

In their often shaky relationships with men, Sondheim's
women struggle with their own conflicting images of self. Their
struggle is often made more difficult, however, by men's unrealistic
image of them. Bobby is unable to commit himself to one *real* woman
in *Company* because he is searching for the unattainable ideal woman,
a composite of all the best qualities of his closest female friends:

My blue-eyed Sarah
Warm Joanne
Sweet Jenny
Loving Susan
Crazy Amy,
Wait for me…. (54)

He does achieve a certain kind of emotional closeness with his women friends, but it is a chaste one. To his girlfriends, he can only relate on a sexual level and nothing more. If only Bobby could combine these two types of relationships with women, perhaps he could commit. But instead, "He is seeking the ideal mate who exists only in the world of myth and fairy tale—or in the never-never land of traditional American musical theater" (Gordon 53).

Ironically, the image of Desirée as the "perfect woman" is the undoing of Carl-Magnus and Fredrik in *A Little Night Music*. "If she'd only been faded,/ If she'd only been fat," they lament (129). "If she'd cried or whatever/ A woman would do in a pinch,/ It would have been wonderful" (130). Rather than taking responsibility for their own foolishness, they blame this ideal woman for their predicament. Obviously, in the imperfect world of a Sondheim musical, a woman cannot win. She is blamed if she is perfect, and blamed if she is not. As he sings "In Praise of Women," the egotistical Carl-Magnus extols "Knowing their place" as one of the womanly virtues (72). In the traditional world where "There Is Nothin' Like A Dame," the women are always pretty and loyal, and they do know their place. Not so for Sondheim's women as they grope their way through life's choices. Although Carl-Magnus expects his wife calmly to accept his own infidelity, he cannot tolerate the same behavior in his mistress. But, to the egotistical count, the notion of Desirée being attracted to another man is unthinkable, and he finishes a song by proclaiming, "The woman's mine!" (73). The two Princes in *Into the Woods* also seem incapable of being true to their image of the ideal woman. For them, she is only ideal as long as she seems unattainable. But once they've conquered, they do not seem so adept at relating to the real flesh-and-blood woman behind the image they've created.

If the male-female relationship is sometimes strained in Sondheim's musicals, women's relationships with each other are not what one usually expects, either. The secondary female lead of traditional musical comedies acted as best friend and confidante, but Sondheim's women generally have only themselves to rely on, fumbling alone along life's path. Their insecurities and doubts about self-image are often manifested in their views of and relationships with other women. *Anyone Can Whistle* pits the rational Fay against the scheming mayoress, Cora. Their feelings toward each other are best summed up in a song that was cut from the original Broadway production, but recently restored to a concert version of the show at Carnegie Hall, "There's Always a Woman."[6] During the number, the two women bemoan the fact that there is always a woman to put a kink in the other one's plans; they then proceed to imagine ways in which to do each other in. *Sweeney Todd*'s Mrs. Lovett shows no mercy to the Beggar Woman and allows Sweeney to believe that his wife is dead so that she can establish the kind of relationship with him that she had always longed for. Old resentments between women also crop up at the *Follies* reunion, where Sally is reunited with an old love who married her former best friend. And *A Little Night Music*'s Charlotte and Anne team up to spoil their rival's conquest of Fredrik by emphasizing Anne's youth over the more mature Desirée.

This sense of female competition can also be seen in the song "Poor Baby" from *Company,* sung by all of Robert's married female friends. Although they tell Robert, "You know, no one/ Wants you to be happy/ More than I do" (93), they then criticize all of his girlfriends. Unable, and unwilling on a conscious level, to consummate their own relationships with Bobby, they nevertheless are jealous of his sexual relations with these other women. Under the guise of being concerned, they sweetly hurl insulting adjectives at the thought of them: dumb, tacky, neurotic, vulgar, immature, and "...tall enough to be your mother" (94).

From the early days of musical theatre, the majority of heroines sweetly sang their way to a fulfilling life as wife and mother. Even the spunkier ones, like Ado Annie in *Oklahoma!* or Carrie in *Carousel*, promised to mend their wandering ways once married and submit to their husbands. The choices were more clear-cut, between the nice men or the more risky ones. Those women who were unlucky enough to fall for the wrong kind of guy usually paid for it with a kind of romanticized martyrdom in which they even seemed to revel. For example, Julie in *Carousel* loves Billy so much that she does not even feel his abusive blows. And this is the message that she hands down to

her own daughter—that loving your man hard enough makes everything all right. But in the past thirty years, the musical heroine has
grown up, as exemplified by the women in the musicals of Stephen
Sondheim and his collaborators. Sondheim's women tend to be more
realistic and multi-dimensional than their more traditional counterparts. Their choices are not so clear-cut, their motivations not so pre-
dictable. They express doubts and fears about life and love and are
not always so sure about what they want, as they proceed haltingly
along the road to greater self-awareness. But right or wrong, the choices
have to be made, the consequences faced: "Where there's nothing to
choose,/ So there's nothing to lose" (*Woods* 64). Dot is all too familiar
with the painful, yet necessary process of accepting and taking responsibility for one's own self. She expresses this eloquently and seems
to speak for so many of Sondheim's women as she sings:

> I chose, and my world was shaken—
> So what?
> The choice may have been mistaken,
> The choosing was not.
> 　　　　You have to move on. (169)

☙

NOTES

1.　In his foreword to *Musical Comedy* (by Raymond Mander and Joe
　　Mitchenson), Noël Coward sums up the often silly and superfluous
　　misunderstandings that created the obstacles to true love in traditional
　　musical comedy: "Either he would insult her publicly on discovering
　　that she was a Princess in her own right rather than the simple com-
　　moner he had imagined her to be, or she would wrench his engage-
　　ment ring from her finger, fling it at his feet and faint dead away on
　　hearing that he was not the humble tutor she had loved for himself
　　alone, but a multi-millionaire" (7–8).

2.　It is interesting to note that George later uses the same melody to
　　describe a dog he is drawing in the park (48).

3.　Shortly after the Baker's Wife has her fling with the Prince, she is
　　killed in the havoc wreaked by the giant. One critic, however, took
　　this as commentary by the show's creators. In his article, "'No One is

Alone': Society and Love in the Musicals of Stephen Sondheim," Robert L. McLaughlin makes note of that critic's reaction: "The implication of the Baker's Wife's death as punishment for her adultery caused Kramer in *The New Yorker* to accuse the authors of misogyny" (411).

4.   Preview of *Passion,* by Stephen Sondheim and James Lapine, dir. James Lapine, Plymouth Theatre, New York, 25 March 1994.

5.   This idea of a woman letting her man win in order to keep his love is a time-honored one and can even be seen in an early musical from the 1890s, *A Contented Woman,* in which a woman runs for mayor against her husband, but allows him to win.

6.   *Anyone Can Whistle,* by Stephen Sondheim and Arthur Laurents, perf. Scott Bakula, Madeline Kahn, and Bernadette Peters, Carnegie Hall, New York, 8 April 1995.

WORKS CITED

Banfield, Stephen. *Sondheim's Broadway Musicals.* Ann Arbor: U of Michigan P, 1993.

Buck, Joan Juliet. "Passion Play." *Vogue* May 1994, 277–79.

Coward, Noel. Foreword. *Musical Comedy.* By Raymond Mander and Joe Mitchenson. New York: Taplinger, 1969.

Goldstein, Richard M. "'I Enjoy Being a Girl': Women in the Plays of Rodgers and Hammerstein." *Popular Music and Society* 13.1 (1989): 1–8.

Gordon, Joanne. *Art Isn't Easy: The Theater of Stephen Sondheim.* New York: Da Capo, 1992.

Hammerstein, Oscar, II. *Lyrics.* Milwaukee: Hal Leonard, 1985.

Holden, Stephen. "A Fairy-Tale Musical Grows Up." *New York Times* 1 November 1987.

Kalem, T.E. Rev. of *Company,* by Stephen Sondheim and George Furth. *Time* 95(11 May 1970): 62.

Lahr, John. "Sondheim's Little Deaths." *Harper's* 258(Apr. 1979): 71–78.

McLaughlin, Robert L. "'No One is Alone': Society and Love in the Musicals of Stephen Sondheim." *Journal of American Drama and Theatre* 3(1991): 27–41.

Sondheim, Stephen, and George Furth. *Company.* New York: Random, 1970.

——, Larry Gelbart, and Burt Shevelove. *A Funny Thing Happened on the Way to the Forum.* New York: Applause, 1991.

———, and James Goldman. *Follies.* New York: Random, 1971.

———, and James Lapine. *Into the Woods.* New York: TCG, 1987.

———. *Passion.* New York: TCG, 1994.

———. *Sunday in the Park with George.* New York: Applause, 1991.

———, and Arthur Laurents. *Anyone Can Whistle.* New York: Leon Amiel, 1965.

———, and Hugh Wheeler. *A Little Night Music.* New York: Dodd, 1973.

Comedy Tonight!
A Funny Thing Happened on the Way to the Forum
Lois Kivesto

> Something familiar,
> Something peculiar,
> Something for everyone—a comedy tonight![1]

The creators of *A Funny Thing Happened on the Way to the Forum*, librettists Burt Shevelove and Larry Gelbart, and composer/lyricist Stephen Sondheim, set out to construct a musical comedy based on the style and spirit of the surviving plays of Titus Maccius Plautus, the third-century B.C. Roman playwright who taught Roman audiences to laugh for the first time at character and situation. Gelbart was pleased to observe the survival of "Plautus' aged, ageless writings based on man's gift for silliness, for pomposity and hypocrisy." Fortified by this discovery, the writers began to reformulate Plautus' material extracting a character here, a relationship there, as well as creating new material based on early twentieth-century burlesque conventions as the connective tissue to bond their work to the Roman antecedent (Shevelove et al. 2). The resultant compilation of characters and situations derives from five works of Plautine comedy: *Miles Gloriosus*, the braggart soldier; *Pseudolus*, the crafty slave; *Menaechmi*, twins separated at an early age; *Mostellaria*, the haunted house; and *Casina*, or the lot-drawers.

Scholar Erich Segal indicates in *Roman Laughter* that Plautus' twenty-one plays constitute the largest extant body of classical dramatic literature (1). Plautine comedy derives from several immediate sources from the fifth and fourth centuries B.C.: the popular *phylax* or gossip plays based on Greek legends; the crude, farcical Atellan plays; the solo mimes with musical accompaniment; and the main ingredient, the Greek New Comedy of Menander and his rival playwrights (Taylor 55–57). The New Comedy style was that of realistic, situational comedy about ordinary people, or "stock characters in stock situations" (Segal, *Comedies* x). Plautus did not invent these characters, but did with enormous skill and interest develop certain types (Segal, *Comedies* xv), which in turn caught the interest of *Forum* librettist Gelbart:

> the sly servants, those wily slaves, scheming and plotting and outwitting everyone in sight, constantly getting the upper hand on the upper class, which was largely composed of senile skirt-chasers and hen-pecked husbands, very often one and the same; domineering matrons, Gorgon-like women past their prime in every aspect of life but possessiveness; lovesick young men, so much in love they were sickening; and, of course, comely courtesans with hair and hearts of gold that you couldn't bring home without fear of possibly offending your mother— and the certainty of arousing your father. (Shevelove et al. 3)

Add the corrupt, greedy procurer and the swaggering, pompous soldier and the *dramatis personae* for both *Forum* and Plautus' many works is complete. It is not by chance that the creators of *Forum* chose the slave, Pseudolus, as their hero. In resurrecting the spirit of Plautine comedy, the ghost of its greatest hero was bound to be reincarnated also (Slater 118). Shevelove felt that although the emphasis on Pseudolus' desire for freedom in *Forum* was "extremely un-Roman" (qtd. in Zadan 68), it was used for stronger relevance to the modern audience.

A successful combination of "Roman convention and American invention" in the words of critic Robert Brustein (qtd. in Gordon 19), *Forum* is a worthy reworking of important dramatic stylistic traits from the earliest roots of comedy, including set design, female roles limited to those of courtesan or older woman (*matrona*), and textual use of prologue, aside, eavesdropping and epilogue. Sondheim has, in turn, considered the "one-set, one-costume" format of *Forum* to be an experimental one in the Broadway musical genre (qtd. in Savran 228).

A significant Plautine convention employed in the musical's adaptation is that of the song or *cantica*. The songs used by Plautus were styled on the popular music hall songs of his time (Law 5), and were in the form of lyric poetry accompanied by a reed pipe or *tibia* (Smith intro 8) Both the songs and recitatives were written in meters different

from the rest of the text in order to provide rhythmic contrast. They
were primarily emotional in content and of little narrative importance (Law 27). Shevelove encouraged Sondheim to use the songs in
Forum in the manner of the original Plautine sources (Sondheim 12),
as musical respites from the farcical action, in which as Stephen Citron has stated, the audience could "massage their ribs aching from
the laughter that zaniness on stage provided" (100n). Sondheim, having remarked, "...*Forum* is the best farce ever written.... It is never
not funny. The reason is, it is based on situations so solid that you
cannot *not* laugh," found it difficult to compose a score in which the
songs were not intentionally character-based in the integrated manner of the Rodgers and Hammerstein school in which he had been
raised" (Sondheim 11–12). In his first Broadway venture as com-
poser/lyricist, he developed a witty score which he has called "a vaudeville sound transmuted through my own style" (qtd. in Gottfried 63),
and "just a musical...a collection of songs...it virtually has no musical design" (Banfield 98).

   This "collection" of songs begins with the ensemble prologue
"Comedy Tonight," fondly dismissed by Sondheim as a "list" number (qtd. in Gordon 22). The direct, nimble lyrics announce the show
and provide what Stephen Banfield has termed "an anticipated rave
review set to music" (93). Just as words were a source of joy to Plautus,
with rich dramatic vocabulary drawn from a colloquial speech colored with puns, invented derivatives, and alliterations (Sandbach 123),
Sondheim's jocular wordplay in "Comedy Tonight" includes

> Nothing with gods,
> Nothing with fate.
> Weighty affairs will just have to wait.
> Nothing that's formal,
> Nothing that's normal,
> No recitations to recite! (20–21)

and

> Something that's gaudy,
> Something that's bawdy,
> Something for everybawdy—
> Comedy tonight! (23)

   The next number, "Love I Hear," is sung by the lovesick young
Hero. Before the comic plot lines have yet become complicated, Hero's

inner turmoil and confusion are reflected in the manner of an integrated song, by the juxtaposition of smooth musical and lyrical phrases:

> Love, they say,
> Makes you pine away,
> But you pine away
> With an idiotic grin.

and fragmented ones laden with clever internal rhymes:

> I pine, I blush,
> I squeak, I squawk.
> Today I woke
> Too weak to walk.
> What's love, I hear,
> I feel…I fear…
> I'm in. (29)

Both the melodic line and the lyrics reflect the sweet, naive qualities of Hero complete with a touch of vulnerability in the harmony. In the one instance of a musical correlation in the score, the counterpoint or second melody in the background of "Love I Hear," is the main melody in the verse of the next song entitled "Free," sung by Hero and his slave, Pseudolus (Gottfried 63).

Banfield has suggested that Plautus' reference to runaway slaves in *Menaechmi*:

> But if you wish to guard him so he won't run off,
> You ought to chain the man with lots of food and drink.
> Just bind the fellow's beak right to a well-stocked table,
> Provide the guy with eatables and drinkables,
> Whatever he would like to stuff himself each day.
> He'll never flee, though wanted for a murder charge.
> (Segal, *Comedies* 142).

is reflected in Sondheim's ironic lyrics in "Free":

> The way I am,
> I have a roof,
> Three meals a day,
> And I don't have to pay a thing…
> I'm just a slave and everything's free.
> If I were free,
> Then nothing would be free. (34)

In early drafts of the *Forum* dialogue, the fragment: "Spell it!...F-R-E-E" and the song cue: "*sing it*" predated the musical number (Banfield 86):

PSEUDOLUS:	Sing it!
HERO:	Free!
PSEUDOLUS:	Spell it!
HERO:	F-r-double...
PSEUDOLUS:	No, the long way...
HERO:	F-R-E-E-
BOTH:	FREE!!! (36)

The grand flourish of this vaudeville ending enhances the song's comic effect (Gordon 23).

Categorized by Banfield as a refrain song, with the title line as the point of arrival, the number is justified by Pseudolus' wish to be free. Throughout the song's discussion, the slave ironically leads while the master follows, although the latter is in control of the former's freedom. Contrasting the refrain song "Free" is the motif song "I'm Calm" later in Act One, in which the title line is the point of departure. Ambiguities in the musical elements of "I'm Calm" parallel the comic situation (Banfield 107–8). There is a hitch in the rhythmic flow of the song's initial $3/8$ time signature. A calm waltz then depicts the desired state of the hysterical slave, Hysterium, who is concealing the liaison of Hero and Philia (Gottfried 66):

> I'm calm, I'm cool,
> A gibbering fool
> Is something I never become!
> When thunder is rumbling
> And other are crumbling,
> I hum. (62)

The next musical number, "The House of Marcus Lycus," was abbreviated from a vivid extended song to an instrumental dance number for the introduction of the courtesans by their procurer. Sondheim has stated that Shevelove wanted this introduction conveyed through either song or dance, and opted for dance owing to the large amount of song in Act One (Shevelove et al. 147).

Citron has pointed out Sondheim's disapproval of the technique of reprises:

> I find the notion that the same lyric can apply in the first
> act and the second act *very* suspect.... In the case of *Fo-*
> *rum*, we did a reprise for comic intent. That is to say you
> heard the song again, but in an entirely different context,
> and in fact with a different lyric. (208)

"Lovely," sung in Act One by the attractive but dim-witted Philia, is
for Lehman Engel, "a love song that makes us laugh at all other love
songs" (qtd. in Gordon 27). For Philia, her loveliness is not a state of
being but rather, an occupation:

> I'm lovely,
> All I am is lovely,
> Lovely is the one thing I can do.
> Winsome,
> What I am is winsome,
> Radiant as in some
> Dream come true. (45)

Building on this subtle comedy, the Act Two reprise of the song depicts the slave, Hysterium, disguised as a dead virgin by Pseudolus,
as:

> ...lovely,
> Frighteningly lovely,
> That the world will never seem the same! (117)

The counterpart of the prologue "Comedy Tonight" is the epilogue
of the same name, in which the plot conclusions are reiterated to
great comic effect. The beleaguered Senex's "a tragedy tonight" provides what Banfield has called "the unforgettable final structural
complement—the last joke, if you like—to all that has been going on
(121).

From an almost identical situation and phrase in Plautus' *Miles*
Gloriosus: "Pretty picture—please proceed" (Segal, *Comedies* 100),
Sondheim develops the song "Pretty Little Picture." In this song,
Pseudolus uses alliterative word-play and imagery to carry Hero and
his love, Philia, on an imaginary journey of escape:

> And far behind
> At the edge of day,
> The bong of the bell of the buoy in the bay,
> And the boat and the boy and the bride are away!
> It's a pretty little picture to share.... (51)

Gottfried has suggested that this song "demonstrates how a composer and a lyricist can inspire each other to higher levels even when they are the same person." He cites as examples the series of alliterations throughout the song on virtually repeating pulses, and the clear introduction to each of the song's three verses by means of a prefatory lyric ("Well"; "Now"; "Think") followed by a musical rest. Banfield has indicated that the melodic and rhythmic components which combine to form a syncopated bass rhythm of three beats against four in "Pretty Little Picture":

> No worries,
> No bothers,
> No captains,
> No fathers! (51)

point towards a rhythmic motif and a "mesh of pointillistic elements cutting across lyrical ones" used in many of Sondheim's later scores (Banfield 106).

"Everybody Ought to Have a Maid" may have begun with Sondheim's notes:

> *Two Fathers.*—Ironic satire on September Song: by the time you've perfected the art of love, it's too late. Or: Giggly remembrances, interrupted phrases—(e.g. Prettiest Girl I ever—darn near broke the chariot—) all left to the imagination. (qtd. in Banfield 97)

This number is, according to Gottfried, "the only old-fashioned showstopper that Sondheim would ever write" (65), and according to Gordon, "the ideal lyric and musical structure to express the style of *Forum* (27). The comic device in this song is the burlesque technique of additive encores as the duet of lechers gradually becomes a quartet. The additive phrasing in:

> ALL: Everybody ought to have a maid.
> Everybody ought to have a serving girl,
> A loyal and unswerving girl
> Who's quieter than a mouse. (58)

supports the encore device which concludes with comic bawdiness (Banfield 97):

> ALL: Everybody ought to have a maid!
> Someone who'll be busy as a bumblebee

	And even if you grumble, be
	As graceful as a grouse!
LYCUS:	Wriggling in the anteroom.
HYSTERIUM:	Jiggling in the living-room,
PSEUDOLUS:	Giggling in the dining-room,
SENEX:	Wiggling in the other rooms,
ALL:	Puttering all around
	The house! (60)

"Impossible" emphasizes similarities and ambiguities in the vacillating views of father, Senex, and son, Hero, as they both long for the same courtesan, Philia:

SENEX:	Just a fledgling in the nest...
HERO:	Just a man who needs a rest...
SENEX:	He's a beamish boy at best...
HERO:	Poor old fellow...
SENEX:	He's a child and love's a test
	He's too young to pass—impassable!...
SENEX:	He's a handsome lad of twenty,
	I'm thirty-nine—it's possible!
HERO:	Older men know so much more...
SENEX:	In a way, I'm forty-four...
HERO:	Next to him, I'll seem a bore...
SENEX:	All right, fifty! (68–69)

Sondheim employs a direct translation from the Plautine original, *Miles Gloriosus*, "I am a parade!" for the introduction of the braggart soldier of the same name in *Forum*. This favorite comic line of Sondheim's (Gottfried 66) is at the center of Miles' strident, blatantly pompous march:

Let haste be made,
I cannot be delayed!
There are lands to conquer,
Cities to loot,
And peoples to degrade! (79)

Banfield has stated that in *Forum*, Sondheim has not as yet started to develop the range of his female characters. In keeping with the reduced status of Plautine female roles, neither Domina nor Philia has a great deal of satisfactory music that is clearly her own (102). The first song in Act Two is Domina's "That Dirty Old Man," a blues number concerning her husband, Senex, whose title gives away its comic punch (Gottfried 66). In the next number, Philia's "That'll Show Him," the humor is in the dramatic action and outside the song itself, as Hero's frustration mounts at Philia's plans to thwart Miles (Banfield 97):

> When I hold him,
> I'll be holding you,
> So I'll hold him ten times as tight,
> That'll show him, too! (114)

At director George Abbott's suggestion, and against Sondheim's wishes, the accompaniment for "That'll Show Him" is presented as a tango rhythm in the orchestration by Irwin Kostal and Sid Ramin. Gottfried has commented that the song is not unified in its construction and, with little musical interest, "is about as workaday as anything Sondheim ever wrote" (66).

The final new musical number in Act Two is the "Funeral Sequence and Dance," set in the Lydian mode and filled with melismatic wailing for Miles' supposedly dead virgin (Banfield 100). Amidst archaism and florid emotions, Miles, ever the military commander, laments:

> Sound the flute,
> Blow the horn,
> Pluck the lute,
> Forward…mourn! (120)

The creators of *Forum* had hoped to prove that Plautus' one-dimensional characters and his complicated style of plotting were timeless (Gelbart in Shevelove et al. 4). Critic Clive Barnes affirmed their achievement in his *New York Times* review:

> This is the funniest, bawdiest and most enchanting Broadway musical that Plautus, with a little help from Stephen Sondheim, Burt Shevelove and Larry Gelbart, ever wrote. (Qtd. in Zadan 76)

In general, the production received the rave reviews, but not the score. While *Forum* won the 1963 Tony Award as Best Musical, Sondheim did not receive a nomination for his first Broadway score, one which Gottfried has termed "a generally delicious score, original yet still traditional, musicianly without pushing a fistful of notes in the audience's face" (66–67). At the time of the 1972 Broadway revival of *Forum*, Shevelove noted a marked increase in the appreciation and comprehension of the score by an audience now attuned to the sparkling musical and lyrical intricacies of other complete Sondheim scores (Zadan 76). Two additional decades of Sondheim's work have developed an even more conversant audience for the 1996 Broadway revival.

Forum, being "neither a musical musical nor a book musical," according to Gottfried, "is a thing of its own kind" (63). Considered by Sondheim, more than two decades after its creation, to be "the only really popular show I ever had" (qtd. in Gottfried 67), *Forum* owes much to its roots in antiquity. Segal eloquently traces the continuum from ancient Rome to the original production of *Forum*:

> The most obvious monuments to her [Rome's] craftsmanship are the aqueducts which still carry water, the bridges and highways which can still be travelled. But when Zero Mostel as Pseudolus trod nightly on his way to the Broadway forum, he was walking another Roman road of astounding durability. (Segal, *Laughter* 14)

ဆ

NOTE

1. Stephen Sondheim, lyrics, *A Funny Thing Happened on the Way to the Forum* by Burt Shevelove, Larry Gelbart, and Stephen Sondheim (New York: Applause, 1991), 19. All subsequent quotations will be from this edition, with page numbers cited parenthetically within the text.

WORKS CITED

Banfield, Stephen. *Sondheim's Broadway Musicals*. Ann Arbor: U of Michigan P, 1993.

Citron, Stephen. *The Musical From the Inside Out*. London: Hodder & Stoughton, 1991.

Gordon, Joanne. *Art Isn't Easy: The Achievement of Stephen Sondheim*. Carbondale: Southern Illinois UP, 1990.

Gottfried, Martin. *Sondheim.* New York: Abrams, 1993.

Law, Helen Hull. *Studies in the Songs of Plautine Comedy.* Chicago: U of Chicago P, 1922.

Sandbach, F.H. *The Comic Theatre of Greece and Rome.* London: Chatto, 1977.

Savran, David. *In Their Own Words.* New York: Theatre Communications, 1988.

Segal, Erich, trans. *Plautus: Three Comedies.* New York: Harper, 1969.

——. *Roman Laughter: The Comedy of Plautus.* Cambridge: Harvard UP, 1968.

Shevelove, Burt, Larry Gelbart, and Stephen Sondheim. *A Funny Thing Happened on the Way to the Forum.* Intro. Larry Gelbart. New York: Applause, 1991.

Slater, Niall W. *Plautus in Performance.* Princeton: Princeton UP, 1985.

Smith, Peter L., trans. *Plautus: Three Comedies.* Ithaca: Cornell UP, 1991.

Sondheim, Stephen. "The Musical Theater." *Dramatists Guild Quarterly* Autumn 1978: 6–29.

Taylor, David. *Acting and the Stage.* London: Allen, 1978.

Zadan, Craig. *Sondheim & Co.* 2nd ed. New York: Harper, 1989.

Company—
25 Years Later
John Olson

Musical comedies have most often been set in fantasy worlds. Their creators have used the art form to carry us into romantic places—the idealized past, far off countries, mythology, fairy tales, exotic big cities, charming rural towns—but rarely the world we actually inhabit. Is that because it may be too jarring to listen to characters who otherwise look and speak like us as they transition from realistic dialogue into song? Maybe it's easier to accept this in a context in which we've already suspended our disbelief while viewing an environment that we've never experienced. Is it that the music helps create these fantasy worlds—making the art form uniquely able to present escapist entertainment? Do the colorful sets and costumes of exotic locales add production values to big-ticket prices? Or are the creators and investors concerned about making the piece "timeless" enough that audiences will want to view it for decades, and increase the chances for profit in a business in which return on investment can take many years?

All of these considerations probably have some bearing on the fact that we have few musical comedies set in the present. Only a handful have attempted to portray, without analogy or disguise, some aspect of contemporary life. (Jonathan Larson's 1996 Pulitzer Prize–winning *Rent* is a rare and recent exception).

Company is one of the few Broadway musicals of the past 30 years to reflect the environment and lives of its original audiences. Like some other shows of its time (*Promises, Promises, How Now Dow Jones, Seesaw*), it presents stories about "present-day" New Yorkers. And while it is revived more frequently than these contemporaries, its original 1970 setting is considered to be problematic and a barrier to successful revival. If not for the reputation of its composer-lyricist Stephen Sondheim and the importance of the piece to his canon, perhaps *Company* would have been similarly forgotten. Had Sondheim left the musical theater after *Company* (as did *Promises* composer Burt Bacharach), or were he viewed less reverentially, as merely an accomplished Broadway composer like *Seesaw's* Cy Coleman rather than a cultural icon, we might not feel compelled to revisit the show. (Although Coleman is one of Broadway's most successful composers of the last 30 years, he has yet to be studied in the manner that Sondheim has. And it is unlikely that we'll soon see a Carnegie Hall performance of Coleman's early work at up to $500 per ticket, as Sondheim enjoyed for his 1964 flop *Anyone Can Whistle* in 1995.)

Company remains one of Sondheim's less-frequently performed works, with the Roundabout Theater Company's 1995 revival being the show's first Broadway production since the original. In fact, as noted by *The New York Times*, it was the first revival of *Company* for a "large audience" anywhere in the New York area (Baldinger). Critical reaction to this production was mixed, but generally positive. A frequently voiced concern about the show was that its book, by George Furth, was dated.

This reaction raises major questions not only about the significance of *Company* in the Sondheim oeuvre, but also to the potential for contemporary-themed musicals on the Broadway stage. For if a show with the pedigree of *Company* was too dated for a successful revival on Broadway, while the 1927 period musical *Show Boat* was playing to capacity audiences just down the street, was it likely that a lesser talent than Sondheim would ever create a musical with a present-day setting that could survive for more than a few years? *Company* was a critical success in 1970, and won seven Tony Awards—the most for any musical in the award's history up to that point. Since then, its songs have been among Sondheim's most performed works in compilation recordings and "tribute" performances. So there appears to be little question that *Company* is an "important" musical, yet it remains one of Sondheim's less frequently produced shows.

Additionally, *Company* is Sondheim's only show as composer-lyricist set in an unambiguous present. *Anyone Can Whistle* is described as a "musical fable" in its published script. Its time frame, while apparently the present, is not specified. Further, it has a surreal quality that distances it from a realistic present. The action of *Follies* occurs both in the 1940s memories of its four protagonists and in a "present" that for logistical reasons must remain the early '70s. Since the characters

Sally and Phyllis were 20-ish chorus girls in the final years (the early 1940s) of a Ziegfeld-like *Follies*, and since they are in their fifties today, the present-day action must, for historical and arithmetic reasons, take place in the early '70s, although that time period has no other significance to the story or characters.[1] The action of *Merrily We Roll Along* occurs over a 25-year period, from 1981 *backwards* to 1956. Sondheim's remaining shows are clearly set in historical or fantasy worlds.

The original script for *Company* describes the scene as "New York City, NOW" (Furth & Sondheim 644) and *Company* is the purest example of a Sondheim show set in the "present," but that isn't the only reason for its importance. *Company* can also serve as a case history for examination of musical comedy as a vehicle for expressing a vision of contemporary life. Sondheim's reputation as master of the art form makes this show a particularly good specimen for study.

The degree to which a musical or play, originally written to depict its time, may still be played as "contemporary," or may even survive as a period piece that has continued relevance to a wide audience, will depend upon several criteria. The following criteria will be used for this analysis of *Company*.

(1) Does the *premise* or *central theme* of the musical remain equally believable, important or challenging to today's audiences?

(2) Does the *specific action* and do the *characters* remain believable and realistic as occurring in the present, in light of contemporary lifestyle practices?

(3) Are there elements of the *dialogue* or *music* that would suggest that the action is occurring in a earlier time rather than the present?

(4) How might the *audience's perspective* toward the material have changed since the show's original production? What experiences do they bring to viewing a production that may be different from those of the audiences of the era in which the show was first produced?

Assuming that there are elements of the show that might be dated, we can also ask the following questions:

(1) How easily *can a production team "update" the musical* without rewriting that would violate the authors' copyright protection? Elements that are generally considered

appropriately the venue of an individual production's director include wardrobe, set design, props and interpretation of the script—both dialogue and blocking.

(2) How could the *authors—composer, librettist and lyricist—update the show* if they chose to? Sondheim and Furth had the opportunity to make updates for two major revivals of the work in 1995—the previously mentioned New York revival by the Roundabout Theater Company which opened in October 1995, and the Donmar Warehouse production in London, which opened in December of the same year. It's illuminating to view the choices the authors made in preparing the show for its first major revivals in 25 years.

The Theme

Company examines committed relationships and marriage from the perspective that adults have the choice to enter or *not to enter* such relationships. It departs from the traditional musical-comedy perspective of meeting-pursuit-and-capture between a male and a female, and instead, looks at five couples who are already in committed relationships when the action begins. These couples are friends of a 35-year-old single man by the name of Robert (or Bobby). He's a best friend to them all and has the opportunity to examine their relationships or marriages from a close distance. They often wonder why he's not married and frequently suggest that he should be, even though the men sometimes envy his singlehood and the women fear losing his friendship whenever he does seem to approach a committed relationship.

Bobby learns, through the course of the musical, that the essence of a relationship is *compromise*. Partners frequently have to give up their independence, their comfort and some freedom in order to maintain a relationship. Sondheim, speaking about *Company*, said "Show me a good marriage and I'll show you a difficult relationship" (Sondheim "Conversation"). The theme is summarized in *Company*'s climactic song, "Being Alive."

> Someone to hold you too close,
> Someone to hurt you too deep,
> Someone to sit in your chair,
> To ruin your sleep…. (114)[2]

In a song cut from the original production, but reinstated for both the Roundabout and Donmar revivals, Bobby pictures an ideal relationship in which he wouldn't have to compromise. He could receive just what he wants from a wife, without any sacrifices.

> Marry me a little,
> Love me just enough.
> Cry but not too often,
> Play but not too rough.
> Keep a tender distance,
> So we'll both be free.
> That's the way it ought to be.
> I'm Ready! (69)

"Marry Me a Little," originally written for the spot in which "Being Alive" now appears, was used in the Roundabout and Donmar productions as the Act I finale. By the end of Act II, Bobby realizes that his ideal vision was impossible—there's no opportunity for a real, lasting relationship without giving up some of himself and putting up with the pain as well as the pleasure. In "Being Alive," he sings of his willingness, finally, to enter such a relationship.

Scott Ellis, director of the Roundabout production, says, "I don't think what any of the couples or Bobby is going through is any different today than it was in 1970" (interview). Indeed, Bobby's imperative to either choose to live his life with another or to *choose not to do so* may be one of the most compelling decisions adults face in the late 20th century. While in earlier eras, the economic structure of society pushed most adults into marriage (job opportunities were limited for women and men were generally unprepared to maintain a household), that phenomenon is no longer true in this era.

In fact, the ability to choose singlehood over marriage is probably greater now than it was in 1970, particularly for women. Career opportunities have improved in the past two decades and it has become easier and more acceptable for women to pursue a career rather than choosing to work in the home in the context of a marriage. Although it might have seemed improbable in 1970, *Company's* indecisive protagonist could now as easily be a Roberta as a Robert.

Census statistics support the theory that audiences may find the challenge of choosing between marriage and singlehood even more an issue and less of a foregone conclusion today than they did in 1970. In 1970, U.S. marriage rates were 10.6 annually per 1,000 population. By 1992, this rate had fallen to 9.3 marriages annually per 1,000 population (Dept. of Commerce 75).

Another dimension to the theme of choosing partnering over monogamy is the decision to *remain* in a marriage as well as enter into one. In fact, one of *Company*'s five couples, Susan and Peter, announce in Act I that they've decided to divorce. Their action mirrors a dramatic increase in divorce rates between the year of *Company*'s Broadway premiere and the early '90s. In 1970, the U.S. divorce rate was 3.5 divorces per 1,000 population. By 1992 that rate had risen to 4.8 divorces per 1,000 population (Dept. of Commerce 75).

The ratio of marriages to divorces is particularly telling. In 1970, that ratio was roughly three marriages to one divorce. In 1992, the ratio was just below two marriages to one divorce, using the data cited above. These census data show that Americans have in fact come to view marriage more as an *option* rather than a *requirement* since *Company* first opened. Based on this trend, it is certainly realistic to assume that Bobby's angst over contemplating marriage must continue to have resonance for audiences in the late 1990s and that *Company*'s theme remains relevant and is not dated. And if so, it merits continued attention and production for current audiences.

The theme may, however, be less revolutionary as a topic for entertainment than it was in 1970. *Company*'s action reflects a number of societal changes that began in the late 1960s. Traditional marriages and family values had begun to be questioned. The practice of couples living together without benefit of marriage was still somewhat avantgarde if no longer scandalous. Adults had begun to wait at least a little later in life to enter into marriage. The term "swinging single" quickly became a cliché, and the concept of "singles bars" began in New York, as typified by places like Maxwell's Plum on the Upper East Side of Manhattan. The decision to delay marriage—at least for a while—had become socially acceptable. *Company* was considered a landmark effort for putting these societal changes on the musical stage.

Most of the successful earlier musicals are based upon the assumption that their characters want, need, and deserve a loving, committed partnership with a member of the opposite sex. Their dramatic tension came from the pursuit of such a relationship, usually with a potential partner that is an opposite in other respects as well. *My Fair Lady*'s Henry Higgins is educated and affluent while Eliza is poor and uneducated. *The Music Man*, Professor Harold Hill, is a flashy conman pursuing plain Marian the Librarian. In *West Side Story,* Tony is Anglo, while Maria is Puerto Rican. And *Brigadoon's* Tommy and Fiona have to deal with a difference in their ages—some 200 years, in fact!

These classic musicals all end with the opposites attracting and falling in love. *Company* challenges this romantic fantasy by examining the difficulties of maintaining relationships between lovers who, regardless of their similarities or "opposite-attractions," are unique and different people who must learn to compromise their personal needs and independence in order to allow their relationships to survive. So even if *Company* wasn't the first musical to depict the difficulty of love among contemporary New Yorkers, it may have been the first to challenge the romantic ideal of committed relationships that formed the basis of most Broadway musical plots.

Part of the charge that *Company* is dated comes from the observation that this unromantic view of loving relationships is no longer revolutionary on the Broadway stage or in entertainment in general. Yet, the fact that this show may have been ahead of its time should hardly make it dated in the 1990s if it now only reflects its time.

Sondheim has also spoken of a secondary theme to *Company*. He writes that the show is also about "the increasing difficulty of making emotional connections in an increasingly dehumanized society" (qtd. in Zadan 177). Scott Miller, who directed a 1995 production of *Company* in St. Louis, believes this theme to be even more valid in 1995 than it was in 1970:

> With more and more technology that allows us to conduct our lives without actually ever talking to people in person—faxes, the Internet, e-mail, voice mail, ATMs, answering machines, etc.—I think Bobby's inability to connect makes more sense now than it did 25 years ago. It's so easy to not connect to other people these days. (Interview)

The Donmar Warehouse production developed this theme in a new opening scene in which Bobby, upon entering his apartment, listens to messages on his answering machine left by other characters. Later, in the title song, the couples' invitations to Bobby in the title song can be interpreted as messages on an answering machine, since they've been, as they sing, "trying to reach" him all day (9), and since the messages are all one-sided. We don't hear Bobby respond to them.

Action and Situations

Given the continued validity of *Company's* theme, we ask whether it is developed through specific actions and situations that will appear true if they are intended to be read as occurring in the present. Three of the scenes involving the five married couples would seem to have no dated elements, while the scenes of the remaining two may be more problematic. The first scene, which involves the competitive and combative Sarah and Harry, should play quite believably in the present. Sarah's trying to eat more sensibly and lose weight. Harry's trying to quit drinking, and may be alcoholic. Both of these health concerns remain common today, although perhaps the recognition of alcoholism as a serious illness has grown to the point where it would no longer be played for humor, as it is here. The scenes involving Susan and Peter—the couple who announce happily that they are getting a divorce—and Amy and Paul—who may or may not be "getting married today" seem to have no dated elements whatever.

The action of the remaining two couples, however, present activity that is not particularly commonplace, or typical in the mid-'90s. Yet, if we look at these characters as individuals and not as '90s archetypes, we can find them to be credible present-day adults. Jenny and David join Bobby for a marijuana-smoking session in the scene that establishes this couple's relationship. Jenny has obviously never smoked dope before. Bobby and David have. In 1970, marijuana was still emerging as a presumably "safe" drug and it was somewhat fashionable, maybe "risqué" to give it a try. In the mid-'90s, the drug seems to have little of this mystique and it would be unlikely for a sophisticated Manhattanite to have never tried it. Yet, the dialogue establishes that Jenny may not be typical. David describes her as "square" (a dated term)..."dumb" (46) and that "she doesn't get things like that" (45). Her dialogue risks becoming dated when she says, in reference to their drug experience, "we were all—trying to keep up with the kids tonight" (45). The audience may wonder what she's thinking. In 1995, it's not unlikely that her parents may have already tried pot, so why would pot smoking be a province of the young? But given David's description of Jenny as "square," maybe *she* would believe that it is. Scott Ellis contends that Jenny's statement is the "excuse that pulled her back into the mode she was more comfortable with, and that she believes her husband accepts" (interview).

The relationship of Joanne and Larry may appear even more atypical in the nineties. Joanne is, in essence, an upper-class housewife. Her husband is rich, and Joanne, like her fellow "ladies who lunch," doesn't work outside the home. Since they presumably can afford domestic help, she probably doesn't have to work much *inside* the home either. The routine of women like Joanne includes, in the lyrics of "The Ladies Who Lunch," going

> Off to the gym,
> Then to a fitting,
> Claiming they're fat.
> And looking grim
> 'Cause they've been sitting
> Choosing a hat —
> Does anyone still wear a hat?
> I'll drink to that. (106)

A later line in the lyric provides one of the more dated references in the show as Joanne describes the women who are...

> Keeping house but clutching a copy of *Life*
> Just to keep in touch. (107)

The lyric would have been even more dated if *Life* magazine had not resumed publication after a several-year hiatus sometime after *Company*'s original run. Still, it's probably not viewed as a vehicle of choice for "keeping in touch" in the nineties.

Working women, particularly professional women, are more common today than in 1970. The rise of feminist thinking in the '70s and '80s has made it unfashionable to live entirely off the career and earnings of one's husband. Today, a "lady who lunches" would probably at least be heavily involved in civic or charitable activities rather than spending her afternoons simply viewing a "matinée, a Pinter play, perhaps a piece of Mahler's" (106). At best, she may have an impressive career and reputation of her own.

Yet certainly, in some circles, particularly upper income ones, women like Joanne must still exist, in spite of the fact that they could pattern their lives after more positive role models. Ellis, a Manhattanite himself who would have the opportunity to meet a Joanne, insists that he does know some of these "dinosaurs surviving the crunch"

(108), to echo a lyric from "The Ladies Who Lunch" (interview).

The greater point to be made about Joanne's life, and the lives of the women like her, is that they exist in the shadows of husbands who have more visible, more lucrative careers than their wives. These wives may feel, as Joanne does, that they are mere "supporting players" in the lives of their successful spouses. In fact, George Furth later wrote a nonmusical comedy, *The Supporting Cast*, which celebrates the contributions made by behind-the-scenes spouses on behalf of their successful mates. Joanne, however, feels uncelebrated and is resentful of her husband's success.

It would seem that in virtually any marriage, one partner will be more successful than the other, and that there is always the risk that the less successful, less visible partner will feel less important. From this perspective, Joanne's experience should still find empathetic audiences.

But like the pot-smoking scene, Joanne's situation may not read as quickly as "NOW" as it did in 1970, and there is probably no easy way to minimize that problem, short of creating a new character and losing the legendary "Ladies Who Lunch" number.

Bobby's scenes with his three girlfriends include only one situation that might be less probable in the '90s. His sexual conquest of a "stewardess" is, for audiences who would remember the era, a depiction of a particularly '60s kind of fantasy—the suave bachelor seducing a hot "stew." Now that stewardesses are "flight attendants" and may also be males or married women as well as single ones, this image seems less appropriate. A younger audience, however, might not share the disadvantage of remembering the old "stew" stereotype and could instead view flight attendant April as simply one example of a working woman who travels for her job. Today, April could as likely be a young businesswoman in town for a trade show as she might be a "stewardess." However, this would make it harder to believe that she could be as "dumb" as she describes herself. If she's traveling to "Barcelona" for her job, as she explains in the song of that title, what kind of job would require a "dumb" woman to travel internationally? Again, we risk undermining one of the musical's signature numbers if the authors had chosen to change April's occupation for this revival.

Perhaps Bobby's promiscuity in bedding April might also be seen as anachronistic given the greater fears in the '90s of AIDS and other sexually transmitted diseases. But who's to say he doesn't slip on a condom before sex? Their sexual activity occurs offstage and there's no need to present the details of the encounter any more explicitly.

Period References in the Dialogue and Music

There are few period references in either the dialogue or music that would anchor *Company* in the late '60s/early '70s. The script is relatively devoid of period slang, and it lacks any references to pop culture, political figures, or "current events" that might set the action around 1970. One slightly dated action, in the second scene of Act I, occurs when Harry offers Robert a Bourbon. Given the decline of "brown" liquors since 1970, it's more likely that today he'd be offered a beer or wine. Yet, Bourbon has hardly disappeared as an alcoholic beverage and it's not improbable that Bobby might be offered one.

In approaching the Roundabout's Broadway revival, the authors might have attempted some updates of the action and dialogue that could have set the show more clearly in the present. Some details might have been easily updated—changing Bobby's drink from Bourbon to beer, or clutching a copy of some other magazine than *Life*. But the nature of Joanne and April's occupations could not be changed without threatening the integrity of two key musical numbers, "The Ladies Who Lunch" and "Barcelona," and without requiring significant rethinking of the Joanne and April characters themselves. Ellis says, "You have to be truthful. You have to serve the piece. The essence of who April is can't change. If you were to stamp (*Company*) as 1995, each change could start a 'domino effect' that would require the whole structure of the piece to change." Ellis had another reason for seeking a timeless setting. "I didn't want it to be 1995. Then in another year it would be dated again" (interview).

Interestingly, the only lyric change for the 1995 production was to change a reference in "You Could Drive a Person Crazy" from "fag" to "gay" (42). This change would not have been necessary for mere updating, and was presumably made to show greater sensitivity to the diversity of theater audiences and society in general.

The music is similarly timeless. Sondheim's score reflects his classical influences, which he describes as Ravel, Britten and Stravinsky ("Conversation"), more than it does any other Broadway scores of the period. He does include two historical pastiches: "You Could Drive a Person Crazy"—a takeoff on the Andrews Sisters style from the

1940s— and "Side by Side by Side," which recalls the songs of vaudeville and the English music halls. But because these numbers were deliberately dated for comic or ironic effect—and never intended to reflect the time of the musical's action—they play in precisely the same manner today as they did when first performed. They are no more or no less dated than they were at that time.

The original orchestrations incorporated electronic sounds that became popular in the late '60s and sound dated today. They were updated for the Roundabout production by the original arranger, Jonathan Tunick, so that they would have less of a period sound.

Production Design

Production design offers directors perhaps their greatest opportunity to personalize a piece. It gives them the chance to update the show without actually rewriting it and violating copyright law. The original *Company* production team clearly worked to establish its action in the present. Costumes reflected ultra-trendy fashions of the time that would probably have been laughable a few years after the Broadway opening.

The Roundabout revival used a neutral design that could play as either 1970 or 1995. Tony Walton's set had a neo–Art Deco appearance reflective of architectural styles that have been popular in New York for many years. Ellis says that all the costumes were chosen to reflect designs that could have been found at retail in either 1970 or 1995. Most of the characters were dressed in classic, conservative fashions. Bobby's eccentric girlfriend Marta, however, wears an eclectic collection of elements that Ellis says could probably be found today in shops in New York's East Village (interview).

The stewardess April was dressed in a '70s-style uniform, complete with a pillbox hat that highlighted the period stereotype of her character rather than minimizing it. Ellis admits that the pillbox hat would pretty hard to find at retail today, and may have skewed audience perception of the character from "timeless" to seventies (interview).

Scott Miller chose to deliberately set his production in the nineties. Without the involvement of the authors or the option of making script and lyric changes, he used props and incidental music to achieve this setting.[3] He describes his approach to the title number: "Instead of a busy signal at the beginning of 'Company' we have contemporary phone dialing and ringing noises. Everyone is holding a cell phone or cordless phone. The disco scene is now in a '90s dance club instead of a 'disco'..." (Miller, Sat. Rev.). To establish this scene, he created an arrangement of 'Company' reminiscent of the techno-flavored version featured in the documentary film, 'Exposed'" (Miller interview).

Changes in Audience Perspective

Scott Ellis says, "I felt that if we focused on the characters and the relationships, the audiences wouldn't be concerned if it was 1970 or 1995." He explains that it was more important for his production to get the audiences "involved with the people...involved with their journey" (interview) than to create a particular era. But even if the characters' journeys are timeless, there may be changes in the audiences' perspective on the piece a generation later.

Today, audiences may be better prepared to analyze and understand the human relationships portrayed in *Company*. There is strong evidence to suggest that Americans have become more "psychologically minded," to borrow a term from the mental health profession. From U.S. Census data, we can infer that expenditures on mental health services have risen dramatically since 1970. In 1970, total expenditures for the census category that includes mental health services (along with other services such as registered nurses, physical therapy, ophthalmology and visiting nurses) were only $1.5 billion. In 1991 total expenditures in this category had risen to $35.8 billion, an increase of nearly 24 times (Dept. of Commerce 110).

In addition to receiving professional mental health services, a large number of Americans are pursuing methods of self-help. An estimated 7.5 million adults participated in a self-help group such as Alcoholics Anonymous during 1992, according to a 1993 study (Lieberman & Snowden). While there were apparently no similar studies conducted in 1970 that would provide comparative data, it seems that the direct participation of some 4% of the adult US population has created some familiarity—either first-hand or through family or friends—with the basic concepts and buzz words of the self-help movement. Further evidence that the concepts of self-help have become widely known can be found in the observation that the popular network television program *Saturday Night Live* began to satirize self-help groups in 1991, when character Stuart Smalley made his first appearance. Stuart is "...a caring nurturer, a member of several twelve-step programs, but not a licensed therapist." He is also, "co-dependent, an adult child of an alcoholic, a recovering overeater, and a perfectionist (Cader 255). He tells audiences "I'm good enough, I'm smart enough, and doggone it, people *like* me!" (Cader 257).

Some of the common terms of self-help literature that might be used to analyze *Company*'s characters are *denial, co-dependency, control, self-esteem, risk-taking, approach-avoidance, people-pleasing,* and *fear of intimacy.* So in 1995, perhaps audiences not only recognized *Company*'s characters from their life experiences, but maybe they also knew how to describe and classify their behaviors.

We can imagine that Sarah already attends an Overeaters Anonymous group. Her husband Harry should be going to AA, but it appears that he's in *denial* (which Stuart Smalley tells us "ain't just a river in Egypt"). Harry still *denies* that he has a drinking problem.

Jenny's husband David could be seen as having an issue with *control.* When he tires of the fling with marijuana that he, Jenny, and Robert share, he makes it clear to her that she should stop smoking now as well.

> ROBERT: Shall I roll another one?
> JENNY: Maybe one.
> DAVID: No.
> ROBERT: I can roll one in a second.
> DAVID: No.
> JENNY: No more?
> DAVID: (*A moment. Then looks at Jenny*) I don't think so.
> JENNY: (*After a pause*) I don't think so either.
> ROBERT: It'll just take a second to make another one.
> (*There is a long pause*)
> DAVID: Listen, you two have one.
> JENNY: I don't want one.
> DAVID: Have one if you want one.
> JENNY: But I don't. (*A pause*) I'll get some food. (*She embraces David*) Isn't he a marvelous man? (674)

David uses a shorthand that Jenny reads quickly, while it takes Bobby longer to figure out what's going on. She acquiesces to David immediately, even though she was clearly enjoying the drug. Is she *co-dependent*, so concerned about maintaining his approval that she foregoes her apparent preference to keep smoking? Or was she only smoking pot to please him in the first place? David even displays some signs of an *abusive spouse*—not only through his efforts to control her action, but in his verbal put-downs of Jenny as "dumb" later on:

> ROBERT: She loved it.
> DAVID: For *me*. She loved it for me. She didn't really love it. I know her. She's what she said… square…dumb…. (46)

The increased attention and presumably greater understanding of spousal abuse that has developed in the past 25 years gives David and Jenny's relationship a new and much more disturbing perspective than audiences probably brought to it in 1970.

The next couple depicted in *Company* provides some comic relief from the unsettling episode of David and Jenny. Poor Amy, the bride who swears she's not "getting married today," merely suffers from problems of *self-esteem*. In that song, she explains her fears that her husband-to-be Paul will suddenly realize he's "saddled with a nut and wanna kill me, which he should" (59).

And what about Bobby? Bobby's harder to read. His girlfriends sing that "He's a truly crazy person / Himself" (42). Are we any better able to understand Bobby and his reluctance to enter into a committed relationship today? If Bobby were to attend some 12-step group meetings in the nineties, what issues would he work on? As many critics and observers of the show have observed, he's a cipher.

Most of the 1995 revisions to the libretto included in the Donmar Warehouse production apparently were written to help clarify Bobby's character. In Bobby's Act One visit to Jenny and David's home, there is a new speech in which Bobby explains why he didn't get married when he was younger.

> ROBERT: I've always had things to accomplish. That's the main reason. First I had to finish school. Then I wanted to get started, to get some kind of security. And, uh—just things I wanted to do before I could even begin to think in terms of marriage. Oh, I know that can sound like rationalization, but it's not. Frankly, I wanted to have some fun before I settled down. (40)

Other revisions in the libretto attempt to dispel the frequent interpretation by critics of Bobby as a closeted homosexual. The Act

II scene at Susan and Peter's apartment now ends with an exchange in which Bobby states explicitly that he's not gay, and ignores a sexual advance from Peter (102–3). Additionally, one of the answering machine messages in the opening scene comes from Marta, who reassures Bobby that she's not pregnant and that he can relax (4)—providing further evidence beyond his sexual encounter with April just before the song "Barcelona," that he is a sexually active heterosexual.

Despite these additions, Bobby remains a character that is, by his own making, hard to read, because he rarely expresses his own feelings. Up until his climactic scene with Joanne, his statements to others seem designed to make the others feel good. When Joanne offers to take care of him, and he answers, "then who will I take care of?" (111) it's the first time he expresses anything about his own needs.

Since Bobby tells us so little about his own feelings, our impressions of Bobby's motives will vary depending upon the interpretation of the character given by the actor and director. Bobby may simply want the others to *like* him—making him a *people pleaser*. When played by a younger actor, such as the Roundabout understudy James Clow, he can very believably be portrayed as earnest, eager-to-please, unsure of himself.

In the first scene, he says to the assembled groups of friends, " I am just indeed lucky to have all of you. I mean, when you've got friends like mine…" (6). At Sarah and Harry's apartment, Sarah has just offered Robert some coffee. We see how Robert is either excessively polite, or simply has trouble asking for what he wants.

> SARAH: Sugar and cream?
>
> ROBERT: Both. May I have lots of both?
>
> SARAH: Of course you may.
>
> HARRY: Do you want some brandy in it, Robert? Or do you just want some brandy?
>
> ROBERT: You having some?
>
> SARAH: We don't drink, but you have some, you darling. Go ahead.
>
> HARRY: Or do you want a real drink? We have anything you want.
>
> ROBERT: Well, Harry, if you don't mind, could I have some Bourbon?
>
> HARRY: Right. (21)

At Susan and Peter's, he falls all over himself trying to be complimentary to Susan.

> ROBERT: In fact she is, without a doubt, the most charming woman I have ever, ever met. You are a lucky guy, Peter. *(Gives her a little hug)* I mean that kind of—oh, Southern graciousness—there just ain't no more of that around. You two are beautiful together. Really. And Peter—if you ever decide to leave her I want to be the first to know. (35)

Bobby's reluctance to enter a relationship may be the result of an inability to know himself and his needs. He's so busy being what he thinks everyone else wants him to be that he's never really himself.

Or Bobby can be played as *manipulative*. Maybe he really wants something from each of these people. The libretto never explains how Bobby met any of his friends, or what the basis of the friendships may be, so we're free to speculate on his motives. Maybe it's a desire for business connections, or networking—"the friends of friends" he can meet through them—or status and prestige. Surely it's fair to term his behavior in seducing April as manipulation. He gets her into bed by telling her exactly what she wants to hear as he describes to her a past encounter with another woman.

> ROBERT: I met a girl, a lovely girl, at a party one night and well, it was like you and me, April. We just—connected. You don't mind my telling this, do you?
>
> APRIL: No.
>
> ROBERT: It just…came to my mind. Anyway, we just connected, in such a beautiful way…exactly like tonight. (89–90)

Bobby can be seen as a selfish man, one who manipulates others into giving him what he wants. Committing to another might mean giving up too much of that self—a marriage partner might want something in return.

His relationships with the three girlfriends provide some insight. "You Could Drive a Person Crazy" suggests that Bobby might suffer from *approach-avoidance* because he "Titillates a person and then leaves her flat" (42). Once he gets too close to someone, it scares him and he backs away. He may have a *fear of intimacy*.

We can understand his reasons for shying away from Marta and April. Marta's fun, but a little bit of a nut case—not his type. And neither is April. He really does seem to find her dumb. When in their duet "Barcelona" we see how badly he wants her to leave after they finish having sex, it's not approach-avoidance. He simply wanted her for a one-night stand—acting on a desire of the moment and not necessarily revealing a general fear of intimacy.

But his failure to connect with Kathy makes us more suspicious. Nothing seems to have been wrong with her. Was he simply afraid that their relationship would develop the problems he's seen in the marriages of his friends? Was it fear of intimacy and approach-avoid-ance? When she asks why he didn't ask her to marry him, he says, "I never thought that you would [want to marry me]" (53). He didn't want to risk rejection.

Throughout the show, we see much evidence of Bobby as a *risk-aversive* person. We never see him initiate contact with his friends or acquaintances. In the title number we hear Bobby's friends calling him with invitations—not accepting his, but making new invitations of their own. Most often, he appears to merely react to the actions of others. In fact, the only risks he takes are asking Amy to marry him (more of impulsive reaction than a deliberate risk), walking in the door of his apartment in the show's opening (which represents no risk because he knows exactly what he'll find inside) and choosing *not* to enter the apartment in the final scene. That final choice shows his ultimate willingness to take a chance on changing his routine and his life.

Margo Jefferson's *New York Times* review of the Roundabout *Company* acknowledged that today's audiences bring a different perspec-tive to the piece than those who saw the original production.

> We have had two and a half decades to watch people like this on talk shows, in the movies, in novels, magazines and newspaper-advice columns. We make speculations and assumptions that the script seems never to have heard of.

There's a lot of familiar human behavior in Furth's book and Sondheim's songs. Much is suggested, little is explained, much like the people in our own lives. Is it less interesting or less fun to have a few more tools with which to analyze Furth's characters, the same ones we may use to figure out our own friends and lovers? For Ms. Jefferson, it apparently was, but each playgoer or reader of *Company* may respond as they like. The ultimate judges of the continued strength of the material should not be the theater historians, dramaturgs and critics who will analyze the piece in excruciating detail, but rather the audiences viewing it for the first time...unaware of its history...as if it were an entirely new show.

Company remains a rare musical in its ambition and ability to be entertaining, but not escapist. Sondheim said that he and Furth and director Harold Prince wanted the audience to "sit for two hours screaming their heads off with laughter and then go home and not be able to sleep" (qtd. in Zadan 119). As Ms. Jefferson's comments suggest, the show may not have been that unsettling in 1995. Audiences may now be less idealistic about marriage and more knowledgeable about the human behaviors that make committed relationships so difficult. They may enter the theater much better prepared for *Company*'s message.

Although musical theater audiences may find it enjoyable to visit someplace new to them, like Camelot, 19th-century Paris, or even rural Oklahoma, it can be fun to see our own world up on the stage as well. Does *Company*, which in its original production was clearly intended to be set in the present, play so quickly as "NOW" when produced in the mid-nineties? No, and in fact the published 1996 edition of the libretto drops that simple description of the time period. Some of the situations and action—particularly as they relate to sex and drugs and rock & roll (or in this case 'disco')—would certainly not be the same situations that today would be chosen to present a snapshot of 1995. Yet, if they're no longer entirely "NOW," they're not so improbable that they read as "THEN," either. We see from the stagings of recent productions that directors of *Company* have a number of options to present the characters' journeys in an environment that does not put the distance of time between the audience and the characters. Bobby and his thirteen friends can still look enough like us, and the people we know, to force us to think about ourselves and our ability to love another person.

We turn to many sources for help in understanding our lives and relationships...to our friends, to psychology, to self-help groups or to religion. With a show like *Company*...we can even turn to the musical theater.

ↁ

The research assistance of Michael Lynch, Ph.D., is gratefully acknowledged.

NOTES

1.   A contradictory opinion on the relevance of the Nixon era to *Follies* is articulated by James Fisher in his essay (p. 69).

2.   George Furth and Stephen Sondheim. *Company. A Musical Comedy*. New York: Theatre Communication Group, 1996. Unless otherwise noted, all subsequent quotations will be from this edition, with page numbers cited parenthetically within the text.

3.   *Company*. By George Furth and Stephen Sondheim. Dir. Scott Miller. New Line Theater, St. Louis. 18 Nov. 1995.

WORKS CITED

Baldinger, Scott. "'Company' Enters A New, Scary Stage of Life." *New York Times* 17 September 1995.

Cader, Michael, ed. *Saturday Night Live. The First Twenty Years*. Boston, New York: Houghton Mifflin, 1994.

Ellis, Scott. Telephone interview. 9 January 1996.

Furth, George, and Stephen Sondheim. *Company. A Musical Comedy*. New York: Theatre Communication Group, 1996.

——. *Company*. In *Ten Great Musicals of the American Theatre*. Ed. Stanley Richards. Radnor, PA: Chilton, 1973.

——. *Company*. Dir. Scott Miller. New Line Theater, St. Louis. 18 November 1995.

Jefferson, Margo. "Listen to 'Company,' Tune Out the Book." *New York Times* 15 October 1995.

Lieberman, Morton A., and Lonnie R. Snowden. "Problems in Assessing Prevalence and Membership Characteristics of Self-Help Group Participants." (Special Issue: Advances in Understanding with Self-Help

Groups). *Journal of Applied Behavioral Science* 29 (June 1993): 266 (15). *Expanded Academic ASAP.* Online. 5 January 1996.

Miller, Scott. "Is 'Company' Dated?" 6 November 1995. Online posting. Saturday Review Online, Sondheim Bulletin Board. America On-Line. 8 November 1995.

———. Personal interview. 18 November 1995.

Sondheim, Stephen, quoted in Craig Zadan. *Sondheim & Co.* 2nd ed., updated. New York: Da Capo, 1994.

———. "A Sunday Conversation with Stephen Sondheim." Chicago Humanities Festival VI. Orchestra Hall, Chicago. 12 November 1995.

United States. Dept. of Commerce *Statistical Abstract of the United States, 1994. The National Data Book, U.S.*

Nixon's America and *Follies*
Reappraising a Musical Theater Classic
James Fisher

> All civilizations rest on myths, but in America myths have
> exceptional meaning. A myth is a way of pulling together
> the raw and contradictory evidence of life as it is known
> in any age. It lets people make patterns in their own lives,
> within the larger patterns.[1]
> — Theodore H. White

> *Follies* was a state of mind which represented America
> between the two world wars: up until 1945, America was
> the good guy and everything was hopeful and idealistic.
> Now the country is a riot of national guilt. The dream
> has collapsed. Everything has turned to rubble and that's
> what *Follies* is about—the collapse of the dream.[2]
> — Stephen Sondheim

The years in which Richard Milhous Nixon rose and fell from the
presidency were among the most turbulent in American history. The
brinkmanship of the Cold War, the turmoil of the Civil Rights Movement, the assassinations of John F. Kennedy, Martin Luther King,
Malcolm X, and Robert F. Kennedy, and the escalation of American
military involvement in Vietnam which led to great social unrest,
sorely tested many of America's abiding social myths. The 1960s and
the early 1970s were marked by an ideological war that challenged
virtually all long-held certitudes, as doubt about the values of Nixon's
generation crept into the minds of the American populace. All of this
resulted, as Theodore H. White writes in *Breach of Faith: The Fall of
Richard Nixon*, in a generational and cultural clash that "ran through
families as well as communities. Fathers against sons, mothers against
daughters, students against teachers, arguing over such matters as dress
and manners and morals and sex and drugs and rioting" (332).

In the midst of this social conflict, Stephen Sondheim and James Goldman's *Follies* opened on Broadway on April 4, 1971 and ran for over a year. Among other things, *Follies* is a searing commentary on the American experience in the middle of the twentieth century. It has been twenty-five years since *Follies* first appeared, making it possible to view its tumultuous era with some historical perspective. The parallels between Nixon, as a symbol of the deterioration of faith in pervasive American myths, and the lives of *Follies'* characters and the sunny myths emanating from the pre–World War II popular stage, add significant dimension to a work remembered more for its dazzling theatrical savvy than for its socio-political themes. In her book, *Art Isn't Easy. The Achievement of Stephen Sondheim*, Joanne Gordon has written that "*Follies* is about time and memory, illusion and reality, dreams and desires, fantasy and truth, theater and life—themes explored through one all-encompassing metaphor: the American musical theater" (76). *Follies* is also about two profoundly significant eras: the pre– and immediately post–World War II epoch and the mid-1960s through Nixon's White House years. In the escapist form of musical theater, *Follies'* "characters—and by extension, the America of the seventies—confront their inner pain and come to terms with the limitations of ordinary life" (Gordon 109).

Follies was certainly not the only Broadway theatrical product to comment on its time, but it must be acknowledged as one of the first, despite the fact that critics and audiences paid scant attention to its social commentary when it opened. Other dramatic works commenting on the struggles of the era claimed greater attention for their themes than did *Follies*. In 1962, Edward Albee's *Who's Afraid of Virginia Woolf?* exposed an horrific marriage filled with deceptions, illusions, and vitriol. Political in the sense of its assault on marriage as an institution, Albee's drama most significantly taps deeply into the disappointments and fears of its characters. This same approach is evident in Jason Miller's Pulitzer Prize–winning drama *That Championship Season*, produced a year after *Follies* opened. Set at the twenty-fifth reunion of a champion high school basketball team, *That Championship Season* is not a warm Robert Bly–style gathering of men. All of the men are in emotional and spiritual crisis, and it becomes clear that, as one of the characters puts it, "we stole that trophy, championship season is a lie" (117). Having cheated to win, the members of the team and their coach find that their "winning is everything—winning at all

costs" mentality has rendered their triumph hollow—and has poisoned their entire lives. Other Broadway and Off-Broadway plays of
the era pointedly criticized American involvement in Vietnam, and
David Mamet, a chronicler of the corrupted soul of modern urban
society, emerged with *American Buffalo* (1975), a drama ostensibly
about contemporary America's business ethics as represented by the
denizens of a junk shop. Critic Michael Billington identified broader
themes in *American Buffalo*, which he viewed as "a deeply political
play [in that it] makes its points about society through the way people
actually behave" (*Guardian*). Mamet himself has said that the play
was "about an essential part of American consciousness, which is the
ability to suspend an ethical sense and adopt in its stead a popular
accepted mythology and use that to assuage your conscience like everyone else is doing" (*Times*). Like *Follies*, the themes examined in the
plays of Miller and Mamet, and the Vietnam plays of the period,
reflect the emptiness of the mythologies of the Nixon generation, but
few did so within the confines of the musical stage. *Hair* (1967), and
its numerous knock-offs, brought counter-culture social criticism into
musical theater, but through the discordant sounds of rock music,
and aimed at the "baby boom" generation—Nixon's children. *Follies*
was unique in that it brought its political and social criticism to an
audience made up mostly of the Nixon generation, and it did so
through the familiar theatrical traditions of that generation's own
musical idiom—"a great, big Broadway show" (Goldman 36). As
Sondheim has described it, the characters in *Follies*, like their true-life
counterparts, discover that "In the thirty years since they've seen each
other, their lives have fallen apart, just as the Follies have, just as the
country has. What was hopeful and promising and naive and innocent back there is now cynical and lost and bitter" (Mandelbaum 67).

Although Sondheim is not typically thought of as a particularly
political artist, *Follies* is not the only Sondheim musical featuring
overtly political themes. As early as 1964, *Anyone Can Whistle* satirized aspects of American politics as seen through the life of a corrupt
woman mayor, *Company* (1970) lampoons many accepted social mores
and attitudes about relationships of the later 1960s, *Sweeney Todd*
(1979) is adapted from a bloodthirsty nineteenth-century melodrama
to expose the dog-eat-dog ethics of the day, and most recently, *Assassins* (1991) returns to many of the themes raised in *Follies* in its look

at the dark underbelly of the American Dream—in this case as represented by the murderers of American Presidents.

The original New York production of *Follies*, despite a year-long
run, is often remembered as a commercial failure due to the expenses
of a large cast and lavish production values. Although many critics
admired Sondheim's score, the production garnered mixed reviews.
The ironic cynicism of Sondheim's lyrics frankly exposes the frustrated yearnings of Sally Durant for Ben Stone, the husband of her
one-time "Weismann Follies" roommate, Phyllis Rogers. Sally and
her husband Buddy Plummer meet Ben and Phyllis thirty years into
their marriages at a Follies reunion. This meeting unleashes a torrent
of memories and recriminations as the characters encounter ghostly
images of their former selves haunting the decaying theatre. Sondheim
and librettist James Goldman had begun their *Follies* collaboration in
1965, inspired in part by Eliot Elisofon's memorable photograph of
Gloria Swanson standing amidst the ruins of New York's Roxy Theater. The original production, co-directed by Hal Prince and Michael
Bennett (with Bennett's choreography), was set on Boris Aronson's
haunting and cavernous set which served, as Joanne Gordon characterizes it, as "an effective theatrical metaphor for the present. The theater and society are in a state of degeneration and decline. The gloss
and artificial glamour, the false values and insincerities are peeling
away; ugly crevices have appeared in the shiny surface of the American Dream" (82). Featuring a large and expert cast, *Follies* was a one-
of-a-kind experience. As Jack Kroll described it, the original Broadway production was a "rousing piece of American show business and
an acute criticism of the psychic, emotional and cultural implications
of show business as an American phenomenon" (121).

Follies has become something of a cult classic. As with such landmark musicals as *Show Boat* (1927) and *Gypsy* (1959), the theatrical
setting of *Follies* provides a perfect showcase for Sondheim's memorable score which captures the musical language of Tin Pan Alley and
the popular stage between the two world wars. Although Sondheim's
A Little Night Music (1973) is more melodic and *Company* more upbeat in its message, the score for *Follies* stands as Sondheim's richest,
combining serious plot songs for the four principal characters along
with delightful and subtle parodies of the songs of vaudeville and
Broadway circa 1918 to 1941. These pastiche numbers serve to comment ironically on the circumstances of the characters and are also sly

parodies of such composers and lyricists as Irving Berlin ("Beautiful Girls"), De Sylva, Brown and Henderson ("Broadway Baby"), Sigmund Romberg or Rudolph Friml ("One More Kiss"), Jerome Kern ("Loveland"), Ira Gershwin ("You're Gonna Love Tomorrow"), and Cole Porter[3]. Other numbers evoke stage luminaries of Broadway, Hollywood, and vaudeville: Maurice Chevalier ("Ah, Paree!"), Helen Morgan ("Losing My Mind"), Ethel Merman ("Who's That Woman?"), Bert Williams ("The God-Why-Don't-You-Love-Me Blues"), Fred Astaire and Ginger Rogers ("Rain on the Roof"), and Astaire again ("Live, Laugh, Love"). Sondheim's rejuvenation of these familiar musical traditions is a powerful thematic device wherein the naive and hopeful sentiments of the songs are set against the grim realities of the failures, regrets, and deep sense of loss felt in a contemporary America surviving an unpopular war, social unrest, and revelations of arrogance and corruption in government—all as symbolized by Nixon's presidency. Even the poster design for the original production, depicting a Follies girl looking like a cracked Statue of Liberty, underscores the socio-political dimensions of *Follies*. Sondheim also provides a set of chilling "star turns" in the fantasy "Loveland" sequence in which Sally, Ben, Phyllis, and Buddy perform their individual emotional dilemmas in an ironic distortion of the Follies star spots of yore; in essence, completely merging plot and character with the musical stage clichés of the middle of the twentieth century.

The connections between Sondheim's score and James Goldman's oft-criticized libretto are important to examine fully to comprehend the complex political and social themes of *Follies*. Critic Stanley Kauffmann's view that the "plot and dialogue by James Goldman, the tuppenny poet of *The Lion in Winter*, are inane" (37) was unfortunately typical of the reviews of the original production. Even some of those involved in creating *Follies* fault the book. When Michael Bennett said that "I think that 80 percent of *Follies* was the greatest musical ever done" (qtd. in Zadan 148), the missing 20 percent in his view was the libretto. In retrospect, Sondheim thought that "there were too many pastiche numbers in the show which hurt the book and subsequently hurt the show. Perhaps if we had used fewer songs and had more book the show would have been more successful" (qtd. in Zadan 150–51). Goldman's script is, in fact, a highly effective framework for the score. As Goldman himself describes it, the book is "very terse and very little was said that didn't have to be said" (qtd. in Zadan

151). More importantly, the book is thematically sharp and economic in its exploration of the characters and the meanings of their actions and attitudes. The lean libretto mirrors the revue structure typical of Follies-style entertainments and, more importantly, permits Sondheim's lyrics to expand, deepen, and reveal the many thematic layers of *Follies*, various of which are expressed in the language, characters, music, and visual elements with remarkable equity. Along with Sondheim's score, Goldman's contribution is, in fact, one of the strengths of *Follies*. It is witty, succinct, darkly cynical, and continually surprising, combining an unsentimental tone with compassion for its characters' all-too-human frailties. It must be acknowledged that the critics and audience of the original production may well have blamed Goldman's book for the fact that, as Joanne Gordon writes, "*Follies* presents audiences with things many do not want to accept: youth denies age, and age glamorizes youth; the American faith that material wealth brings emotional maturity is inherently deceptive" (121). Ken Mandelbaum seems to agree with Gordon when he asserts that "Audiences didn't want to hear the message of it, and didn't want to face its portrayal of ferocious relationships and of foolish illusions destroying lives. It was not that audiences couldn't follow the book; they were unwilling to listen to the unpleasant things *Follies* was saying" (75). It seems likely that audiences and critics objected to the political and social overtones in *Follies*, too.

Follies captures poignant reflections on the lives of Sally and Phyllis as youthful Follies chorus girls and Ben and Buddy as their stage-door Johnnies at the outset of World War II then set these against images of their middle-aged selves in Nixon's America. Their backgrounds and experiences are the same ones that shaped their generation and Nixon, whose public life spanned an age marked by challenges to values constructed as much from the myths of Broadway, vaudeville, and Hollywood as from any other source in American life. Nixon and his stage counterparts in *Follies* were conditioned by the fears and hardships of the Depression of the early 1930s and the war years, as well as the inflated optimism of the years immediately following the war. The theatrical device of the present-day characters sharing the stage with images of their younger selves provides a multi-layered view of the ramifications of these conditions and the characters' personal choices. Sally and Buddy, married and living a lower- middle-class life in the Southwest, represent the failure of the

"American Dream" of economic success in the postwar years for some of their generation. Sally and Buddy have grown apart (he has a mistress in another town), if indeed they were ever truly together, and Sally drifts further into reveries of her past. She lives on fantasies of her long-ago affair with Ben, whom she views as the lost love of her life. Ben and Phyllis, married and living a materially successful existence in the upper echelons of New York society, have each lost their way, spiritually and morally. Although director Hal Prince referred to Phyllis and Ben as being like the Kennedys (Sally compares Phyllis to Jackie Kennedy when they meet again), Ben, a foundation president, particularly evokes Nixon. A political and social icon wearing a mask of public propriety, Ben cannot completely believe in himself in this role. Clearly he has been willing and able to do anything required to get where he is, but the result is that he cannot keep the illusion alive. As the energy he has put into his public image flags, his emotions unravel. Hal Prince has described Ben, the character he most related to while working on the musical, as "the perfect 1970's monolith approaching menopause on the cusp of a nervous breakdown" (159). Ben and Sally also represent a Nixonian brand of suspended ethics, as their behavior is continually counter to their words. They maintain images of propriety and mouth platitudes about marriage and love, but they both move toward their individual goals without any anchor in the values and morality they espouse.

Phyllis, on the other hand, despairing over the failure of her marriage to Ben and longing for greater understanding of her conflicted feelings, has come back in hopes of finding some answers. As Ben and Phyllis mingle, Dimitri Weismann, a character evoking the flamboyant Florenz Ziegfelds, Earl Carrolls, and George Whites of Broadway's golden age, welcomes the guests and characterizes the evening as "a final chance to glamorize the old days, stumble through a song or two and lie about ourselves a little" (7). He ushers forth Roscoe, an aging tenor, and invites the ex-chorines to parade down the grand staircase one final time as Roscoe sings "Beautiful Girls," Sondheim's first pastiche number in the show. The song, obviously inspired by Irving Berlin's Ziegfeld Follies anthem "A Pretty Girl Is Like a Melody," sets the tone for what is to come and establishes the metaphor that the stage world represents an America where your "Reason is undone" (9). Sally's ability to reason has been tragically undone for a long time. She flees home to attend the reunion against Buddy's wishes. He has followed her to New York and when they run into Ben and Phyllis the reminiscences—and self-delusions—begin. Buddy's lie is also his wish—for a quiet, comfortable life with a loyal and loving spouse. He pretends to Ben that this is what he has, but moments later Buddy is flirting with an attractive young waitress. When Ben and Sally steal away to talk, Sondheim's lyrics suggest her fears and longing to return to her youth. She wonders, "What were we like, it's so hazy!" (19)—the real memories have gone and she has replaced them with illusions. Phyllis, clearly the most honest character among the foursome, is blunt about her present life. Following the Nixonian model, appearances mean everything to Ben and Phyllis in a life otherwise devoid of emotion or action. Phyllis, like Sally, has lost touch with her beginnings—she even remarks that when she sees a photo of herself from the past that it seems like a stranger.

The characters are drawn back to the past remembering the early days of their relationships in one of Sondheim's outstanding plot songs, "Waiting for the Girls Upstairs." The song was suggested by *Follies's* original working title, *The Girls Upstairs*, and allows the couples to ruminate on the hopes and dreams that shaped one of the seminal turning points of their lives. They remember a time when:

> Life was fun, but oh, so intense.
> Everything was possible and nothing made sense
> Back there when one of the major events
> Was waiting for the girls,
> Waiting for the girls,
> Waiting for the girls
> Upstairs. (31)

The song is interrupted midway by the first significant appearance of the younger visions of Ben, Phyllis, Buddy, and Sally, and with great subtlety Sondheim's lyrics and Goldman's libretto expand the blurring of past memories and present realities. It is most effectively in Sondheim's lyrics that the past and present converge, and the depths of self-deception inherent in the characters' lives emerge. Ben, who has never figured out what he really wants except fame and material success, is without the spiritual or emotional resources to survive. His predicament—one undoubtedly experienced by many men of his and Nixon's generation—is most effectively explored in "The Road You Didn't Take." Here he wonders about choices and mourns for the "Ben I'll never be" (40), evoking the dark side of the American Dream.

Having lived according to the rules of its myth, Ben, like Arthur Miller's
Willy Loman,[4] is disoriented, needing love but not knowing where
or how to get it or give it. Ultimately, Ben begins to realize his life is
a lie and that despite his material success, he does not have what he
wants. He speaks of meaningless affairs, which he pursues hopelessly
seeking the love he believes Phyllis does not feel for him. This leads to
a renewed attraction to Sally, whose self-delusion, which borders pre-
cariously on madness, reaches a peak as she tells Ben of her life since
Weismann Follies days. Like Buddy, she creates an image of simple
domestic bliss, but betrays her profound unhappiness with Buddy
and the jealousy she feels of the life she imagines Ben and Phyllis
have. The lyrics of "In Buddy's Eyes" portray a Sally who remains
"young and beautiful" in her husband's eyes and contented with a
simple, domestic life. However, Sondheim incisively includes a lyric
passage revealing Sally's pain through her rose-colored lie:

> So life is ducky
> And time goes flying
> And I'm so lucky
> I feel like crying,
> And…. (44)

This song effectively permits the actress playing Sally to interpret it in
different directions, all with chilling results. Dorothy Collins, the original Sally, performed the song with a vivid sense of anguished regret,
but Barbara Cook, who performed the role in a 1985 concert version,
stresses that Sally's song is a lie: "The character is trying to convince
herself that all this idyllic stuff that she is singing about is really true,
though she doesn't really believe it. But I decided to perform the song
as if she meant every word of it…from the bottom of her heart" (qtd.
in Zadan 329). Either way, the result is a Pirandellian collision
between reality and illusion.

In another pastiche, Sondheim constructs a "shady lady" song
that might have been sung by Ethel Merman in the 1930s. For "Who's
That Woman?", brassy Stella Deems gathers the "girls" to perform
the number as they had thirty years before. In the midst of the vigor-
ous routine, the women are joined by the ghostly images of their
former selves in a remarkable visualization of the musical's central
metaphor. Their older, stiffened bodies struggle to meet the demands
of the choreography and the effect is exaggerated as their younger

selves appear and effortlessly dance in the shadows. Often referred to
as the "mirror" number, Michael Bennett's choreography of "Who's
That Woman?" is rightly regarded as a classic moment of modern
musical theater. In tandem with Bennett's staging, Sondheim's lyrics
point up the shock of recognition as the woman in the song catches a
glimpse of her true self in a mirror of reality. Phyllis's desire for finding
truth leads her to attempt to get Ben to share his feelings. He will
not—or cannot—and the fact that their marriage is on the rocks—
and that they cling to it merely for the sake of appearances—becomes
vividly apparent. This emptiness is set in counterpoint to the appearance of Carlotta Campion, an ex-Follies girl who has had an up-and-
down career on stage and television. Like the dizzying highs and lows
of Nixon's political career, "I'm Still Here" reflects the vicissitudes of
life's journey from a tough survivor's point of view. Ben is not so
resilient, and he dreams an impossible dream—like Sally's—of start-
ing life over. These two unhappy characters seem to yearn for a lost
love in Sondheim's lyric, but a scene between Young Ben and Young
Sally interrupts the song and shows all too clearly that their affair was
brief and insignificant from Ben's point of view, despite Sally's wish
that it had meant more. Ben panics when he realizes that Sally seri-
ously believes they can start over together and Phyllis, hurt by Ben's
attentiveness to Sally, confronts him. Ben confesses angrily, but with
rare honesty, some of his fears in a charged moment from Goldman's
libretto:

> PHYLLIS: I thought you needed me.
> BEN: For what? To tell me I'm a fake? I don't need
>   you for that. I know it. Doesn't everybody? Jesus,
>   can't they see it? Are they blind? They look at
>   me and I keep waiting for them all to point and
>   say, "You! Stone! I know what you are" (75)

The characters collide in a shouting match of anger, despair, and re-
crimination. As they argue, their youthful counterparts join the fray
and reality explodes to be replaced by "Loveland," a show biz
fantasyland where the characters must play out their emotional turmoil in the aforementioned "star turns" that, as Martin Gottfried
writes, are "grotesque and horrific" (*Times*). This transformation has
been the ultimate goal of *Follies* and the characters from the start,
"with its growing impression of smallness and banality in the characters.

Since it's exactly this inevitable side of ourselves—the petty and grudg-
ing, the self-concerned and self-pitying—that the American popular
song-and-dance tradition—with its style and rue and humor—re-
deems and transforms at its best into something large and elegant and
free" (Harvey 240). As James Harvey wrote of this transition in
Commonweal:

> When suddenly and startlingly the stage flares into light,
> a lot of candy-box Valentine scenery descends, and a
> troupe of pseudo-Fragonard boys and girls come pranc-
> ing out, get into place, and sing: "In love land, where
> everybody loves!" In the middle of this blinding explo-
> sion of inanity stand the two couples, four haggard
> middleaged wrecks—stunned and gaping—while the
> chorus boys and girls trill and pose relentlessly around
> them. It's a moment of such complicated brilliance, such
> triumphant soaring wryness that I can't honestly think of
> a parallel to it—except in other parts of *Follies* itself. (240)

Each of the characters must confront themselves in the language of
the Follies traditions. The first myth shattered is the materialistic hope-
fulness that Nixon's generation believed in as a result of the post-war
boom. It is played out by Young Ben and Young Phyllis in Sondheim's
subtly cynical "You're Gonna Love Tomorrow," where "Tomorrow's
what you're gonna have a lifetime of / With me!" (89). Each of the
four characters has their "Loveland" moment, with the hapless Buddy
depicted as a baggy-pants vaudeville comic, Sally as a torch singer in
the manner of Helen Morgan, Phyllis as a flashy dancing lady *à la*
Eleanor Powell, and Ben as an Astaire-esque "man-about-town," all
familiar images from the entertainments of the Nixon generation.
Buddy, Sally, and Phyllis perform comparatively honest visions of their
personal dilemmas, but Ben's turn, "Live, Laugh, Love," is still an
absurd lie. As Ben moves through his number he seems to lose
confidence and begins to forget the words and dance steps. His song
crumbles and the characters are hurtled back to the reunion, while
the rising sun of a new morning—and reality—flows through the
cracks in the theater's walls. Buddy finds Sally in total despair. Buddy
tries to create hope for their lives together, but Sally must face a startling realization that a tomorrow without the comfort of her illusions
has arrived. She thus becomes the ultimate "American Dreamer," rep-

resenting a nation that must awaken from the dream of its own myths to face the realities of political dissention and social chaos of the era. Ben, similarly despairing in the face of reality, insists that he cannot go on. However, Phyllis will not permit any more delusions, either for herself or for Ben. As the most resilient of the foursome, Phyllis confronts the shallowness of her life and the failure of her marriage. She is steeled to begin anew by firmly putting the past behind her. As the two couples stagger from their *Walpurgisnacht* of self-revelation, their own voices from the past call to them from the dark corners of Weismann's ruined theater. Phyllis, representing those in the social order prepared to face their fears of an uncertain future, leads the way out into the bright new day.

Follies finished its year-long run and an aborted tour before fading into the memories of those fortunate enough to have seen the Broadway production. An abbreviated original cast recording was issued, eliminating or cutting down much of the score and including almost nothing of the libretto except part of Weismann's introduction to "Beautiful Girls." For nearly fifteen years, *Follies* would be considered only an ambitious failure. Why? Michael Bennett believed that "the idea and the visual metaphor became stronger than the material, or more interesting. That's why it was not successful" (qtd. in Mandelbaum 75). Brendan Gill asserted that "what has proved unworkable in *Follies* is its subject matter and not his great themes" (67). Few shared James Harvey's view that *Follies* "is in fact a remarkable original show, whose originality defines itself against strikingly conventional limits, both of sensibility and form" (239).

In 1985, with an eye toward securing *Follies* its rightful place in the canon of musical theater classics, one *Follies* admirer, RCA record producer Thomas Z. Shepard, arranged for two all-star concert performances of *Follies* at Lincoln Center's Avery Fisher Hall. The reactions to the concerts suggest that, as Frank Rich believed, audiences "were not unaware of how time and history had at last caught up with the perceptions of *Follies*" (*Times*). More importantly, the two significant eras of *Follies* asserted themselves vividly thanks, in part, to the perspective of time. As Stephen Banfield notes, the concerts were "almost as nostalgic and triumphant a celebration of the era of 1971 as was the original production of 1940, or 1940 of 1908" (212). The concerts resulted in a superb live—and virtually complete—recording, as well as a PBS documentary. The enthusiastic critical response and the brisk sales of the new recording encouraged British producer Cameron Mackintosh to mount a first-ever London production for which Sondheim contributed four new songs (and eliminated a few of the originals) and, unfortunately, Goldman significantly rewrote the book.

When *Follies* opened in London billed as "A Broadway Legend," it had an entirely different, and significantly more optimistic, tone. Goldman's revised book offered some small improvements over the original. More emphasis was placed on the intertwining relationships of the four main characters and Sondheim's best new song, "Country House," wherein Ben and Phyllis wittily exchange suggestions for resuscitating their failing marriage, added some dimension to aspects of these characters. Unfortunately, Goldman and Sondheim opted to eliminate or downplay the more bitter and unsympathetic qualities of the characters. For example, Ben's admission of random infidelities in the original libretto was reduced to Phyllis asking him if he had ever been unfaithful. To this, Ben offered only an ambiguous response. The cynical, almost Brechtian quality of the original book helped to showcase the irony of the musical clichés Sondheim brilliantly parodied. However, the sweetened book undermined the effect of several of the pastiche sequences, and "One More Kiss," "Broadway Baby," "Beautiful Girls," and "Who's That Woman?" seemed closer to the familiar old chestnuts they satirized than the searingly ironic comment that Sondheim surely intended. While some vestiges of the show's edgy strength remained, the under-development of many of the secondary characters made this *Follies* seem more like a geriatric version of *A Chorus Line*. In effect, this version seemed to sell out to a new American myth, the false optimism of the Reagan years. Even Buddy, the broken down salesman of the original version, is nearly as prosperous as Ben; at one point, Sally shows off a huge diamond ring Buddy has given her. Whereas Ben and Phyllis seemed to be political conservatives in the original version, both couples appear to be much the same in the London revision.

Other changes were less distressing, including "Social Dancing," a sequence in which many of the secondary characters drop one-liners about themselves. Phyllis's original "Loveland" number, "The Story of Lucy and Jessie" was replaced by "Ah, But Underneath…," a mock striptease, but the song was similar in its intent and not an improvement on the original. Ben's original "Loveland" number, "Live, Laugh,

Love" was also gone, replaced by "Make the Most of Your Music" which, unfortunately, also eliminated Ben's breakdown and the striking explosion of the "Loveland" fantasy which in the original version served to carry the main characters back to reality. Other excisions from the original score included the memorable opening music that accompanied the arrival of the reunion party guests, Ben's "The Road You Didn't Take" and "Bolero d'Amour." There were also slight lyric changes in several songs to accommodate changes in the book. All of these changes, however, had significant impact on the themes so clearly presented in the original libretto. Sondheim's songs retained their bite, but without the supportive framework provided by the original libretto, a delicate balance was lost. The pastiche songs become the most interesting feature of the London version, which seems to exploit the nostalgic qualities of both the era Sondheim's songs evoke and the legendary reputation of *Follies* itself.

Critics of the original Broadway production remarked on *Follies'* "camp" qualities, undoubtedly viewing it as another of the nostalgia shows featuring aging stars, like the "new 1925 musical" *No, No, Nanette* starring Ruby Keeler, which had opened months before. However, as Martin Gottfried writes, "any criticism of *Follies* as camp is really missing the point—there is nothing gay in this realism. Prince has snatched away the gauze curtain from our nostalgia to reveal the present as a crumbling monument to the past, a decaying body painted over with flaky primary colors" (*Times*). However, the London production, with the cooperation of Sondheim and Goldman, seemed to give in completely to the sort of camp and nostalgia the original production had savagely debunked. Rather than confronting the political and social realities of the day, as the original version of *Follies* had done, the new *Follies* embraced the *status quo*.

Even in the weakened state of the London production, the richness of *Follies* remained unforgettable. The critical dilemma in approaching Sondheim's more ambitious works is that he combines traditional musical theater techniques and a film composer's sense of the emotional power of underscoring, with an operatic scope. As such, his works do not fit comfortably into any immediately recognizable niche, and like virtually all of his canon, Sondheim's *Follies* score offers few compromises in any area. Joanne Gordon writes that "In both the music and lyrics of *Follies*, Sondheim lays bare the contrasting and conflicting Weltanschauung of American society from the end of

World War I to the present" (77).

The last decade has seen a revival of interest in *Follies*. If Sondheim's score might only be heard again within the context of Goldman's original libretto, *Follies* could again, as Ken Mandelbaum writes, show "how the tinsel, glamour, and gaiety of show business past provided a false set of standards, which resulted in a disillusioned postwar America. In its way, *Follies* addressed the idea of the American Dream as strongly as Arthur Miller's *Death of a Salesman*" (67).

ↄ

Notes

1. Theodore H. White, *Breach of Faith. The Fall of Richard Nixon*. New York: Atheneum Publishers, 1975, p. 322.

2. Stephen Sondheim, quoted in Craig Zadan, *Sondheim & Co*, Second Ed. New York: Harper & Row, 1986, p. 136.

3. This number also parallels "The Saga of Jenny" (Kurt Weill and Ira Gershwin, *Lady in the Dark*, 1941), an earlier song about an ambivalent woman.

4. The leading character in Miller's *Death of a Salesman* (1949).

Works Cited

Banfield, Stephen. *Sondheim's Broadway Musicals*. Ann Arbor: U of Michigan P, 1993.

Billington, Michael. "Review." *The Guardian*, 29 June 1978.

Gill, Brendan. "Casting Out Remorse." *New Yorker* 47 (10 April 1971): 67.

Goldman, James (book) and Stephen Sondheim (music and lyrics). *Follies. A Musical*. New York: Random House, 1971.

Gordon, Joanne. *Art Isn't Easy. The Achievement of Stephen Sondheim*. Carbondale: Southern Illinois UP, 1990.

Gottfried, Martin. "Flipping Over 'Follies'." *New York Times*, 25 April 1971.

Harvey, James. "Original Follies." *Commonweal* 94 (14 May 1971): 240.

Kauffmann, Stanley. "Stanley Kauffmann on Theater." *The New Republic* 164 (8 May 1971): 37.

Kroll, Jack. "Backstage in Arcadia." *Newsweek*, 77 (12 April 1971): 121.

Mamet, David. Quoted in *The Times*, 19 June 1978.

Mandelbaum, Ken. *"A Chorus Line" and the Musicals of Michael Bennett.* New York: St. Martin's Press, 1989.

Miller, Jason. *That Championship Season.* New York: Atheneum, 1972.

Prince, Hal. *Contradictions. Notes on Twenty-Six Years in the Theatre.* New York: Dodd, Mead, 1974.

Rich, Frank. "Sondheim's 'Follies' Evokes Old Broadway." *New York Times,* 15 September 1985.

White, Theodore H. *Breach of Faith. The Fall of Richard Nixon.* New York: Atheneum, 1975.

Zadan, Craig. *Sondheim & Co.* Second Ed. New York: Harper & Row, 1986.

The Last of Sheila
Sondheim as Master Games-Player
Douglas Braverman

Stephen Sondheim's fascination with games and puzzles is not merely an interesting tidbit of Sondheim lore; his enjoyment of these brain-teasers is clearly reflected in his work as a composer and lyricist. One can almost sense his game-player's delight in his inventive rhymes (*Night Music*'s The hands on the clock turn,/ But don't sing a nocturne/ Just yet.), his plays on words (*Gypsy*'s...any IOU I owe, you owe.), his echo songs (*Follies*'...A fellow she prefers. Furs. Furs.), and his fun with alliteration and interior rhyme (*Forum*'s I pine, I blush,/ I squeak, I squawk./ Today I woke/ too weak to walk.). Musically, Sondheim, the puzzle-worker, sets up and successfully meets his own challenges, whether creating a style to emulate the pointillism of Seurat's paintings in *Sunday in the Park with George,* or composing a score in which the musical themes develop backwards chronologically in *Merrily We Roll Along.* Yet, for all the intellectual wizardry found in his music and lyrics, none of his work is a more direct demonstration of his love of games and puzzles than the only original screenplay he has thus far written, the filmscript of the murder mystery *The Last of Sheila,* co-authored with his friend, actor Anthony Perkins. An examination of *The Last of Sheila* not only illustrates the master games-player at work, but also reveals interesting parallels with his writing for the musical theatre.

As Craig Zadan reports in his book *Sondheim & Company, The Last of Sheila* was inspired by the elaborate party games which Sondheim and Perkins often designed to entertain their friends. Herbert Ross, the eventual director of the film, participated in one of their Halloween treasure hunts, and was intrigued by the cleverness of the project: "We'd know we were in the right location when we saw a poster of a woman who was running for Congress. In one place on West 48th Street, we saw the poster and beside it was a woman who invited us upstairs. When we got there, she served us cake and tea. If you put the slices of cake together, the icing spelled out the next clue. Lee Remick's team lost...they ate the cake" (187). Ross especially enjoyed Sondheim's murder mystery game in which the party guests were given typically tricky clues and asked to solve a murder case. Envisioning the dramatic possibilities of the game, Ross convinced Warner Brothers to commission Sondheim to write a screenplay in which both the audience and the characters could play along.

After considering the project, Sondheim eventually invited Perkins to collaborate on the script. Not surprisingly, Perkins, an alumnus of Alfred Hitchcock's *Psycho*, was primarily interested in developing the suspense scenes, whereas Sondheim's main concern was creating the puzzles and clues. The two agreed to concentrate on their separate areas of expertise, often writing scenes individually and then mailing them to each other for comments. Their dual objectives resulted in a screenplay that contains some wonderfully suspenseful moments, as well as some of the most diabolically complex plotting in American cinema.

In brief, the film deals with Clinton Green (James Coburn), a somewhat sadistic movie producer, married to Sheila, an equally vicious Hollywood gossip columnist. After a party at their home, Sheila is accidentally killed by a hit and run driver. Clinton, suspecting that her death was really murder, invites the party guests to spend a week's vacation aboard his luxurious yacht in the Mediterranean, where he plans to have them play a detective game similar to those which Sondheim and Perkins were fond of devising. The game is based on Sheila's profession as a gossip columnist: each guest is given a card with one dirty secret on it. The point of the game is for each of the guests to deduce which dirty secret has been assigned to the others. Midway through the game, however, it becomes clear that Clinton is using their deductions to try to unmask Sheila's murderer. In the midst of the game, one of the participants is found dead, and the guests must now use their game-playing abilities to solve a real murder while stranded aboard the yacht with a killer.

Examining *The Last of Sheila* provides an interesting glimpse into Sondheim's creative process. In all of his work for the musical theatre, the plots and characters have been created by others. However, *The Last of Sheila* is an entirely original script and allows the viewer to

sample pure, undiluted Sondheim, with an emphasis on his characteristic craftsmanship and wit, and his uniquely dark view of the world.

Sondheim's joy in games is evident throughout the movie.
Clinton's yacht is decorated with an array of game boards and toys.
("Who did this room?" one of the guests quips. "Parker Brothers?"),
and the idea of a murder game turning into reality, requiring the
game-players to solve the now-real mystery, surely appealed to
Sondheim's own game-playing instincts.

The clues used both in the gossip columnist game and in the
solution of the actual murder are clearly kin to the intricate wordplay
for which Sondheim is famous. During the game, for example, players are confronted with a bottle of perfume. One of the game-players
recognizes that the brand, Chanel Number Five, is an indication to
switch the television in the room to Channel Number Five, where a
videotape supplies him with the information necessary to solve that
round of the game. (Chanel Number Five becoming Channel Number Five recalls Lee Remick's deliberately artificial French accent as Ze
Lady From Lourdes in *Anyone Can Whistle*.)

As the film continues, the clues grow in complexity. Even the
title takes on multiple meanings, referring to Sheila's death, to the
name of the movie Clinton plans to produce about Sheila, to a weary
remark made by one of the guests: Will we ever hear the Last of Sheila?,
and, most importantly, to a clue which is crucial to the mystery's final
solution.

Sondheim obviously takes great delight in devising these multi-
level brain-teasers, and, as the game-players try to identify the real
murderer, they must contend with acronyms, a visual crostic in a
group photograph, and a deduction relating to the adjective *little* which
only a wordsmith such as Sondheim could have conceived or appreciated. Just as Sondheim's work in musical theatre possesses an intelli-
gence and an inventiveness which are uniquely his, so too does *The
Last of Sheila* boast an intricacy and a delight in the cerebral which
sets it apart from most other screenplays, and identifies it as a work by
Sondheim.

It should come as no surprise that a man renowned for the intricacy of his lyrics should be able to create the complex clues and elaborate twists and turns that comprise the plot of *The Last of Sheila*.
However, upon watching the film a second time, an interesting parallel with his musical work becomes discernible.

Sondheim has often stated that his primary method for composing a complete score for a show is to create individual themes for particular characters or plot points. As the show progresses, Sondheim continues to develop these themes until by the end of the evening they mature into a fully unified score.

The pattern of assigning and developing themes is also evident in *The Last of Sheila*. Upon the initial appearance of every character, Sondheim introduces a leitmotif for each of them, which, on first viewing, probably goes unnoticed. Lee (Joan Hackett), the wife of the screenplay writer, is observed with a drink when she first receives her invitation; Phillip (James Mason), a fading film director, makes his initial appearance on the set of a dog food commercial, directing ringleted little moppets; Anthony (Ian MacShane), the husband of glamorous movie star Alice (Raquel Welch), brutally punches a member of the paparazzi who is annoying his wife; and Christine (Dyan Cannon), a loudmouthed super-agent, first appears chattering on the telephone. All of these actions are both in character and not especially extraordinary, but Sondheim continues to develop these themes throughout the screenplay.

Finally, when the characters' true dirty secrets are revealed during the murder investigation, observant viewers will realize that the introductory scenes actually foreshadowed these secrets: Lee turns out to have a drinking problem; the garrulous Christine is revealed to have been an informer during the McCarthy hearings; Anthony has done time in prison for assault and battery; and Phillip has a predilection for very young girls.

This development of character leitmotifs works not only to unify the film in the same way in which it unifies Sondheim's musical scores, but also enhances the consistency, and hence, the reality, of the characters and their motivations, especially necessary in a murder mystery.

Another major theme that Sondheim develops throughout *The Last of Sheila* is the idea of games and game-playing. Sondheim introduces this concept almost immediately by having the film open with Clinton, surrounded by his games, typing the letters that invite his guests to participate in the gossip columnist game aboard his yacht. The concept of games runs throughout *The Last of Sheila* almost as if it were a musical theme, with the gossip columnist game itself comprising most of the story, and individual references to games such as

Clinton's collection of game boards and puzzles developing it further. Sondheim continues the game theme right up until the end: a final murder attempt is made when one character tries to strangle another using a pair of brightly colored hand puppets from Clinton's game collection; and the final plot twist clearly divides the surviving characters into the winners and losers.

Just as Sondheim uses identifiable themes to give each of his musical scores its own unique flavor (the rollicking burlesque feel of *A Funny Thing Happened on the Way to the Forum*; the abrasiveness of contemporary city life in *Company*; the Oriental sound of *Pacific Overtures*; the graceful waltzes of turn of the century Sweden in *A Little Night Music*; the operatic grandeur of *Passion*), the game theme adds a through-line which gives *The Last of Sheila* its own quality of both the fun and dangers of game-playing.

The characters themselves are also representative of Sondheim's work. Each is as efficiently and distinctly drawn as if he or she had been given a solo to sing, and their dialogue is as witty and as in character as a Sondheim lyric.

Sondheim's dark view of humanity so evident in such musical works as *Sweeney Todd*, *Into the Woods*, and *Assassins* also permeates *The Last of Sheila*. Sondheim seems perfectly at home writing of Hollywood heartlessness. All of the characters are hoping to profit in some way from the film that Clinton is planning to produce about the death of his wife, and there is an undercurrent of gleeful sadism running throughout the picture as Clinton forces the others to participate in his games.

The end of *The Last of Sheila* is actually darker than that of *Sweeney Todd*. The killer in *The Last of Sheila* literally gets away with murder, and then, in a burst of irony typical of Sondheim, receives just desserts by being consigned to a personal hell far worse than if the killer had simply been turned over to the police.

Another interesting point about *The Last of Sheila* is that Sondheim worked on the script while writing the score for *A Little Night Music*. Although Sondheim was probably not conscious of it at the time, there are several distinct parallels between the two projects. In both, a flamboyant theatrical type (Desirée in *Night Music*, Clinton in *Sheila*) invites a group of guests to a luxurious, isolated setting (the Armfeldt mansion, Clinton's yacht) with the idea of manipulating the lives of the people involved. In each case, the hero is an intelligent working man (Fredrik the lawyer in *Night Music*, Tom the screenwriter in *Sheila*), as opposed to their wealthier hosts. The men arrive with their more ingenuous wives (Anne in *Night Music*, Lee in *Sheila*). The other participants include a blustering, macho birdbrain (Carl-Magnus in *Night Music*, Anthony in *Sheila*) accompanied by his glamorous, and far more intelligent spouse (Charlotte in *Night Music*, Alice in *Sheila*; although Raquel Welch's portrayal of Alice tends to emphasize her physical charms rather than her intellectual prowess, it is Alice who first realizes the true motivation behind Clinton's gossip columnist game, and who first understands the significance of the secrets assigned to each of the players); and a sexually rapacious woman whose presence adds largely to the comic relief (Petra in *Night Music*, Christine in *Sheila*). Wisdom in both shows is represented by an older character with a sexually checkered history (Madame Armfeldt in *Night Music*; and, in *Sheila*, Phillip, the director, who provides much of the detective work necessary to unmask the killer.) *Night Music* includes an attempted suicide; *The Last of Sheila* contains an apparently successful one. Even the theme of games and game-playing, so prevalent in *The Last of Sheila*, appears in *Night Music*, where the characters who arrive to spend a weekend in the country admit that "We'll be laying our plans/ While we're playing croquet..."; and, as Craig Zadan reports in *Sondheim & Company*, an earlier incarnation of *A Little Night Music*'s book depicted Madame Armfeldt as a witch-like figure playing solitaire. Each time she would reshuffle her pack of cards, the play would revert to the beginning, and the characters would have another chance to find a satisfactory partner from among the other guests (202).

Although *A Little Night Music* is set in bucolic, turn of the century Sweden, and *The Last of Sheila* deals with the dog-eat-dog world of contemporary Hollywood, there are noticeable similarities between the two projects, and it is interesting to wonder, from the point of view of film history, whether Ingmar Bergman's *Smiles of a Summer Night*, the classic movie on which *Night Music* is based, is actually the forerunner of Sondheim's *The Last of Sheila*.

Film critics were not kind to *The Last of Sheila*, complaining about its nearly indecipherable clues and extremely convoluted plot. However, this criticism also places *Sheila* firmly in the canon of Sondheim's work, for upon first exposure to his scores, many critics have denounced the characteristic complexity. It is only upon second and third hearings that one can fully appreciate the skill, beauty, and richness of the construction of Sondheim's music and lyrics.

First-time viewers of *The Last of Sheila* may indeed be overwhelmed by its intricacy; however, now that the film is readily available on video cassette, a second viewing permits the audience to appreciate how deftly Sondheim plants his clues, how skillfully he constructs the plot and develops the characters, and how fairly he plays throughout the film—the hallmark of a true connoisseur of games.

As with his scores for the musical theatre, repeated viewings of *The Last of Sheila* serve only to increase the audience's enjoyment of a complex work that is uniquely by Sondheim, and evidence of his skills as a master games-player.

ᘓ

Work Cited

Zadan, Craig. *Sondheim & Co.* New York: Macmillan, 1974.

On Performing Sondheim
A Little Night Music *Revisited*
David Craig

While the creators of musical theater (the composer, the lyricist and the librettist) toil in a climate of accordant, if not always benign, consensus, the subsequent rehearsals of the production of their efforts can only be described as monuments of departmentalization. The Director, the Choreographer, the Scene Designer, the Costume Designer, the Music Director, the Orchestrator, the Lighting Designer, pianists, stage managers, stage-hands and, in recent years, the elevation of the Sound Engineer to peer status, all work away, separate and apart, on the stage, in lobbies, anterooms of restrooms and, in extremis, in rented ballrooms and studios. Midway in rehearsals, their individual contributions begin to come together in a kind of alchemy and, with the help of the gods, even fit. Arbitrary entrances ("Here comes Joey, now"—John O'Hara) and exits ("I smell something burning in the kitchen"—John Van Druten) conjoin like magic to make their own kind of sense. Dances gain context, cross-overs that appeared arbitrary in execution now are integral, and unresolved scenes that ended precipitately segue sensibly into song. Never mind how organic their creative birth, the production of musicals, unlike plays, is a mechanistic construct of stunning complexity.

Leaving aside the mini-armies of artists and artisans who make up the production team, it is of some interest to note that in our time there never has been, nor is there now, a staff-member whose sole duty is to stage the sung score. When we consider how much text in a musical is sung, this can be considered, and with some justification, a missing person.

Once upon a time, the performing skills of the great stars who appeared in musicals during the first half of this century would have made the job redundant. The success of a musical hung on two, and only two, elements: the score and who sang it. The "book" was for-mulaic; the entire enterprise designed to amuse and to entertain. In John Lahr's disturbing and strangely elegiac essay on the work of Stephen Sondheim, he mourns that "once upon a time" when "people [didn't] walk, they dance[d]." And they sang. Singers were stars (Helen Morgan, Ethel Merman, Vivienne Segal, Ethel Waters, Dennis King, Al Jolson, Maurice Chevalier), dancers could sing with ease (Fred and Adele Astaire, Marilyn Miller, George M. Cohan, Gene Kelly, Avon Long), comics sang for their laughs (Eddie Cantor, Bert Williams, Danny Kaye, Phil Silvers) and so did clowns (Bert Lahr, Beatrice Lillie, Eddie Foy, Fanny Brice, Nancy Walker). Nor was their singing con-sidered second-class. A virtual pantheon of composers and lyricists willingly wrote for them. The musical theater (more aptly labeled musical comedy) in which these eminences toiled is long gone, al-though today's passion for reviving it appears to be Broadway's effort to mark time by marching backward. It is of some interest that these revivals lean heavily on lavish physical design as compensation for the absence of those performers who, more often than not, were the *raison d'être* for the original productions.

As "what" is on the stage replaces "who," a new breed of performer works the musical boards. Unlike those artists who once engaged and held an audience by virtue of their singular imprint on the songs they sang, "cross-over" actor/singers, dancer/singers and, paradoxically, singer/singers do not nor cannot be expected to possess such expertise. Their time on the musical theater stage is too desul-tory, too sporadic. In consequence, the standard procedure today is to allot the task of shaping vocal performances to the Choreographer or, should the song require less "fixed" staging, the Director. This may or may not be an aesthetic plus. When a song calls for a set pattern, choreographers can make it a show-stopping experience but when a knowledge of how to make a song "work" in its dramatic context is needed, their skills are arguably irrelevant. The Director, working on a macro-canvas, may have neither the time nor the facil-ity to be of sufficient aid to a performer whose sense of self in song is betrayed by an all-too-evident self-consciousness. Of course, there are exceptions—in particular when choreographer/directors are or have been performers as well. Tommy Tune, Patricia Birch and the late, gifted Michael Bennett come to mind (the last two were, at one time, students of mine. I mention this to establish that they were dancers who also sang). Too often, however, I find myself ill at ease when, in an otherwise beautifully conceived and executed production, I become conscious of sung performances that are awkward or, worse, disserve a song.

The essential thrust of what I have taught for almost fifty years and written about at length is simply stated: just as well-articulated dialogue is not the actor's sole concern, songs that are merely sung (*told*) to an audience, whether outside of or within the context of a set score, I consider unsung. Rejection of "playing" the words is basic to the early study of the actor's art and yet the cross-over actor who moves into the lyric theater reverts to his or her earliest amateur beginnings at the mere sound of a musical introduction. The conflictive pressures and confrontational tensions that lie beneath a *sung* script (in the case of Stephen Sondheim's textured work, these can interface as well as interlock) remain uninvestigated and, worse, disappear behind an infantile indication of the lyric. What we hear and witness, too often, are charaded performances of what is being sung. In general, this may be considered the root cause of the physical self-consciousness that afflicts cross-over actors, dancers and, sadly, concert singers when they first begin a life in song. My thesis, then, is this: Concern yourself only with the words and the music of what you sing and you have joined the audience by becoming the reactor *to*, rather than the creator *of* the song. Simply stated, the subject and the predicate have reversed themselves: the song sings you.

The actor who first moves into the musical theater arena takes up an uneasy residence. His discomfort impels him to ask, not unreasonably: why are *speaking* and *singing* such disparate activities? Shouldn't there be a common utility factor present in song as well as in speech? Sadly, the answer is this: not at the start and only fractionally at the finish. To begin with, those who seek to sing what they might have elected to speak now live in the world of music and music is a stringent dictator. Its binary components, melody and rhythm, confine the singer. Whereas the melodies and rhythms of *speech* are self-created, the rise and fall of what is *sung* and the tempi in which it must be delivered are rigidly set down by the composer. There can be no argument for argument would play havoc with the orchestra. The actor may be the final arbiter of when he or she chooses to speak and how it will be inflected, but alter the speech into song and the singer forfeits these freedoms. Furthermore, the *explicit* cue which, in the exchange of dialogue, is the actor's source of reaction is denied him in song. Nevertheless, sung or spoken speech (on the stage) cannot be, indeed dare not be, the result of memorized words. Just as the soliloquies in Elizabethan drama are dependent upon an internalized flow of sub-textual thought, the need in song for *implicit* cues is mandatory. What makes singing so difficult are the prescribed rhythms that dictate the speed of the flow of the internalized ideation. It is the graceful *timing* of this sub-textual continuum that is, for me, the primary element of great performing and defines that elusive word: style.

It can be seen, then, that when, in late 1990, Gordon Davidson asked me to stage the score of *A Little Night Music* in his production of the piece in Los Angeles, the opportunity to leave the classroom was instantly alluring. Mr. Sondheim is one of a dwindling few whose works require dramatic, as well as theatrical, performances. There is no over-larding of productional excess to give validity to what is sung unless, of course, it is relevant, e.g., in *Follies*. Dramatic verity and not decoration informs his scores. The performer is required to hold the stage solely by virtue of his or her ability to do so. Mr. Sondheim's wit can capture the ear of the audience but it can, and often does, upstage a pedestrian performance. The singer must claim pre-eminence over him when the show is on. Here, then, was a chance to work on a score with which I was familiar and for which I had enormous regard; a rare opportunity to work the songs in their natural habitat rather than, as is the custom in my classes, to approach each one as a discrete entity that owes its allegiance solely to an effective performance whether or not the performance matches the imperatives of the original context.

Furthermore, Lee Remick was to play Desirée and Miss Remick was a cherished friend whom I had taught many years before. In what we all considered a minor *coup de théâtre*, Glynis Johns was willing to play Mme. Armfeldt (thereby appearing as both Armfeldt *mère* and *fille* within a span of almost twenty years) and, as an added enticement for me, John McMartin, a Sondheim alumnus whose work I keenly admired (he was the "first" and, for me, the definitive Ben in *Follies*), had already signed to play Fredrik. So, there we were, a wedded troika of sorts: Onna White, our choreographer, Gordon and I; each of us working within our own defined domain and I, in my innovative role, who had until then never been a member of the wedding.

The experience, from almost the beginning to the end, was exhilarating. "Almost the beginning" trivializes the early chronology for, during pre-production proceedings, we sustained the shocking news of Miss Remick's terminal illness (she died three months after opening night). Paralyzing despair and the realization that we had to move on hurled us into thirteenth-hour auditioning anyone and everyone who was able to play the role—and a few who were less than able. We chose Lois Nettleton (again, an actress whom I had taught) but rehearsals began with Lee's absence hanging heavily over the entire affair. Miss Nettleton behaved impeccably. Further weighted down by the presence of Miss Johns and pressured by the implied comparison, she was doughty and determined to bring her own signature to the work. In Miss Johns's defense, it was the first time she had performed the piece since its New York run and then, of course, "...Clowns" had been hers. Although it could not be considered a "signature song," one felt she entertained a kind of proprietary ownership of the song and, indeed, quite possibly the role.

There is a singular joy in working on a Sondheim score. He is an iconoclast who nevertheless can write a solid ABAB song ("Anyone Can Whistle") should he care to; invent new language to sing about: "A Bowler Hat" (*Pacific Overtures*); juxtapose seemingly disparate subject matter: "Children And Art" (*Sunday in the Park with George*) and achieve heightened dramatic effects by employing ever-changing rhythms: "The Ballad Of Booth" (*Assassins*) is scored, in one ten-bar sequence, in $\frac{4}{4}$, $\frac{6}{4}$, $\frac{4}{4}$, $\frac{6}{4}$, $\frac{5}{4}$, $\frac{6}{4}$, $\frac{7}{4}$, $\frac{6}{4}$ and $\frac{4}{4}$ time signatures! In the case of *A Little Night Music*, a minor miracle is achieved: the entire piece, with one exception, was conceived in $\frac{3}{4}$ time or its equivalent extensions. Only "A Weekend In The Country" gallops along in $\frac{6}{8}$ rhythms but even here, although the conductor beats *two* beats to each measure, each beat contains *three* eighth notes or their equivalent. Straight waltzes, valses tristes, Viennese waltzes, tumble off the page in unlimited variety. Even "Send In The Clowns," with its broad, Brahmsian melodic theme on the third line of the first, second and last "8":

> Me here at last on the ground, you in mid-air...
> One who keeps tearing around, one who can't move...

and:

> Losing my timing this late in my career…

is written in multiples of threes (shuttling between 12/8 and 9/8) although one can barely discern a waltz anywhere in its exposition.

From the start, the prospect of staging four songs, in particular, intrigued me:

(1) The Trio that comprises "Now" (sung by Mr. McMartin), "Later" (Franc D'Ambrosio) and "Soon" (Michelle Nicastro) in Act One, Scene One;

(2) "Liaisons" (Miss Johns) in Act One, Scene Four;

(3) "In Praise of Women" (Jeff McCarthy) in Act One, Scene Five; and

(4) "Send in the Clowns" in Act Two, Scene Six.

This is not to imply that the entire score is not challenging but:

a) "The Glamorous Life," like "A Weekend in The Country," depends on "picture" staging, placement of groups and impeccable diction to make its points;

b) "You Must Meet My Wife," with its intentional by-play of jokes, is virtually foolproof;

c) "It Would Have Been Wonderful," truly a "book" song, works to the degree that the men resist clowning and remain true to their characters;

d) In "Every Day a Little Death" (sung by Marcia Mitzman and Miss Nicastro), the most personal of soliloquies—albeit there are two women on stage—they live (and sing) in two worlds separate and apart from each other. The lyric is ravishing in its allusions and requires next to no "staging." Sub-text is all and this internalized sub-text acts like an engine that drives and makes possible the outpouring of Charlotte's revelations. In apposition to the intensity of her pain is Anne's coming-of-age and subsequent disillusionment, all of which occurs within the margins of her vocal participation. However, once that sub-text is defined for the singers, the director's work is done. The physical appearance of the performance is, and must be, as simple as the internal life is dense. The lyric can afford only a minimum of

> body language at peril of upstaging what must be
> heard and, finally,

e) "The Miller's Son" (sung by Katherine Rowe
   McAllen) has always presented a problem. It arrives
   at that moment in the second act when the first plot
   line is all but over and, despite its brilliance as a set
   piece, suffers, I think, from a length far in excess of
   the importance of the character who sings it. Before
   the butler, Frid, lost "Silly People" in the out-of-town
   pre-Broadway surgeries, there may have been an aesthetic balance for Petra's aria but with that balance
   no longer present, one can do little more than sing
   the devil out of it (and the role is always cast to
   make that a certainty) while paying lip-service to post-
   coital positioning.

The trio "Now," "Later." and "Soon" presents an enormous challenge. One is impelled to find a way to give theatrical life to each of
the parts without sacrificing the inevitable whole of the trio, to make
certain that the audience hears each of the three elements before the
parts cohere and to set forth as clearly as possible each character's
problem—as sung. To begin with, the placement of the bed upon
which Fredrik sits and inevitably lies down upon presents a major
problem. He will be "napping" yet singing when "Now" becomes a
third of the trio. The final bars in which "later…," "soon…," and his
"now…" arrive, seriatim, in harmonized succession are not the ultimate last words we hear. Fredrik, supposedly deep in sleep, dreamily
whispers "…Desirée." This slip of the tongue must be audible to the
entire theater in order to understand the sudden wide-awake reaction
from Anne who, shaken from her drowse and in profound shock, sits
up in bed to perform her "take." The moment can be said to intro-
duce the attack of the play in the muttering of one word. To make all
this possible, the bed must be raked but not so obviously that the
audience is aware of the reason that dictates the angle, and even
Fredrik's positioning when supine requires some faking. In the original production the vanity table at which Anne sits was far upstage
center, thereby making it virtually impossible to understand what was
being said and sung since she was quite literally facing the left upstage
wing. We moved it downstage, almost "in one" below right of the bed
placement. By this means we not only heard her running babble that
accompanies "Now" but her subsequent "Soon" promises and, more

important, contrived to get her into the bed in time for the trio's finish without resorting to awkward staging. Henrik and his cello remained where they have always been—stage left of the bedroom.

I was fascinated by the task of inventing and timing the physicalization of "Now" (Fredrik is undressing and preparing for his nap while he sings) so that the audience would never be in doubt when they were to watch and when they were to listen. Mr. McMartin's task was not made easier by the rapid tempo in which "Now" is scored. To begin with, he began his undressing standing downstage of the bed during the orchestral introduction (which has a "safety"), took off his jacket and folded it over his arm in time to freeze and sing the problem of the moment:

> Now, as the sweet imbecilities tumble so lavishly
> On to her lap

He remains in place, a lawyer working it out:

> Now, there are two possibilities: A, I could ravish her,
> B, I could nap…

Then, moving upstage to the clothes rack, he hangs up his jacket and turns front, still working it out, working it out and, at the last possible instant, getting closer to a plan of action for:

> Say it's the ravishment, then we see the option
> that follows, of course:

He has begun to take off his tie but this time, pleased with himself that a jurist's thought processes are being put to good use, he stops to explain to the audience (the jury?):

> A, the deployment of charm, or B, the adoption of
> physical force.

He sits on the foot of the bed and continues the pro's and con's with a certain pleasure he derives in the clarity of his argument:

> Now B might arouse her, but if I assume
> I trip on my trouser leg crossing the room…
> Her hair getting tangled, her stays getting snapped,
> (*Slow realization that the argument may be leading to
> inevitable doom*):
> My nerves will be jangled, my energy sapped…

He stands and begins undoing his shirt, while coping with the grow-ing realization that B won't work (there is a two-bar musical fill here):

> Removing her clothing would take me all day
> And her subsequent loathing would turn me away,

The dead end reached—another tack must be taken:

> Which eliminates B
> And which leaves us with "A."

What all this achieves is that Fredrik's thought processes are what we *see*. The song is not only *about* now. It *exists* in the now. We are finally free of being "told" the tale and instead, can watch its evolution and hear its revelations at the same time that they occur to Fredrik. In the end, he opts for the nap.

This can be described through to the end but suffice it to say that, at the conclusion, he had undressed down to his period under-clothes, pulled down the coverlet, and half-sitting and half-lying down during the four-bar fill that precedes

> Bow as I must to adjust my original plan…
> How shall I sleep half as deep as I usually can?
> When now I still want and/or love you
> Now, as always,
> Now, Anne!
> (*He falls asleep*)

"Later" is not an easy aria to sing and when a production is fortu-nate enough as we were to boast a Henrik whose tenor is unfazed by its demands, one is only too willing to give preeminence to the score, in particular the high B-natural in the final apogee:

> How can I wait around for later,
> I'll be ninety on my deathbed
> And the late, or rather later,
> Henrik Egerman!

And yet, at the same time, I was determined to make Henrik's cello accompaniment credible (he plays his own) as a secondary action to the primary one: the singing out of his frustrations. The rapid-fire fingering of the cello obbligato that accompanies his held high B-natural on: "For God's sake!" as performed by Mr. D'Ambrosio was so perfectly fingered that, at our first music reading, the entire orchestra, led by the lead cellist, burst into applause.

"Soon"'s implicit problem is getting Anne away from her vanity table where the script finds her at the top of the trio. When she rises to begin "Soon," she moves around the rear of the bed caressing his side of the headboard as she passes upstage of him and downstage for the pivotal moment in the lyric, directed to a straight-front focus, her tremulous sexual awakening:

> Even now,
> When you're close and we touch,
> And you're kissing my brow,
> I don't mind it too much.

and subsequently back to and into the bed in time for her above-described "take" preceding the blackout. Again, all this without upstaging the lyric.

And, finally, when the trio came together, to give each part enough activity without menacing the primary effect of the whole: Henrik merely talking in his sleep, Anne dealing with the sequence of lying down beside him and making herself comfortable beneath the counterpane, while Henrik continued his frustrated "duet" with his cello.

"Liaisons" afforded me the most pleasure. In the original, Hermione Gingold who, as the aging Mme. Armfeldt, had been wheelchair-bound whenever she was on the stage, experienced a stunning, if temporary, cure that allowed her to perform the song as vertical as a vaudevillian, albeit with a cane if not a straw hat. I was hell-bent to keep Miss Johns in the chair where her physical condition had consigned her and to create a language for the chair that would enliven as well as enhance the performance. By the end of rehearsals, Glynis became a veteran at the game. She was able to manipulate the chair up, down, laterally and, as a device to get into second and third choruses, to achieve "double takes" by the quick application of the brakes followed by a slow reverse course. I shall never forget her sweep downstage center, arms spread wide as if embracing the audience, that accompanied the arrival of the quite thrilling key change into E-flat major that elevates the final words into a kind of apotheosis:

> In a world where the kings are employers,
> Where the amateur prevails and delicacy fails to pay,
> In a world where the Princes are lawyers,
> What can anyone expect except to recollect liai...

So moved was the audience by the performance that our only problem became the timing of the butler's hasty entrance in order to wheel the lady off without killing her hand.

"In Praise Of Women" requires a singer who is able to stay implacably in the instant of each line of the song so that its performance is experienced in the immediate present. Since Carl-Magnus is something of a dolt, the task is made more difficult; he must not only appear to be dim-witted but, at the same time, be sharp enough to perform double-takes that occur in rapid-fire sequences:

> She wouldn't...therefore they didn't...
> So then it wasn't....not unless it...
> Would she?...(etc).

as well as shuttling between the out-and-out sensual pleasure he takes in limning his own perception of the virtues of the female sex:

> Capable, pliable women...women
> Undemanding and reliable,
> Knowing their place. [etc.]
> Durable, sensible women...women...
> Very nearly indispensable creatures of grace. [etc.]
> The world would surely be a poorer—if purer—place.

and on to the niggling dilemma: "How can you slip and trip into a hip-bath?", "Where were the papers?", "She wouldn't....Therefore they didn't...," until the solution to overlook the hip-bath is arrived at: "Of course, he might have taken back the papers..." which in turn transforms the interrogative tone at the top of the lyric into the ringing exclamatory that summates the regaining of his masculine pride: "The woman's mine!" The song is a virtual tour de force that, when performed well does not, in fact must not appear to be so. Carl-Magnus the actor must be no less a dolt than Carl-Magnus the singer.

"Send in The Clowns," within the body of the score, is an undisputed masterpiece. It has an inevitability that makes it seem to have been plucked in its entirety out of space. How, indeed, had no composer not plucked it out before Mr. Sondheim? Everyone loves this perfect song and that is the good of it. We wait for it with a kind of delicious anticipation. The bad of it? How to make the audience hear it and attend it as if for the first time. It is an "eleven o'clock" number (or almost) that arrives in the penultimate moments of the play and "sings" revelations that occur to Desirée at the very moment that they are revealed to the audience. (In that regard it resembles another "perfect" song: "I've Grown Accustomed To Her Face" from *My Fair Lady*). Again, Miss Nettleton and I were chary about larding the performance with an excess of physical language for we felt that Desirée would be virtually paralyzed by the shock of Fredrik's back-tracking from commitment. There was, too, her distaste for sentimentality that would impel her to dissemble the heartbreak resulting from the failure of her plotted "weekend in the country." We felt that she would be impelled to accomplish this confession of autumnal regret with an overlay of her innate wit (Mr. Sondheim's innate wit). We risked one move of her hand toward his lap (they are seated at the foot of her bed) immediately following the lines

> One who keeps tearing around,
> One who can't move.

but before it came to rest there, she withdrew it guiltily as if intimacy of any kind between them was no longer permissible. We worked, too, on which lines belonged to her (an internalized focus), which to the audience (an objectivized focus) and which ones could be risked to him (very few, indeed). After his exit, rather than keep her sitting there, I felt strongly that the song had been honestly served and now, in deference to the audience's affection for it and a desire to have them share in its final reprise, I asked Miss Nettleton to rise and move slowly downstage where, lighted by the tightest of pin-spots, she sang the final "eight":

> Isn't it rich,
> Isn't it queer,
> Losing my timing this late in my career?
> And where are the clowns?
> There ought to be clowns.
> Well, maybe next year…

as the pin-spot irised out with the slowest fade we could manage.

I do not mean to suggest that the score of every musical theater production should be separately serviced as it was in this instance. As I have said above, the task of many of today's musical theater productions is to astound. The physical aspect is primary. As I write this, there are sung performances on the Broadway stage that are but a small element of the total stage picture. Their effect upon the audience is the same whether the star, the understudy or a replacement is singing. The ticket buyer attends the event with the same expectations one brings to any gaudy event. Stephen Sondheim's work demands something more of the audience. They spectate but, more important, they are asked to become involved; not only to look but to see, not only to hear but to listen to the comedy as much as the tragedy of what we are about: the Passion, betrayal, first love, missed connections, painful memories, social behavior both frivolous and destructive. All of life is being sung about. In my own case, it was a stimulating adventure to present not only what the score of *A Little Night Music says* but, more important, what the score *means* (to me). Further reward was the gratitude expressed by the actors and singers for an outside "eye" to help in the shaping of their interpretive performances. In an interview with Tony Roberts (relative to another musical he had been in), he had this to say about the difference between the rehearsal process of a play and a musical:

> [In a musical]…one depends more on a "third eye" to tell you when you are in your own world—one that no one will go to with you—or what you need to do to take the audience with you to that level of experience. You know, somehow, innately what an audience will buy when you are talking to another actor because you know whether the other actor is buying it…[but] when you are out front with a song, [you need] someone who will give you specific anchors through the song. Gradually, through that direction, the song is broken down into units. You need this…because you are flying free out there. It goes back to the need to have to be wound up and motivated in order to sing. [To be free to do it] you cannot watch yourself closely at the same time…You need that third eye. (1997)

If departmentalism is inherent in the rehearsal process of a musical production, when the words and music demand primacy there may be argument in favor of an added staff member to service what is, after all, the quintessential element of all great musical theater: its score.

‿

WORK CITED

Roberts, Tony. Personal interview. In David Craig. *On Musical Theater Stages.*
　　New York: Applause, forthcoming (1997).

"More Beautiful Than True" or "Never Mind a Small Disaster": The Art of Illusion in Pacific Overtures
Leonard Fleischer

Although *Pacific Overtures* (1976) has been called by Frank Rich a "one-of-a-kind experiment in the annals of the musical theater" (qtd. in Zadan 224–25), and in style of presentation resembles no other work by Stephen Sondheim, its relationship to other Sondheim musicals is far closer than might initially appear. It is true that none of his other works utilize elements of the Japanese Kabuki theater or were written for what is essentially an all-male cast. In addition, Harold Prince's comment to Hugh Wheeler, "This [*Pacific Overtures*] is not about people. This is a musical about the clash of two cultures, which means do not emphasize the human aspects of it" (qtd. in Zadan 214), applies to no other Sondheim show. Yet despite the undeniable uniqueness of *Pacific Overtures* in the Sondheim canon, its links to his other works do exist and reflect a continuity of thematic focus.

The original 1976 production—as well as the more favorably reviewed revised 1984 version—lost its total investment. John Rockwell has written that the work was "hard for audiences to identify with—all that foreignness in the musical and dramatic idioms, the lack of a single romantic hero or heroine, the distance from contemporary life" (217). As Joanne Gordon has pointed out: "[F]or all its intellectual audacity, many feel the dimension of emotional commitment, so poignant and powerful in *Company* and *Follies*, is absent" (175). She added that "the subliminal cry of outrage, which gave such resonance to the other works, is missing" (175). Yet though *Pacific Overtures* was not the most financially successful or audience-pleasing of Sondheim's works, its many virtues and its daring approach to the "Broadway musical" render it worthy of close scrutiny, particularly as it reflects his continuing exploration of certain themes.

The genesis of *Pacific Overtures* has been well documented. It began as a straight play by John Weidman who submitted it to Harold Prince. Prince felt that the material could be musicalized and brought in Sondheim. Despite initial reservations, Sondheim agreed to proceed and explained his approach to the materials:

> What we actually did was to create a mythical Japanese playwright in our heads, who has come to New York, seen a couple of Broadway shows, and then goes back home and writes a musical about Commodore Perry's visit to Japan. It's this premise that helped give us tone and style for the show. (Qtd. in Zadan 210)

Its score and lyrics reflect both Japanese and Western influences. Indeed, as the show progresses and the impact of the Western invasion is evident, the haiku-like lyrics of such tender Act I songs as "There is No Other Way" and "Poems" give way to more colloquial language, culminating in the final song, "Next," a jarring industrial show–like "tribute" to modern Japan. In "Poems," Kayama and Manjiro, walking to Uraga, conclude each of their brief alternating verses with the gracious line, "Your turn" (41–44). "Next," with its emphasis on speed and movement, and performed by anonymous modern characters (including, for the first time, women), ends each stanza with "Next!," a word which is repeated thirty-five times (102–7).

The Westernization of Japan is foreshadowed in the brief wordless Act I finale with Commodore Matthew Perry doing a combination of the "traditional Kabuki lion dance and the American cake walk" (65). Early in Act II, in "Please Hello," admirals from five "invading" nations (United States, Great Britain, Holland, Russia, and France) each perform a number in a style indigenous to that country (71–85). "A Bowler Hat" preserves some of the haiku-like quality of earlier lyrics, but is filled with such modern images as "umbrella," "pocket watch," "cigars," "monocle," and "bowler hat" (91–93). And the penultimate number of the musical, "Pretty Lady," performed by three British sailors in a cockney dialect, includes such words as "ain't," "wontcher," "'alf," and "cantcher" (95–98).

The major focus of *Pacific Overtures* is the metamorphosis of Japan as it becomes more influenced by Western culture and technology, a theme echoed by the changes in its two main characters, Manjiro and Kayama. Underlying this surface theme, however, is a broader

Sondheim concern which, despite the diverse source materials of his musicals and his collaboration with different book writers, seems to permeate his work. Such a preoccupation involves a movement from a state of innocence, self-delusion, or avoidance of reality to a cathartic shattering of illusions, and/or a more mature acceptance of the world (or people) as it (or they) really exists. This progression in the narrative or in the psyches of his characters is sometimes informed by the oft-noted ambivalence of the composer/lyricist toward both the comforting illusions held at the beginning of the work and the painful reality found at its conclusion.

In *Anyone Can Whistle* (1964) the line distinguishing the patients in a mental institution (The Cookie Jar) from the "sane" ones outside is a thin one. Further, the townspeople believe in a "miracle"—that water is gushing from a rock. As Sondheim has noted: "Though organized religion may be dead, there is an enormous need in people to think that something beyond them and not explainable in terms of ordinary human activity is going on" (qtd. in Zadan 88). The need to believe in miracles (or illusions) is a powerful emotion. *Company* (1970) examines the tension between the illusion of happiness secured through marriage or "involvement" and the virtues of emotional detachment. In "Sorry/Grateful," three of the five married men in the show convey this ambivalence, concluding that

> You'll always be what you always were,
> Which has nothing to do with,
> All to do with her. (36)

Although Robert becomes "disillusioned" by the marriages of the five couples, he sees no alternative and, in his final song, "Being Alive," pleads,

> Somebody crowd me with love,
> Somebody force me to care,
> Somebody make me come through,
> I'll always be there as frightened as you. (116)

Follies (1971) is in part an affectionate look at the American musical theater between the two World Wars and provides Sondheim with an opportunity to use the traditional conventions of the genre to reveal the hollowness and falsity of his characters' dreams and illusions. The emotional highs generated by the reunion of the Follies girls ultimately give way to anger, disappointment, and a weary resignation to reality. *A Little Night Music* (1973) also deals with the illusory nature of romantic dreams, but concludes on a far less bitter note. True, the maid Petra sings of marriage to the Prince of Wales, yet understands that she may have to settle for the Miller's son. But the mismatched Fredrik and Anne end their "innocent" unconsummated marriage; Anne runs off with Fredrik's son, Henrik, a more suitable partner; Carl-Magnus returns to his wife, and Fredrik to his former mistress, Desirée. But as Joanne Gordon shrewdly points out, this uncharacteristically "happy" ending in a Sondheim musical is partially undercut by the rigid conventions of "the unreal environment of operetta" (152) which structure the work. It is only in that artificial world that "happily-ever-after romances can occur" (152).

Early in Act I of *Sweeney Todd: The Demon Barber of Fleet Street* (1979), the young sailor, Anthony Hope, sings the praises of the city of London:

> I have sailed the world, beheld the wonders
> From the Dardanelles
> To the mountains of Peru,
> But there's no place like London!
> I feel home again. (5)

His paean to that city, however, is followed soon thereafter by Sweeney Todd's characterization of it as a "hole in the world/ Like a great black pit/ And the vermin of the world/ Inhabit it" (9). Mrs. Lovett may amuse us by her romantic illusion of a cozily domestic life by the sea with Sweeney:

> Every night in the kip
> When we're through our kippers,
> I'll be there slippin' off your slippers
> By the sea.... (137)

But her casual amorality is no less repulsive than the barber's rage, and her ultimate fate's a grim one. Tobias believes that he can protect her from any harm, an illusion soon destroyed when Sweeney discovers the truth about his wife, Lucy. Anthony and Sweeney's daughter, Johanna, despite their travails, do manage to survive, but by witnessing the mayhem at the conclusion, their romantic innocence is unlikely to be sustained. Sweeney's shock and grief at discovering that the beggar woman whose throat he has just slit is, in fact, his wife, whom he had presumed long dead, is genuine. That *he*—not just "society"—bears some responsibility for what has happened to him—and to Lucy—suggests the destruction of a different kind of illusion.

Because of the reverse chronological structure, the appealing innocence of the main characters in *Merrily We Roll Along* (1981) is not fully dramatized until the end of the musical. Unlike *Follies*, which continually interweaves ghosts of the past with the present, *Merrily* moves steadily backward in time from the sour realities and broken friendships of the present to a more hopeful period, years before, when it was "our time," and doors could open. Extending beyond the examination of personal relationships, *Merrily* also evokes the idealistic spirit of the Kennedy years. Even the cynical modern incarnation of Georges Seurat in *Sunday in the Park with George* (1984), lacking the fiercely uncompromising integrity of his nineteenth-century predecessor, is laboring under an illusion. Content to spend his time "putting it together" with aggressive grantsmanship and clever cocktail party chatter (instead of "finishing the hat"), he believes that success gained by repeating chromolume triumphs will bring him happiness. Only after he encounters the ghost of Dot is he able to "move on" (169), creatively and emotionally.

The Baker and his wife in *Into the Woods* (1987) are deluded into assuming that once having achieved their goals in the woods (obtaining Red Riding Hood's cape, Rapunzel's hair, Cinderella's slipper and Jack's cow) they will—in typically "fairy tale" fashion—live happily ever after. What they (and other characters) learn, however, in Act Two is that the results of their amoral or unethical actions in attaining their objectives cannot be ignored. Characters make choices that have consequences. To make the right choice and survive, they must abandon the illusion that they are "alone," that others are not influenced or affected by what they do. To assume that "pure" motives (being able to bear a child) justify "bent" actions, as the Baker's Wife claims, violates the social contract implicit in the work (30). As Stephen Banfield points out:

> The dynamics of choice are not self-sustaining, as with the "free" artist or the married couple, but lead to fruitful or damaging consequences for the whole community. Self-

interest is a liability, and once wronged, the giant returns
and must be appeased or destroyed. (388–89)

Assassins (1991)—like *Pacific Overtures*, a collaboration with the
politically attuned John Weidman—confronts a related kind of illusion: the notion that

> Everybody's
> Got the right
> To be happy.
>   ...
> If you keep your
> Goal in sight,
> You can climb to
> Any height.
> Everybody's
> Got the right
> To their dreams.... (7)

What the actual and would-be Presidential assassins have in common
is a belief in "another National Anthem" (84), one that reflects their
status as "those who never win" (85). The Balladeer repeatedly tries to
defuse their anger with the hopeful bromide that "the mailman won
the lottery" (82–85), but, like the Narrator in *Into the Woods* (who
also tried to impose order on the other characters), he is driven off the
stage.

While not justifying the evil actions of the assassins, the authors
try to shatter our conventional assumptions about them. Some are
treated comically (Sara Jane Moore, Squeaky Fromme, and Samuel
Byck), while John Wilkes Booth, Giuseppe Zangara, Leon Czolgosz,
Charles Guiteau, and Lee Harvey Oswald are given a more human
dimension and placed in a context that permits us to understand,
though not condone, their deeds. When the ghosts of Booth and the
others convince the suicidal Oswald not to take his own life, but instead shoot the President, we see how the tantalizing illusion of "family" evoked by the assassins,

> We're your family...
> You are the future...
> We're depending on you...
> Make us proud... (102)

affects the lonely and distraught Oswald.

The lure of illusion and its potentially destructive consequences are perhaps expressed most dramatically in *Passion* (1994) when Fosca sings:

> There is a flower
> Which offers nectar at the top,
> Delicious nectar at the top,
> And bitter poison underneath.
> The butterfly that stays too long
> And drinks too deep
> Is doomed to die. (22–23)

She bitterly adds:

> I do not dwell on dreams.
> I know how soon a dream becomes an expectation.
> How can I have expectations?
>   ...
> I do not hope for what I cannot have!
> I do not cling to things I cannot keep! (23)

Before long, Fosca abandons her restraint and pursues her "dream" (Giorgio) with a fierce passion that has fatal consequences for her, but leaves her with the priceless knowledge that for once she is genuinely loved. By the close of *Passion*, we see that the real self-delusion existed earlier between Giorgio and his mistress, Clara, both of whom assumed that their passionate, yet ultimately shallow, affair was more than just "another love story" (4).

What seems evident, therefore, is that the price of disillusionment is a painful and heavy one, but necessary if reality is to be faced and truth told. Such a cathartic experience can lead to very different outcomes for the characters involved. For Fosca and the Baker's Wife in *Into the Woods*, for example, it is death. For Ben, Phyllis, Sally and Buddy in *Follies*, it means giving up long-held hopes and dreams (their personal "Follies") that things might have been different, that the past, or least their vision of it (accurate or not), could somehow be recaptured. Characters in other works similarly suffer the shock of discovering that their beliefs and illusions—the enduring value of fame and success, the limitless potential of the American Dream, and the "happily ever after" coda to marriages and fairy tales—only impede their ability to know themselves and the world around them.

In *Pacific Overtures*, personal and national illusions complement and reinforce each other. Its narrative lines are, in one case, political—the transformation of the nineteenth-century isolated "floating island" into a modern industrial powerhouse—and, in the other, personal—the story of a fisherman (Manjiro) and a minor samurai (Kayama), whose individual transformations mirror the tumultuous events taking place in Japan. The original 1976 large-scale Broadway production may well have overwhelmed the stories of Manjiro and Kayama. When a revised version was produced off-Broadway in 1984, several scenes were cut so that the musical, according to Sondheim

> [B]ecame more of a personal story about two men. What made it less so on Broadway was that we tried a scrapbook technique in which the personal story would be interrupted with scenes of what was going on politically in the country and then we'd return to the personal story. (Qtd. in Zadan 222)

Although Sondheim's musicals are not usually considered as political or social criticism, they have often included such a dimension. *Anyone Can Whistle* satirized small town venality, political corruption and the dangers of conformity. *Follies* viewed American society through a theatrical metaphor, but was not just about show business and two unhappily married couples. Ben's "breakdown" number in the original 1971 version reflected his inability to reconcile his desire to "live," "laugh," and "love," with the "success" ethic that prevails in American society:

> Success is swell
> And success is sweet,
> But every height has a drop.
> The less achievement,
> The less defeat.
> What's the point of shovin'
> Your way to the top?
> Live 'n' laugh 'n' love 'n'
> You're never a flop. (106)

Such a destructive ethic, which exalts fame and material wealth, while restricting creativity, is also examined in *Merrily* and *Sunday*. *Sweeney Todd* deals with personal revenge, but is, in Harold Prince's words, about the "class struggle—the terrible struggle to move out of the class in which you're born…the Industrial Age and the incursions of machinery on the spirit" (qtd. in Zadan 245). *Into the Woods* uses fairy tale characters to make larger statements about personal responsibility to the larger community, and, as noted above, *Assassins*—Sondheim's most directly political musical—examines real and would-be killers to remind us that the American Dream can be a nightmare for those who feel betrayed by the system.

The "national" illusion permeating the Act I of *Pacific Overtures* is that the turbulent events occurring in the outside world will have no impact on the "floating" island of Japan. What is changing is happening "Somewhere out there, not here" (4). In the static, changeless world of Japan, "the realities remain remote" (4). Although "Gods are crumbling somewhere," and "machines are rumbling somewhere" (4), in Japan the people are preoccupied with planting rice, painting screens, viewing the moon, and stirring the tea. "Tomorrow" will be arranged to be like "today" (5).

The overriding illusion that such isolation can be maintained permanently is seen in the behavior of individual characters. Kayama is commanded by the Shogun's councilors to invoke a seventeenth-century sacred decree and order the invading Americans to return home immediately, an impossible mission that not only reflects the cowardice and corruption of the Japanese rulers, but also ultimately results in the suicide of Kayama's loyal wife, Tamate.

The apocalyptic fears of a fisherman who spots the four American warships—"Four black dragons/ Spitting fire" (15)—are, in a literal sense, illusory, but the arrival of the Westerners *does* represent the end of a changeless, insulated existence for Japan. Their world *is* about to end. But the national self-delusion that the country is a civilized land threatened by foreign barbarians, is dispelled when a thief sings how he "was rifling through the house/ Of some priests/ In Uraga" and having "finished with the silks…was hunting for the gold" (18). The thief then steals a lacquer box from one of the fleeing townsmen, justifying his action by pointing out that the invaders "can be no worse than the merchants who have bled us dry, or the samurai who cut us down in the street if we fail to bow when they go by" (21). A samurai does come by, notices the stolen goods, and cuts off the thief's hand. Earlier in the scene, a merchant is ready to abandon his aged mother so that he can take his possessions with him instead.

Although Kayama fails in his mission and is humiliated by the Americans who will "speak only to great men" (23), he realizes that anyone dressed in a Councilor's robes would be seen as a Councilor. The *illusion* of power is, in his mind, as effective as holding *real* power. Manjiro, given this task by Kayama, dons a "splendid robe" (26), speaks with "tremendous authority" (26) and, initially at least, appears to succeed. Commodore Perry, however, insists that arrangements be made within the next six days to greet him on Japanese soil and accept President Fillmore's "friendly letter" (28). If not, a cannon will be turned on Uraga and will "blast it off the face of earth!!" (29). The illusion that the American invasion can somehow be forestalled now seems to be threatened.

The delightfully sardonic "Chrysanthemum Tea" renders absurd illusions held by the Priests advising the Shogun, as well as by the Shogun's mother. The Priests believe that

> No foreign ships can break our laws.
> That also is illusion.
> Our laws are sacred.
> It follows there can be no ships.
> They must be an illusion.
> Japan is sacred. (34)

The illusory power of the Shogun fades as he succumbs to the poisoned tea served him by his mother. Her rationale for killing her son is particularly bizarre:

> I decided if there weren't
> Any Shogun to receive it [Fillmore's letter]
> It would act as a deterrent
> Since they'd have no place to leave it,
> And they might go away, my lord.... (37)

Yet the American ships remain, and Kayama and Manjiro face death for failing to drive the foreigners away. Again, the ingenious Kayama comes up with what appears to be a rational solution. Have the Americans land at Kanagawa, cover the sand with tatami mats and build a special treaty house for the delivery of the letter. "When the Westerners are satisfied and have departed, we destroy the house and burn the mats.... The Americans will have come and gone, without setting foot on our sacred soil" (40). The Reciter comments ironically on this latest scheme: "If the Councilors can no longer pretend that the Americans are not coming, they have not yet given up the hope of pretending the Americans were never here" (40). Such a pretense, based on the technicality that the Americans never actually "touched" Japanese soil, constitutes another desperate self-delusion as the reality of a foreign invasion becomes more and more likely.

Kayama (promoted to Governor of Uraga) and Manjiro, now attached to Kayama's service, begin their journey back to Uraga. To ease their trek, they gracefully and with much warmth of feeling exchange haiku, likening elements of the natural world (rain, haze, moon, wind, the nightingale, dawn, leaves, the sun) in Kayama's case— to his wife—and, in Manjiro's case, to Boston and America. Several ironies and illusions are reflected here, some not perceived by the audience until the conclusion of the show. Kayama wrongly assumes that Tamate is alive, thus rendering his loving poem more poignant to audiences who know her tragic fate. As we later learn, the illusion of friendship seen here will be ultimately shattered. Manjiro, now sympathetic to America and perceiving the Japanese as the real barbarians, will be transformed into a traditional samurai and Kayama, as dramatized in "A Bowler Hat," becomes metamorphosed into the epitome of a Westernized bureaucrat, in effect, an exchange of political ideologies. It will be Manjiro, later allied with the Lords of the South in opposition to the Shogun, who will kill his former friend.

"Welcome to Kanagawa" is a bawdy interlude with drag show humor that even Hal Prince felt was not "as good a piece of material as the rest" (qtd. in Zadan 208). The Madame, faced with the loss of her regular girls ("flowers") who are "disappearing in alarm" (48), has replaced them with young ladies from the farm. Using pornographic fans, she tries to teach them the erotic techniques that will convince the invading foreigners that the girls are, in fact, sexually experienced, a comedic example of faith in the power of illusion.

In the brief Scene Eight, a samurai charged with the task of defending his city against the Americans, describes how he ordered canvas screens stretched across the cliffs of Kanagawa and concealed 5,000 armored swordsmen, all on horseback, equipped with enormous bows. But the assumption that the invaders would assume that the canvas is hiding two or three times as many warriors turns out to be yet another illusion for the Japanese. The Americans, seeing the screens, laughingly ask the warriors to pull down the drapes, crying out: "What kind of army hides behind a parlor curtain!" (53).

Scene Nine contains perhaps the most memorable song in the show, "Someone in a Tree," a partial "account" of what happened inside the Treaty House during the negotiations between the Shogun's Councilors and the Americans. Because the Councilors kept their story secret and the official American version is not credible to the Japanese, the only information given is from an observer watching in a tree (who can see what is happening, but cannot hear) and a samurai hidden under the floorboards of the Treaty House (who can hear the conversation above him, but is unable to see what is transpiring). What further complicates the effort to determine what "really" happened in the Treaty House is that the observer in a tree—who was ten years old at the time—is now an old man with a somewhat faulty memory.

The significance of "Someone in a Tree," however, is not limited to its immediate dramatic context. The Old Man and his younger self sing: "Without someone in a tree,/ Nothing happened here" (59), implying that our knowledge of historical events is really shaped by those who witness them. "Objective" reality is one more illusion. It is the perceivers—here the boy in a tree and the warrior under the floorboards—who become "part of the event" (57). Further, history is seen in terms of individual and separate details, or as Joanne Gordon puts it, "random fragments of experience arranged in order to reveal a partial truth" (191).

These individual fragments—the ripple, beam, stone, and someone in a tree—bring us closer to "reality" than anything else. This acknowledgment, in "Someone in a Tree," of our limited ability to really "know" the truth, while humbling, may account for Sondheim's remarkable compassion, even for the rejected outcasts of our society.

The past, therefore, may be ultimately irretrievable and our knowledge of it limited to fragments of experience. Yet the power of memory—flawed as it may be—and the pull of nostalgia can create deceptive and dangerous illusions. How the past interacts with the present and influences behavior is a familiar theme in Sondheim's work, sometimes shaping the dramatic structure of his musicals. Although *Pacific Overtures* is basically linear in structure as it moves from the mid-nineteenth century to the present, its last moments find Kayama and Tamate, in traditional garb, passing silently through the modern-dressed Company. What is evoked here in this brief glimpse of the past is the price of progress. In *Follies*, where past and present continually intersect, Young Buddy and Young Sally sing in the "Loveland" section that

> Love will see us through
> Till something better comes along. (91)

And Young Phyllis cheerfully tells Young Ben that

> You're gonna love tomorrow,
> As long as your tomorrow is spent with me. (89)

But looking through the prism of nostalgia only reveals the deceptive power of our romantic popular songs.

Merrily moves inexorably backward in time as we gradually see what Franklin, Charley, and Mary were—and perhaps might have been. But, as Mary sings:

> Trouble is, Charley
> That's what everyone does:
> Blames the way it is
> On the way it was.
> On the way it never was.

Night Music's Madame Armfeldt constantly evokes the past, contrasting its remembered grandeur with the banal realities of contemporary life.

> In a world where the kings are employers,
> Where the amateur prevails and delicacy fails to pay
> In a world where the Princes are lawyers,
> What can anyone expect except to recollect. (68)

Her peaceful death at the conclusion, after the night has smiled at one who knows too much, implies a final separation from the inhibiting force of memory.

Company exists, in a sense, outside of time, although the narrative is structured around a birthday party for Robert given by his married friends. Its non-linear nature, the absence of a traditional narrative line, does not, however, suggest the absence of growth or development in its main character. Besieged, as he is, by the entreaties and experiences of his friends, he ultimately makes a choice, sensing that though the "happily ever after" notion of a contemporary marriage may well be illusory, his only real alternative (at least in the world of *this* musical) is emotional involvement of some kind.

Reconnecting with the past can also be liberating. In *Sunday in the Park*, what appears to be a concluding action at the close of Act I—the completion of a great work of art—is only an interim ending. For the modern George to understand his ambivalence toward his life and work, he must re-establish that link with his ancestral past (Dot) that served as the source of Seurat's creativity.

As for the Treaty House negotiations in *Pacific Overtures*, we learn that the letter from President Fillmore was finally delivered and that the "satisfied" Americans have left. The house was torn down and the mats rolled up. Kayama's scheme had apparently worked. No foreigners ever touched Japanese soil. As the Reciter declares: "The barbarian threat had forever been removed" (64), yet another illusion of the ability of the Japanese to maintain their isolation.

Such an illusion is short-lived, however, as dramatized in the final wordless moments of Act One when Commodore Perry performs "a strutting, leaping dance of triumph" (65), described in the revised version of the work as a "combination of the traditional Kabuki lion dance and an American cake walk" (65). The Americans have not abandoned their efforts, and the transition of Japan from its adherence to traditional culture (Kabuki theater) to its inevitable capitulation to Western influence has begun.

Act Two begins with the Japanese Emperor, literally and figuratively a puppet, rewarding Kayama and Manjiro for preventing the Americans from defiling the sanctity of Japan's ancestral soil. "Goodbye America. Come back in another two hundred fifty years!" (71), laughingly (and inaccurately) declares Lord Abe, now formally acknowledged as Shogun.

The remainder of Act Two, however, punctures this illusion, beginning with the arrival, in "Please Hello," of American, British, Dutch, Russian and French Admirals, all of whom try to compete with one another in securing exclusive rights and concessions from Japan. The Admirals make their case in vaudeville-like numbers, the surface lightness of which barely conceals the martial threats underlying their appeals. In unison, they complete "Please Hello" by singing, while dancing the Can-Can,

> By the way, may we say
> We adore your little nation,

And with heavy cannon
Wish you an un-
Ending please hello!!! (85)

Here again, as in songs from *Assassins* and *Follies*, Sondheim transforms romantic or comic material, often echoing familiar-sounding
melodies, into something much darker. The contrast between the
upbeat melodic surface—a comforting "illusion" conveyed through
music—and an ironic or even sinister vision expressed through his
lyrics gives his work extraordinary resonance. This technique is used
here in "Welcome to Kanagawa" and "Chrysanthemum Tea," as well
as in "Pretty Women" and "A Little Priest" (*Sweeney Todd*), "The Little
Things You Do Together" (*Company*), and "You Must Meet My Wife"
and "The Glamorous Life" (*A Little Night Music*).

In "A Bowler Hat," the details of Kayama's changing mode of
dress and shifting values mirror the larger changes occurring in
Japan. The scene begins with Kayama and Manjiro in traditional robes,
but concludes with Kayama in a cutaway, and Manjiro in samurai
dress. As articulated in "Someone in a Tree," the small details help us
understand the larger picture. Over the ten-year period covered in
the song, Kayama secures a wife and then leaves her. He sees the
Dutch Ambassador as "no fool," "most rude," and finally, "a fool"
who wears a bowler hat. Acquiring a monocle, Kayama begins to take
imported pills, drinks too much white wine, and smokes American
cigars (90–93).

The fatal consequences stemming from cultural differences are
poignantly dramatized when three lonely British sailors, mistaking
an innocent young woman for a prostitute, offer money for her
favors. Their appeals, conveyed in the ironically tender ballad "Pretty
Lady," only result in her samurai father killing one of them, and slashing another. Where in the comic "Kanagawa" song, the Madam *hoped*
that the invaders would mistake her inexperienced protégés for the
real thing, "Pretty Lady" ends tragically *because* the sailors held the
same kind of false illusions about the woman, another example of
Sondheim juxtaposing comedic and dramatic material.

The violence at the conclusion of "Pretty Lady" foreshadows the
mayhem contained in the next scene. Following the murder of the
Shogun, the assassins responsible for killing him are slain by a samurai who, in turn, is murdered by the now xenophobic Manjiro. Manjiro

kills his old friend, Kayama and, as one of the Lords of the South exclaims, "Japan will be Japan again" (101). Foreigners will be banished and the past restored. However, that illusion is soon shattered as the puppet emperor discards his puppet sticks and begins to speak for himself. He orders samurai to relinquish their swords and crested robes. Feudal forms will be cast aside. An army and navy with modern weapons will be organized. Japan will do "for the rest of Asia what America has done for us" (102)!

In the final number, "Next," Japan, no more a sleepy, isolated nation, is now influencing and, to a considerable degree, dominating much of the world. Confident of its powers, it ignores the less benign results of industrialization and its elevation to a world power:

> Streams are drying—
> Mix a potion.
> Streams are dying—
> Try the ocean.
> Brilliant notion—
> Next!
>
> Never mind a small disaster.
> Who's the stronger, who's the faster?
> Let the pupil show the master—
> Next! (105)

"Next" includes prose references to the successes of modern industrial Japan—223 Japan Air Lines ticket offices in 153 cities; eight Toyota dealerships in Detroit; Seiko as the third best-selling watch in Switzerland; the proliferation of sushi bars in New York City; the high-speed wonders of the Tokaido Express; and, most ironically, the availability of Mitsubishi video cassettes of cherry trees. In the original 1976 production of *Pacific Overtures* some of the above accomplishments of modern Japan were not included. Instead, there were references to Japan's exporting such chemicals as monosodium glutamate and polyvinyl chloride, as well as negative comments about the quality of Tokyo's air and the beaches on the Inland Sea, all of which were cut from the revised script. The ultimate impact of *both* versions is, however, negative. Interestingly enough, *Pacific Overtures* omits any reference to Pearl Harbor, World War II, or Hiroshima. Whether "political correctness" or a desire to defuse potential hostility between Japan and the United States was a factor in these omissions is not clear. But the creators of *Pacific Overtures* were not writing "history," and their selectivity in ignoring or re-arranging events is irrelevant.

Perhaps the most significant illusion in *Pacific Overtures* is one held implicitly by the United States—that it could in perpetuity dominate the world and impose its expansionist policies on other nations. There may be no "real" Americans in the musical, only caricatures of an arrogant and imperialistic Perry and his crew. But the national illusion of a trans-Pacific "manifest destiny" driving the Americans is very much a motivating force in the work. Given what is dramatized about feudal Japan, it would be oversimplifying matters to accuse *Pacific Overtures* of an anti-American bias. Seeing the rulers of Japan continually deluding themselves into believing that the country could forever remain a "floating island," isolated from the rest of the world, provides a ironic perspective on events. But ultimately, the dramatic emergence of Japan as a world power shatters our illusions about that nation, as well as about our own. The real shock of recognition in *Pacific Overtures*, therefore, occurs not in the mind of any single character, but rather in the audience. As is typical in Sondheim works, the cathartic event results in painful truths being exposed. The price of "progress" (industrialization, pollution, dehumanization) is heavy, but clinging to the illusion that time can be stopped and the past preserved is simply impossible.

John Rockwell has pointed out that "As a man of today, Sondheim refuses to accept the pat, sweet directness that once defined our national character, at least as that character was projected in musicals and musical films" (218–19). Such "sweet directness" may be rare in Sondheim's work, but one must treasure his tough-minded and courageous willingness to upset what is conventional and comforting not just in our popular culture, but in our minds and hearts.

℘

Works Cited

Banfield, Stephen. *Sondheim's Broadway Musicals.* Ann Arbor: U of Michigan P, 1993.

Gordon, Joanne. *Art Isn't Easy: The Theater of Stephen Sondheim.* Updated ed. New York: Da Capo Press, 1992.

Sondheim, Stephen, and Arthur Laurents. *Anyone Can Whistle*. New York: Random House, 1965.

——, and George Furth. *Company*. New York: Random House, 1970.

——. *Merrily We Roll Along*. RCA Victor. CBL 1-4197.

——, and James Goldman. *Follies*. New York: Random House, 1971.

——, and James Lapine. *Into the Woods*. New York: Theatre Communications Group, 1987.

——. *Passion*. New York: Theatre Communications Group, 1994.

——. *Sunday in the Park with George*. New York: Applause, 1991.

——, and John Weidman. *Assassins*. New York: Theatre Communications Group, 1991.

——. Additional material by Hugh Wheeler. *Pacific Overtures*. New York: Dodd, Mead, 1977. New York: Theatre Communications Group, 1991.

——, and Hugh Wheeler. *A Little Night Music*. 1973. New York: Applause, 1991.

——. *Sweeney Todd: The Demon Barber of Fleet Street*. New York: Dodd, Mead, 1979.

Zadan, Craig. *Sondheim & Co*. 2nd ed. New York: Harper, 1989.

Psychology, Evil, and *Sweeney Todd*
or, "Don't I Know You, Mister?"
Judith Schlesinger

We go to the theater hoping to experience madness—at least in the sense of brief surrender to an alternate reality. For a few hours, we can enter a new world created by other minds and made only of sound, shapes, movement, and light.

If these other minds are clever enough, their vision will hold us and make us believe that the light is really sun, the shapes are truly places, and the characters are just like us, struggling with dilemmas we can share and understand. We make a willing trade: some of our critical judgment and reason in exchange for the pleasure of the journey away from ourselves.

And we take this journey with others, even as some people enter madness. Back in the more romantic days of psychiatry, there was a mental disorder called *folie a deux* (craziness for two). While it's now called "shared paranoid disorder"—an idea of considerably less charm—it's still two people bound by mutual madness, sharing a skewed view of the universe and bolstering each other's distortions, very much like Mrs. Lovett and Todd, warbling happily about pies made out of people.

This happens on a larger scale as well, between the artist and the audience. Let's call it *folie partagée*—still a shared craziness, but with the number of participants unspecified. And there is the same beckoning, the same pact: come, I will show you another world; yes, we will follow and believe.

We have followed Sondheim from ancient Rome to the opening of Japan. We've been invited into paintings and fairy tales, guided through obsessive passion and introduced to the frustrated anger of assassins. However foreign or exotic the worlds may be, there's always just enough familiarity to ground the vision and give it power.

Within this vision, the characters' concerns must resonate with our own before we care what happens to them. Whether they agonize or gloat, we are up there too, informing their struggles with our own. The fictional world can be so compelling that we're no longer tourists, but come to inhabit the place. And in *Sweeney Todd*, there is no curtain to separate our fact from their fantasy.

Such a *folie partagée* may be so intense that when the lights come up, we need a moment to adjust our sense of self and place; its impact can be so profound that another page is forever folded back for us.

True madness is not nearly so voluntary, and has no intermission. And like real insanity, which rarely provides complete oblivion, there may be glimmers of reality in the greasepaint, dissonant moments when skepticism returns. The more attention we pay to the proverbial "man behind the curtain"—the craft that creates the spectacle— the less easily we can dissolve into the show's cosmology. Thoughts like "I don't believe this" or "This couldn't happen" may intrude to break the spell.

If the show is light, this is only a moment of incongruity, a mild skirmish between fantasy and reality. But if the show is dark, the clash can be a psychological nightmare in which we lose our moral footing and our clarity about good and evil. And if the show is not only dark, but brilliantly designed and laced with ambiguity and contradiction, we are at once drawn in and swept away.

Such is Sweeney Todd, the Demon Barber of Fleet Street.

The Sound of Stress

Sweeney Todd is more than a remote fantasy world: it's an intense and slippery universe where tension and release are carefully manipulated to keep us off guard and in a constant state of suspense. The more slippery the footing, the greater the need to grab for support. An audience kept off-balance is more vulnerable to the artist's vision, and there are a hundred ways to set them wobbling. Two of the best are twists in the plot and dissonance in the music: the book challenges our higher thinking centers, while the music works on us below, sneaking past the intellectual guardposts and heading straight for the viscera. Both devices take advantage of the fact that, in this alternate reality, we can afford to relax our usual defenses.

People are more susceptible to brainwashing—even the voluntary, theatrical variety—when they are under stress. This is a protracted state of mental and physical arousal in response to a challenge, and *Sweeney Todd* is full of them: ambiguity, twists, and sudden mood shifts, all paced and scored to make us feel that we are plunging toward something awful with no escape and no time to reflect. There is too much danger and confusion to stay vigilant and safely apart, and even if the intellect tries to pull us back, we cannot fight the sound.

Within the first 30 seconds of *Sweeney Todd*, as we are lulled and gradually puzzled by an increasingly demented organist, we are hit with a shrieking blast, which returns throughout the show at unexpected intervals. These shrieks, together with thunderous bass lines and nearly continuous dissonant music, combine to keep us vulnerable throughout the play.

In designing the music for *Sweeney Todd*, Sondheim turned for inspiration to Hitchcock's favorite composer, Bernard Herrmann. "I thought, 'Bernard Herrmann,' and out came that kind of music, filled with unresolved dissonances that leave an audience in a state of suspense." (Gottfried 125). Even the beautiful love ballad, "Johanna," has a blue note in it. Such devices make the music a source of anxiety all by itself, even in the absence of any other information.

Like every sensory stimulus, music causes physiological arousal; like any arousal, the pleasure comes with its relief. Different patterns of tension and release will vary the intensity of the reaction. For example, high arousal, suddenly relieved, is quite literally orgasmic; protracted tension, sustained with limited, carefully-timed releases, is the power source of *Sweeney Todd*.

One component of musical arousal is our expectation that dissonances will be resolved. Even untrained listeners anticipate that jangly chords will finally come to rest, and the notes will "match" in a full, harmonious sound (hard rock fans are excepted from this premise). The longer the ride back "home"—or the more frequent the intrusion of incongruous notes—the higher the tension. And this works nicely whether or not the listener understands it.

Similarly, it's intriguing but not necessary to know that the Dies Irae theme, used throughout *Sweeney Todd* to emphasize the sinister significance of the action or commentary, is taken from the Catholic Mass for the Dead, and literally means "Day of Wrath." Nor is it important to recall it from the works of Mozart, Berlioz, Liszt, Saint-Saëns, and Rachmaninoff, or from its more recent, powerful incarnation in Stanley Kubrick's film, "The Shining." The Dies Irae works primarily because of its foreboding sound, not its history, and how well it serves as the bridge over the dark and plunging "Ballad of Sweeney Todd."

The sounds of *Sweeney* pull us in right from the beginning. (Even the name is suggestive: the long screech of "Sweeeeeney" followed by the dull thud of "Todd."). In fact, everything in the initial moments heralds dread and doom—especially the gravediggers dumping a body. At the same time, there are also flashes of dry wit; we learn that "for neatness [Sweeney] deserved a nod," and that, though his victims lacked salvation, "They went to their maker impeccably shaved."

The audience, primed by the cavernous set, gloomy lighting, ominous, galloping Prologue, and years of horror movies, is not expecting humor. Though the lighter note is fleeting, it's enough to trigger uncertainty, adding cognitive dissonance to the musical kind. Next we are disoriented by strange chirping sounds which, after a moment, we realize are Johanna's birds. Though at this point we are still safely distant, the walls have begun to shimmer.

Signposts and Switchbacks

The slippery universe of *Sweeney Todd* is not linear. For everything we think we learn, there is a caveat, a switchback, a puzzle. We cannot settle in anywhere for long, since our moods and perceptions are likely to be upended in the next moment, either by new information or a sudden shift in tone.

With the arrival of Anthony Hope, the handsome hero with his homecoming rhapsody ("There's no place like London"), the audience can relax—but not for long. Todd replies with a dark warning to him (and us): "You will learn," and describes the cruelty of London, rather bizarrely, as "wondrous." Before we have a chance to file this story, the beggar woman appears with her plaintive cry for alms, shifting the mood from dread to poignancy to aggressive obscenity. Her antique dirty words are funny, yet coming so close on her melancholy plea, they seem insane rather than humorous. Which is, after all, the point.

By now, the style is set, the message clear: leave your preconceptions at the door and expect to be surprised. From the very beginning of the show, we understand we must pay close attention. There is evil and madness about, and—like the pies—nothing will be served up plain.

Things get stranger when Todd croons a passionate, intimate ballad to his razors, while Mrs. Lovett listens in a sensuous swoon, imagining that his rapture is meant for her. Lovett has just sung her perky and peculiar tribute to "The Worst Pies in London," and our smiles have barely faded before Todd's razors start to glint. It's clear that our journey through this world will not be an easy one.

A major hurdle is the irony Sondheim keeps throwing in our path. Todd is a bitter and obsessed man who is literally (but not actually) rescued by Hope, the young sailor who plucked him from a bobbing raft. Todd's salvation is only temporary, as the Dies Irae and the Greek chorus keep reminding us. Meanwhile, the person charged with safeguarding justice is venal and lecherous, and most of the comic relief is supplied by bouncy Nellie Lovett, she with the jolly music-hall name and pure, devious greed where her conscience should be.

Sondheim's legendary fondness for puzzles gets free play here, as he dispenses the pieces slowly, all at once, or not at all. *Sweeney Todd* was originally a 19th-century melodrama, a form known for clearcut villains and heroes. In 1973 Christopher Bond revived it in London, and Hugh Wheeler, who wrote the book for the musical, remembers that "the audience would hiss and throw hot dogs" whenever Todd would come in (Zadan 246).

This time, as drawn by Sondheim, it becomes much less certain when to cheer, and whom to hiss. One reason is that the characters are all morally or mentally challenged. Aside from being vile and vicious, the Judge is also sexually kinky, as the song cut from some productions but left on the album clearly demonstrates. He sings himself to orgasm while spying on Johanna and whipping himself, and heightens his pleasure with a perverted religiosity, panting "Mea culpa! Mea maxima culpa!" on his way to ecstasy. This is the perfect expression of anguished, deviant sexual excitement; without it, his lechery is soft-pedalled down to leers and his suggestive contribution to "Pretty Women": "silhouetted" (i.e., backlit so their dresses are transparent, as in the whipping song).

Mrs. Lovett is charming, and a textbook sociopath (currently the somewhat clunkier "antisocial personality disorder"). In her loopy, crafty self, Sondheim has created the perfect comic villain, much funnier (and deadlier) than Lady Macbeth. Mrs. Lovett's crimes are more subtle than Todd's: they are crimes of ice, rather than blood. He does all the slashing, she only makes the pies; though he actually cuts Lucy's throat, Lovett's lie makes her complicit. And while she claims to love Todd, her first reaction to his unravelling is to devise a way to make money from it. When she claims she has "a maternal heart" the irony congeals into repugnance.

Everyone on Fleet Street is warped in one way or another. Pirelli is hilarious, yet a liar and a cheat. The Beadle is a vain dandy who sings beautifully and holds Lucy down for the judge to rape. Even Mrs. Mooney, whom we never meet, defrauds (and possibly poisons) the public with her pussycat pies. Meanwhile, characters in various states of addlement include the raving Lucy, Sweeney's lost wife; the impossibly naive Anthony; the babbling, improbably coiffed Johanna, self-described as "a silly little ninnynoodle"; and the dim Tobias. All the players are askew, bizarre, variously comical and disturbing, and just to complicate things further, most of them will also change as the play unfolds. This adds to our stress, since we can't just make our decisions about them and move on.

The hymn of reassurance ("Not While I'm Around") is sung by the most improbable hero. As Tobias vows to protect Mrs. Lovett, she humors him with "what a sweet child it is." Yet when the plot heaves around again he really does murder Todd, and by then, he is transformed as well: white-haired, vague, and utterly lost.

Custom leads us to expect that Todd's lost daughter will be admirable, but when we meet her she's as loopy as her curls, ready to marry a stranger whose name she doesn't even know. In "Kiss Me," we pray that Anthony will still that babbling mouth with a kiss—or anything else that's handy. But just when we think we've pegged her, Anthony botches her rescue and she's the one with the steel to kill. (No ninnynoodle, she.) Pirelli's truth is a complete inversion of the clownish fop we first encounter. The mad beggar-woman turns out to be Todd's beloved wife, and even Mrs. Lovett gets progressively less lovable.

In fact, it seems that all the labels we pin on these characters end up sliding off. The story unfolds backwards as well as forwards, with each new piece changing the puzzle. Unlike most creators working in Broadway—or anywhere else, for that matter—Sondheim gives his audience credit for the ability to appreciate characters who aren't cartoons. They may be extreme, but they're not stock. Such complexity increases the show's power, as well as our vulnerability to it. After all, we cannot stay on top of (and therefore distant from) the action if we can't make reliable predictions. And Sondheim does everything to make sure that we can't.

It's a measure of his skill—and our need for release—that we laugh so hard at the outrageously macabre and punny "Little Priest." It follows the stunning darkness of "Epiphany," in which Todd has snapped his last tether, shouting "we all deserve to die!" Now, as he gradually comprehends Mrs. Lovett's scheme, the music gathers as well, cresting into a wholly satisfying resolve and a bouncy little waltz.

We are released from the recent tension as these two giggle about what kind of person makes the best pie. But the song also sizzles with satire when Todd divides humanity into two classes: those "…who gets eaten and who gets to eat." And the gaiety is topped with a discordant, warning note. We are released, but not for long.

In fact, the eaters/eaten distinction reprises the injustice theme of Todd's first song, and with a new and disturbing undercurrent. Todd's vengeance has moved from specific to indiscriminate: any innocent man who needs a shave may be next. The laughs continue, but now they are shadowed with the image of spouting blood.

As the show picks up speed, the bizarre moments pile up against each other. Mrs. Lovett thinks "a nice bowl of gillies" will "brighten up" Todd's execution chamber, and sings the tender "Wait" about his yearning to kill. A promise of safety is immediately followed by the thump of the next corpse; a rape scene is introduced by an elegant minuet. Johanna bitterly addresses the Judge as "dear Father," even as we see his intentions are carnal, not paternal. Mrs. Lovett sings another goofy song about her romantic future with Todd ("By the Sea"), while he sits sodden and unresponsive. Johanna's suspenseful rescue turns corny with the shout "Unhand her!," and Miracle Elixirs are nothing but piss.

Then there's Todd, dreamily musing about his daughter while slitting a throat, and praising "Pretty Women" in a luscious duet with his intended victim. Are we still on his side? Or has Todd become as despicable as the Judge, who in fact tells him he is "a fellow spirit?" Despicable or not, he gets madder every moment, sharing the bizarre news that "it's always morning in my mind" and inverting the classic lover's sentiment to "I think I miss you less and less/ As every day goes by."

The original Epiphany was the moment when Jesus is recognized by the Magi. In his, Todd also recognizes a god—but this one is dark and delusional. The mood swings are now compressed and intensified, as his rage and yearning spill over each other. And even as Todd discovers his power and justification, he forfeits his ability to distinguish between vengeance and salvation, joy and pain. Meanwhile, the music itself goes mad—clashing and chaotic—and there is literally no rhyme as he loses his reason.

The evil and insanity are fully unleashed now, as the chorus warns us in dark, newly-psychotic metaphors: "Stirrings in the ground/ And the whirring of giant wings!/ Watch out!/ Look!" In this climate, even simple statements take on a sinister meaning: Anthony thanks Todd for offering sanctuary, and says "I shall be grateful for this to the grave." Does this bass note mean he is next? We may guess where the rapids are headed, but the last bend is still out of sight.

And we can't even identify and trust the usual signposts. For example, the Greek chorus that summarizes the plot for us—helping to distance and protect us from it—deteriorates into the all-lunatic choir in Act II. The plot and character motifs that recur throughout the show are evocative but not always instructive, given the growing level of anxiety; in fact, they serve to heighten the tension by drawing on the power of earlier scenes.

The awful factory whistle that opens the play must be a warning, but it's used too variably to be a reliable precursor. It marks the beginning of both acts and the end, but it also functions to open the humorous shaving contest, signal the first murder, extend the sound of the Beadle's whistle, and make us jump when Johanna paces alone, nervously waiting for Anthony in Todd's shop.

Unlike the bass rumbling in the movie *Jaws* (itself an echo from the Herrmann score for *North by Northwest*) the screech is not restricted to one event. But it works even better this way: the sound itself is aversive, and since we're not sure what it means, it becomes a highly effective mechanism to frighten and unsettle us. In fact, once we are conditioned to the shark motif, there is a point in *Jaws* when the theme appears without the shark; this is perhaps the most terrifying moment of all.

The only character who knows exactly what's happening is the one least likely to: the mad Lucy, who screams "City on fire! Mischief!" and alone recognizes that "evil is here!" It's nervewracking as well as ironic that the person with the most important news is also the one with the least credibility. Her neighbors are so accustomed to dismissing Lucy that although she says, quite clearly, "Somebody,

somebody look up there!... Tell it to the Beadle and the police as well!" no one will listen.

The show gallops toward its final moments with menace and comedy racing together. The tension is unbearable as the Beadle, as insect-like as his name, calmly plays little ditties on the harmonium and urges the frantic Mrs. Lovett to sit down and sing with him. Oblivious to the gathering darkness around him, the Beadle tootles about "Sweet Polly Plunkett" and enlists Mrs. Lovett and Tobias in a daft, repeating chorus of "ding dong, ding dong." Once again, a song functions on multiple levels—silly as it is, we can't help wondering for whom those bells toll.

Don't I Know You, Mister?

This is the question Lucy asks, through her fog, as she recognizes Todd. What are we to make of the demon barber himself? Is he hero or villain, victim or perpetrator? Neither? Both? Are we supposed to identify with him and root for his vengeance? Why does he keep describing himself as "naive"—could he have done something to save his family? Is he blaming himself, as well as the Judge? What does the "demon" in "demon barber" really mean? And when Todd finally snaps under the weight of his obsession, are we to pity his madness or condemn his evil?

The ever-pragmatic Nellie has no such confusion. Hers is a simple, selfish concept of morality and madness. When she discovers that Todd has killed Pirelli, she is shocked until he explains Pirelli had threatened to blackmail him for half of his pay. "Oh," she says, greatly relieved, "I thought you had lost your marbles."

For the rest of us, the answers are not so clear. Are serial killers mad or bad? This is a tough question, in or out of the theater. The June 4, 1995 cover of *The New York Times Magazine* proclaimed "Evil's Back!" (No, it hadn't been away, it was just up for general discussion, again. And still.) Author Ron Rosenbaum quoted Hitler expert Hugh Trevor-Roper as saying that Hitler was not evil because "he was convinced of his own rectitude" (39). Rosenbaum then explains the different categories of evil, with "wickedness" being the worst because of its deliberate, conscious intent (43). This makes sense, but leads straight into another dilemma: how do you define and determine intent?

Such questions have been around as long as evil itself, and answered in the cultural context of the time. The 1979 *Sweeney Todd* opened in a very different social and psychological climate from what we have today. Back then, the public appetite for deviation hadn't grown to the point where it required daily feedings, such as the pathology parade on afternoon T.V. The media had not yet made armchair psychologists out of the public, or turned serial killers into cultural heroes.

The result is that we are more comfortable with evil and madness now than we were then; at least, we seem to be more conversant with them both. But we still have trouble telling them apart—whether on the news or on the stage of *Sweeney Todd*.

Insanity and the Law

Since the courts are better at prying evil from madness, perhaps they can help us understand Todd. The legal requirement for insanity turns on the 1843 McNaughten rule about responsibility, or the ability to judge right from wrong. A murderer who was insane (mad) is different from the one who knew the act was wrong, but did it anyway (bad). The punitive consequences differ as well.

Although many believe indeterminate confinement in a mental hospital (mad) is worse than a measured sentence in prison (bad), at least a successful insanity plea precludes the death penalty. By the McNaughten criterion, Hitler's "sense of rectitude," which self-exempted him from normal moral judgments, made him insane, and therefore not culpable for his crimes.

Is Todd "convinced of his own rectitude" as well? (The Prologue warns us not to engage in this kind of discussion, since "Freely flows the blood of those / Who moralize!" But we press on, nevertheless.) At first, Todd's crime is identified by Mrs. Lovett as "foolishness," and he continues to refers to himself as "naive" (victimized?). In "The Epiphany" he begins by differentiating himself from the wicked, whose lives should be "made brief," but soon works himself into a righteous rectitude, condemning the whole world—including himself. By the end of the song, he's lost the capacity to make rational distinctions, crying "I'm full of joy!" even as he brims with anguish and hatred. As the last note finally resolves, his fate is sealed.

Like other laws, the criteria for madness are subject to argument in their application. Yet they are positively crystalline in contrast to what comes next: trying to determine the defendant's state of mind at the moment the crime was committed.

Making this decision requires the psychologist to diagnose a total stranger, and backwards as well. Was s/he insane last year? Five years ago? The definition has been expanded to include the possibility of "irresistible impulse," which covers the schizophrenic who has command hallucinations (serving "a dark and vengeful god" falls smack in this motivational ballpark). Yet, even with the broadest possible guidelines, making the judgment still requires the magical ability to read a crystal ball in reverse, when diagnosing can be difficult enough in real time.

The insanity determination is usually made with the traditional psychological tools of interviews and testing, unless the prisoner refuses to cooperate. And many do. The head of forensic psychology at Bellevue Hospital in New York City once told me that if a defendant refuses to talk or take a test, the judgment must be based on body language alone.

Given the stakes involved, this is rather disturbing. And even if the accused does cooperate—sketching his childhood, responding eagerly to ink blots—the task is still inherently formidable. Psychological testing is not like DNA testing (and even that, as we've learned, is open to suspicion). Madness has no visible marker. There is nothing tangible to measure or throw up on a lighted screen. So while there is much science in psychology, there is still not enough fully to understand madness. Or evil.

Todd is "diagnosed" in the first few lines of the Prologue: "his skin was pale and his eye was odd." "Odd eye" is hardly an official disorder, but it's much more evocative than anything in the manual. To be fair, the psychiatric guidebook is designed to homogenize understanding, while Sondheim invites each of us to connect our own dots. And every time we use our minds and hearts to complete the sketch, we are drawn in even further, in what is surely the original interactive technology.

Sometimes psychologists are not only asked to exhume the past, but predict the future as well, as in "will the killer strike again?" After a terrorist act, microphones are stuck in the nearest professional face to ask: "why?" And the answer everyone wants to hear is: "because this person is not like the rest of us."

The villain in Thomas Harris's novel *The Silence of the Lambs* is the ultimate nightmare of perverted power: an evil psychiatrist. Like Sweeney Todd, Hannibal Lecter killed; unlike Todd, he ate. And also unlike Todd, who's clearly tormented, Lecter is not only comfortable with what he has done, but also mocks the feeble attempts of his own profession to explain it. When the young FBI agent, Clarice Starling, offers him a questionnaire to elicit "what happened to him" to make him a serial killer, Lecter's informed contempt is especially chilling:

> Nothing happened to me, Officer Starling. I happened. You can't reduce me to a set of influences. You've given up good and evil for behaviorism, Officer Starling. You've got everybody in moral dignity pants—nothing is ever anybody's fault. Look at me, Officer Starling. Can you stand to say I'm evil? Am I evil, Officer Starling? (21)

As an FBI agent, Officer Starling can easily stand to say "evil." Most psychologists cannot. We have a long tradition of avoiding this word as well as any others that reflect moral judgment (clinical judgment is supposed to be neutral, though there are diagnoses that are just as pejorative as epithets). Even benign terms like "good" and "bad" are carefully replaced by "appropriate" and "inappropriate."

This prohibition stems from the worthy original purpose of psychology: to create an objective science of behavior. Therapy was also intended to be neutral, providing a safe place to confess where the goal was understanding, rather than subjective judging and subsequent penance. The irony here is that, in prying moral considerations loose from human conduct, psychology ends up doing just what the Christian church advised people to do: hate the sin, love the sinner.

Does all this imply that madness is the ultimate refuge from personal responsibility? When Todd says, "A madhouse! A madhouse! Johanna is as good as rescued!" for a moment, we wonder what he means. Certainly he himself has retreated into madness, and it brings him no comfort and no peace at all.

The Blind Men and the Elephant

Every explanatory system has something to say about evil: history, philosophy, psychology, sociology, biology, religion, literature, art. Even physics addresses primal causation; we can say this implies

God, and therefore the Devil. Conversely, we may need to address evil because without it, there would be no need for God.

Of all our diverse efforts to understand evil, art has the greatest freedom to illustrate its nuances and disguises. In *Sweeney Todd*, we meet a full range of demons, from Todd and Lovett to the Judge and Fogg, the smarmy, aptly named asylum keeper, from the Beadle to the onlookers at the rape. Each is a different shade of evil, but all share the same spectrum. Similarly, while each profession clings to a different piece of the elephant, their angles have to intersect.

We must gather every approach if we're ever to understand the horror, both on and off the stage. Perhaps it's an artifact of our ubiquitous and graphic media (there were, after all, no camcorders at the Crusades), but it does seem that things are getting more sinister out there. The elephant appears to be growing.

Maybe this is why, in recent years, psychology and religion have been inching closer together. For the first time in history, the new American Psychiatric Association manual—the bible of all mental health professionals—includes religious and spiritual problems among its 381 mental disorders. Moral anguish and confusion, even visions, are now considered a proper focus for psychological inquiry and treatment.

In April of 1995 there was an historic conference at New York Hospital in White Plains, New York. Pastoral counselors and psychiatrists came together to find some common ground, discussing such things as how to handle a patient who claims to have seen God. In the old days, the diagnosis was rapid—paranoid schizophrenia—and the treatment was simple: medication and confinement. Now, clinicians are asked to consider each case more carefully, since religious ecstasies may not automatically indicate pathology. Some people may actually be sincere, and not insane. If this is true, then the door to evil's realm has been opened as well.

Although psychology may be creeping toward the concept of evil, it still wants to call it something else: "malevolence." At the annual convention of the American Psychological Association in August of 1995, Carl Goldberg, Ph.D., who has spent nearly 30 years working with patients who have committed murders, rapes, and other forms of "malevolent mayhem," suggested that evil deeds are "no more a product of mental illness than they are compelled by Satan" (*Monitor* 13).

Goldberg's theory of "malevolent personality" includes six elements: self-contempt, contempt for others, rationalization, justification of feelings of superiority, inability or unwillingness to examine one's "dark side," and magical thinking, e.g., the belief that one already knows all there is to know. This formulation doesn't fit Todd at all, though it does capture some of Mrs. Lovett. And whether Goldberg's theory will advance professional or public understanding remains to be seen. But at least it's an attempt to touch the fire—even with an oven mitt and a very long stick.

Meanwhile, there is no consensus or resolution about evil, either in the bright light of science or the dark world of Sweeney Todd. The questions remain: is he to be forgiven because he's lost his mind, or damned because he knows what he's done? If Todd was "convinced of his own rectitude," is he off the moral hook? Does his history of being wronged find sympathetic echoes in today's "abuse excuse?"

Related to this is the issue of retribution. Does Sweeney Todd's punishment—the death penalty—fit his crime? (If he were truly mad, the law, at least, would have spared him.) Surely his accidental killing of his beloved Lucy—"his meaning and his life"—is far worse for him than death. If so, does this mean he is absolved and released? And while we're at it, does Mrs. Lovett's utter lack of remorse make her the more evil of the two? Once again, we must figure this out for ourselves, since Sondheim never gives us the cover of the puzzle box, where the picture is complete and clear. The only sure lesson of Todd's anguish is that there is nothing worse than the punishment we inflict on ourselves.

Then again, sociologists might disagree. Seen from their side of the elephant, Todd looks more like a victim of society. As such, the true villain is the exploitation and class inequities of the Industrial Revolution, as symbolized by the sunless set with its ominous and idle factory. In fact, when director Hal Prince was asked, "What does it make?" His answer was "they make Sweeney Todds" (Gottfried 127). Whether this is humor or social commentary—or both—the sociologist is more likely to identify the plot's motor as external oppression, rather than internal obsession.

In Sweeney Todd's 19th-century landscape, questions about evil and madness were complicated enough. Now we not only wrestle with the same questions but have new complications to consider, like the role of biology.

Jeffrey Dahmer—Lecter and Todd's real-life brother—killed and ate his victims. He was imprisoned, beaten to death by fellow inmates, and cremated—except for his brain, which Dahmer's mother wants studied to "determine the impact of biological factors on his actions" (Associated Press, 18 September 1995), and probably to give herself some absolution as well.

Well, of course biology had an impact—as it must on everything we do—and eventually we'll be able to measure it. Every day researchers learn more about the role of neurotransmitters and inherited wiring in both normal and abnormal function. The answers are getting closer, but for now the old nature/nurture debate still flares in classrooms and conferences all over the world, with new champions, new jargon—and the same lack of resolution.

And does it really matter anyway, what made Sweeney Todd? Not really. Perhaps all the etiological whodunnits are finally irrelevant at the bottom line: the behavior itself. For the audience, the construction of Sweeney is more personal than philosophical—what matters most is what he evokes in each of us, what we recognize in him, and what we take away. And this, in turn, depends on how deeply we are lured into his world. Todd's real name is Barker, a term for the one who entices people into a carnival. By the end of the show, the more rapt and moved we are, the more successful the Barker (and Sondheim) have been.

City on Fire

By now it's clear that to understand evil and madness we must use all the tools at hand. Musical theater is a powerful implement, since it engages the senses and emotions as well as the intellect and life experience of the audience. It shakes us up, opens us to new possibilities, and makes us think. And, as always, real life obliges us by keeping the issues in play.

Recent headlines have added more nuances to the concept of evil. The Unabomber killed three people and hurt 23 more "to warn us" about the dangers of technology. He promised that if the newspapers printed his 35,000 word Chicken Little manifesto, he wouldn't hurt anyone else. After much breastbeating and no little government pressure, the *New York Times* and the *Washington Post* caved in, counting on him to keep his part of the bargain.

This deal has many ominous implications, one of which is the presentation of evil as compartmentalized, muffled, and restrained. Sure, the Unabomber may be a vicious, indiscriminate killer, but this doesn't mean he won't keep his promises, right? The looking glass has shattered once again, leaving yet another facet: the honorable evil man.

Well, maybe he's just mad, and not evil. Maybe his passionate, plausible ideology justifies his crimes; after all, he too seems "convinced of his rectitude." But when a murderer's agenda is accorded such respectful attention, does that make the media his accomplices? Just what is going on here?

What is going on is precisely the sort of ethical confusion that invites more evil. The Unabomber case—and the Oklahoma bombing, and Susan Smith, drowning her babies in a lake—all such events and their ensuing debates slam against the basic moral underpinnings of our society. With each blow, our moorings are loosened a bit further. And the more we drift, the riper we are for a charismatic leader who promises stability and salvation but delivers precisely the opposite (Nostradamus, call your service!).

As we approach the millennium, the old questions get louder and more urgent: what/whom can we trust? Believe in? What is madness—or evil, or justice? And in one of those little ironies that historians find pivotal in retrospect, our distress is increasing just as managed care reduces our access to qualified psychological help.

He Is Us

In *Sweeney Todd*, Stephen Sondheim has created a theatrical Rorschach where we must use our own experience to make sense of the shapes. What we projected into it in 1979 is very different from what stares back at us today. The good news is that *Sweeney* will always be fresh and relevant; the bad news is what our current resonance to it may reveal about where the world is going.

Sweeney is brilliantly crafted to keep us hungry for answers and therefore deeply involved. From the very beginning, we are kept off guard: alternately jarred and comforted, delighted and horrified, saddened and triumphant. Swept along by a gorgeous score but continually nagged by its dissonance, we are drawn in by compelling characters who both appeal to us and push us away.

Both the ambiguity and the emotional whiplash keep us vulnerable, blurring the distinction between Todd's world and our own. At the end, the chorus makes the merge explicit, warning us that "Sweeney waits in the parlor hall,/ Sweeney leans on the office wall." We are surrounded by Sweeneys—today, now, and here—as the front page of any newspaper will confirm.

But the worst news is saved for last: Sweeney is not only closer than we think, he may very well be us. When the Company finally sings, "There he is, it's Sweeney!" they are pointing straight into the audience.

At last the *folie partagée* is complete: any one of us could be a Sweeney, confusing light and dark, good and evil, salvation and vengeance. Any one of us could start out naive and end up murderous, convinced of our own rectitude. And any one of us could snap if the pain gets deep enough.

Don't I know you, Mister?

WORKS CITED AND BIBLIOGRAPHY

Gottfried, Martin. *Sondheim*. New York: Harry N. Abrams, 1993.

Harris, Thomas. *The Silence of the Lambs*. New York: St. Martin's, 1988.

MacDonald, J.M., ed. *Psychiatry and the Criminal: A guide to psychiatric examinations for the criminal courts*. Third Ed. Springfield, IL: Charles C. Thomas, 1976.

Monitor. "Psychologist posits the origins of evil." Washington, DC: American Psychological Association, October, 1995, p. 13.

Rosenbaum, Ron. "Staring into the Heart of Darkness." *New York Times Magazine*, 4 June 1995, pp. 36–74.

Schlesinger, Judith. "Will mental health field finally address 'evil'?" *Gannett Suburban Newspapers*, 29 April 1995, p. 10A.

———. *Music and Madness: A guide to music's power over mind, mood, and motivation*. Unpublished manuscript. 1995.

Sondheim, Stephen. *Sweeney Todd: The Demon Barber of Fleet Street*. Book by Hugh Wheeler. New York: Dodd, Mead, 1979.

Wadlow, E.C. "Is the insanity defense totally invalid?" *Barrister* 5 (1978): 38–56.

Sondheim: The Idealist
Mari Cronin

Confronted with *West Side Story*'s gang warfare, driven Mama Rose, rivalry between conformity and non-conformity in *Anyone Can Whistle*, *Company*'s study of urban romance and marriage, middle-aged disenchantment in *Follies* or *Sweeney Todd*'s revenge, few theatergoers or critics have thought (or think) of Stephen Sondheim's musicals as idealistic or Sondheim as an idealist. Over the years his work and, by inference the composer/lyricist himself, have been found by most to be just the opposite, misanthropic and pessimistic. It is a charge Sondheim has never been able to escape. Indeed, a new collaboration and more personal and philosophical meditations on art and artists, ethical and community responsibility and obsessive love in *Sunday in the Park with George*, *Into the Woods* and *Passion* still failed to dispel the old criticisms.

But both audiences and the critical community have been too quick to label Sondheim's work. Restless, fretful and constantly experimenting, Stephen Sondheim is a chronicler of twentieth-century anxiety. He is an idealist who continually asks, "How better can we live our lives?" and who, in posing the question and urging his audiences to ask it of themselves, has, throughout most of his career, confronted theatergoers with unexpected and innovative shows, musicalizations of topics related directly to their own lives.

Conditioned to expect musicals to reconfirm greeting card platitudes, the majority of theatergoers have resisted Sondheim's work. Preferring their musicals be escapist entertainment, they believe Sondheim's, and his collaborators', serious approach has taken the fun out of musicals, turned them into work instead of pleasure. They want their musicals to be pretty and safe and easy. For them no idea should be probed too deeply, historical accuracy must be safely distanced by overwrought scenic effects and all things resolved happily by 10:30 or 11:00. Fearful of confronting their own emotional lives, morality and actions, they turn a deaf ear to Sondheim, paying only superficial attention to his voice and misinterpreting his intentions. It is easier and safer to turn one's back on Sondheim's musicals than it is to see *Company, Follies, Sweeney Todd* or *Into the Woods* and face one's own marital concerns, mid-life crisis, desire for revenge or questionable ethics.

For Sondheim however confronting such concerns, even if unsettling, is not to be shunned. It leads to solace and maturity. Only by facing our problems, emotions and desires head-on, he believes, can we come to terms with them. In each of his shows he questions the way we live. Is it *possible*, he asks, to stop the heartbreak caused by clashes of race and culture or prevent persecution and demand for conformity? Aren't romantic relationships, difficult as they are, worth fighting for? Isn't it valuable to explore youthful hopes in order to cope with middle-aged angst? What can be done about the ever-increasing prevalence of corruption within the law and government which leads to injustices producing those who kill indiscriminately or are compelled to assassinate our presidents? And why are ethics and morality of so little importance to today's citizens? The characters in his musicals strive to resolve their dilemmas instead of making believe everything is all right.

Sondheim doesn't pretend to have all of the answers to the questions he raises but as he presents them for contemplation he warns, advises, cajoles and consoles, wanting his audiences to acknowledge their worlds, to act, to "Take one step / And see what it gets you" (*Anyone Can Whistle* 160), to consider that... "Love is Company!" (*Company* 18) and as well "...what you earn, / And return" (*Passion* 91), to avoid falling into that world where "...its morals aren't worth / What a pig could spit" (*Sweeney Todd* 8–9) to recognize that

> There are vows, there are ties,
> There are needs, there are standards,
> There are shouldn'ts and shoulds. (*Into the Woods* 18)

and to contemplate the other national anthem

> For those who never win,
> For the ones who might have been.... (*Assassins* 85)

At the heart of the many complex issues in Sondheim's shows is the consideration of action and the consequences of action taken within the context of one's relationship with oneself, with business associates, romantic partners and friends. How people treat one another is paramount in Sondheim's musicals. Kindness, decency and humanity are always to be adhered to as are loyalty, integrity and morality. In order to warn and advise or to make their points, however, Sondheim and his collaborators often expose audiences to varying views of the issues and self-serving or base human behavior. People fight with or want to institutionalize those who differ from themselves. Couples rage, threaten to leave one another and sometimes do. Judges dictate sentences for their own gain and people kill indiscriminately. Characters lie, cheat, steal and obsessively pursue to obtain their objectives. Audiences then turn away from *West Side Story*, *Anyone Can Whistle*, *Follies*, *Sweeney Todd*, *Into the Woods* and *Passion* mistakenly convinced that it is these repugnant acts which Sondheim advocates.

But Sondheim's vision is a complex one. He sees all sides of an issue. There are no easy solutions to the characters' problems in his musicals. There are no "happy" endings. In asking "How better can we live our lives?", in struggling to come to terms with their problems and in striving for solace and maturity his characters lose their youthful fantasies, endure strained relationships, suffer the loss of loved ones to others or to death, attempt to overcome fear of commitment and fight fiercely to be loved. There is gallantry in the characters' facing of their dilemmas and in their belief that in so doing and in taking action life will improve. But Sondheim doesn't leave his audiences reassured that his characters will live happily ever after. For most of them at show's end the struggle will continue or has just begun. Hope is evidenced, however, in these small steps toward bettering their worlds. One can imagine Fay Apple still struggling to overcome her inhibitions despite knowing she needs Hapgood; Bobby continuing to fight his desire to commit to someone or the couples in *Follies*, who face the dawn determined to make the best of their situations, often doubting their decisions. But as Dot, who chose to leave George for Louis the Baker in *Sunday in the Park with George*, sings:

> I chose, and my world was shaken—
> So what?
> The choice may have been mistaken
> The choosing was not. (196)

This philosophy, Sondheim's great wealth of feeling for the human plight and his complicated life views, displayed within his characters' witty, ironic or bitter lyrics, escapes many theatergoers. Audiences responding to the irony or bitterness and not wanting to contend with his characters' travails, which may resemble their own, or to be told they have to work to try to right matters, convince themselves that his approach signifies heartlessness and his work is cold. But wit, irony and anger are potent forces and Sondheim uses them to dramatic effect. Theatergoers may wince at many of his characters' angry diatribes or be annoyed by other's ambivalence. They may want to turn their backs on his characters' rueful contemplations of midlife anxieties or escape the revenge-seeking characters, but Sondheim, in expressing his sophisticated moral and ethical view, in his desire that that view prevail and in attempting to persuade his audiences that it should prevail, has forced them to consider these issues.

The prevalence of darker tones and adult perspectives in his work gives rise to the misconception that Sondheim is unromantic. But his pragmatism, his wit and ironic approach do not negate his characterization of romance. For Sondheim, love and romance are much more complicated than simply boy meets girl and by show's end wedding bells will ring. They involve May-December relationships, reconciliation of former lovers, romantic attachments that never existed, characters fighting the need to commit to someone or leaving someone for a less seductive companion who needs the person more.

But Sondheim can also write the reassuring romantic numbers audiences seek. This is evident in songs such as "What More Do I Need?" from *Saturday Night* in which a young girl sings of not minding the inconveniences of apartment living—including her grimy window pane—since

> ...I see you, [the boy she loves]
> So the view is bright. (*Sondheim Evening* 2)

in "With So Little To Be Sure Of" as Fay Apple sings to Hapgood

> I need you more than I can say.
> I need you more than just today. (*Anyone Can Whistle* 176)

and in "It Takes Two" as the Baker and his Wife realize how much they rely on one another:

It takes two.
I thought one was enough,
It's not true:
It takes two of us. (*Into the Woods* 13)

These unabashed sentiments are accompanied by melodies as easy to
follow as any by Broadway's more commercial composers. Sondheim's
melodies always capture his characters' romantic sensibilities but audiences like to feel secure. When they know where a melody is going,
when a song resembles a traditional show tune and when it reinforces
already held beliefs, they are comfortable. The increasing ferocity of
"What More Do I Need?" as young love is expounded upon, the
heartfelt melody echoing Fay Apple's surprise and happiness at finding
herself in love with Hapgood and her insecurity, and the Baker and
his wife's tender soft shoe revealing their affection and need for one
another, reassure audiences. From *Follies* to *Sweeney Todd* to *Sunday
in the Park with George* to *Passion* Sondheim has written a wide range
of romantic scores and songs, but his use of subtext and counterpoint, his contemporary realistic vision (even when a show is set in
another period) and the melancholic undercurrents in his music lead
audiences to overlook the romance and turn away from it, as they do
his shows.

Just as much as the tone of his songs contributes to convincing
theatergoers that Sondheim is a cynic, so too does his music, which is
often characterized as unmelodic. But Sondheim's music, like his words
and the subjects of his shows, captures twentieth-century anxieties.
Just as he forces audiences to confront the reality of what he has to say
verbally, he subjects them to the emotional equivalent musically. Anx-
ious, sensual, angry or tender, his music evokes his characters' emotional states or the conflicts in their situations. The phones, buzzers
and door chimes in the score of *Company* echo the jangled nerves of
frenetic New Yorkers and the effort it takes to make personal relationships work. The aural equivalent of the dots with which Seurat created his canvases in *Sunday in the Park with George* paints a portrait of
George's obsession with his work and Dot's increasing impatience
with his inattention. Comments on plaintive Civil War ballads, stirring John Philip Sousa marches or 1970s folk-pop characterize the
destruction caused by the dispossessed in *Assassins* and woven around
one another, *Passion*'s romantic and sensual themes reveal Fosca's crav-
ing for love.

In all of his scores Sondheim yearns musically, just as he does verbally, for a better world. Nowhere is this subtle, complex verbal and musical longing, the question of the living of lives and the contemplation of action, taken more in evidence than in *Merrily We Roll Along*.

Merrily was conceived when Harold Prince, acquiescing to his wife's suggestion to create a musical reflecting the future concerns of teenagers, remembered he had enjoyed the Kaufman and Hart play as a young man. It, he thought, and Sondheim and George Furth concurred, could be adapted to explore preoccupations with friendship, success and the achievement of goals and could also serve as a warning about the seductive power of success. Adapting Kaufman and Hart's character, playwright Richard Niles, who abandons his dreams of writing plays of consequence to turn out Boulevard comedies, into Franklin Shepard, Sondheim, Prince and Furth examined the effects of such action. In the musical, loyalty and integrity are the issues. Friendships, collaborations and marriages are at stake. The desire for career and success collide with the way in which they are obtained. Musicalizing the Kaufman and Hart play was a chance for Sondheim to warn, advise, cajole and console about matters personally important to him. For *Merrily We Roll Along* encompasses all of the tenets by which Sondheim has lived his own long career. A glance at those forty years will reveal that they have been ruled by loyalty and integrity. Again and again he has returned to the same handful of collaborators. He has had the same orchestrator and conductor for years. Often the same designers design successive musicals and the same actors appear in show after show. And he has had the same agent, Flora Roberts, throughout his career. In addition, he has committed to projects which have attracted him artistically without regard to their commercial potential.

Sondheim, Furth and Prince's attempts to explore the moral imperatives of success did not work out as planned, however. To critics and theatergoers, focusing on Franklin Shepard's self-serving behavior, *Merrily*'s creators appeared to be griping, cynically equating success with compromise and corruption. And what did Sondheim and Prince, with their string of artistic (if not always financial) successes unequaled in the musical theater, have to complain about?

But this perception of *Merrily We Roll Along* and Sondheim and Prince's intentions is a mistaken one. The musical is not a cynical take on success. Rather, it is a meditation. It asks, "What is success?" Is it money? Fame? Satisfaction found through love of one's work? Pleasure taken in personal relationships? *Merrily* is concerned with how success is achieved, with guarding integrity, self-respect and dreams.

For Sondheim success is committing, tirelessly, to what one loves to do. Franklin Shepard's tragedy is not that he became a movie producer but that he let go of the one thing he wanted to do. Seeking fame and fortune, he let himself be talked into a second singing of "Good Thing Going" at his first celebrity packed party, became involved with Gussie who offered entree into the world he coveted and put projects with Charley on hold.

Each of these acts led to hurt and betrayal of friends and collaborators and self-betrayal as well. And each action became a regret to be considered when celebrating the premiere of his movie. Charley Kringas, on the other hand, adhered to his dreams, kept his self-respect and integrity intact and was just as successful. He is Sondheim's voice.

Charley Kringas exercises a certain nobility in adhering to his dreams, in his stubborn insistence on upholding his moral imperatives and his refusal to be Franklin Shepard's part-time partner. In the tug-of-war between him and Franklin Shepard, Sondheim sets up an ethical quest both for the characters and the audience. Repeatedly he questions Franklin Shepard's living of his life and asks, "How did you get there from here, Mr. Shepard?" (4) prodding his audiences to examine their own actions and reminding them to watch for the moment dreams start to slip away as when the chorus in the title song sings

> How does it happen?
> Where is the moment? (3)

Through Charley and Franklin's standoff Sondheim implores that loyalty and integrity to others as well as oneself be upheld; that honesty and consideration prevail in the treatment of friends and collaborators; that one's work be enjoyed for itself not for the gain it might bring, and he examines the losses that occur when such moral imperatives are breached. In *Merrily* Franklin and Charley have both lost a friend and collaborator and Mary has lost the security of the threesome to which she belonged.

The contrasting of Franklin Shepard's opportunistic behavior with his youthful commitment to writing great musicals and the presence of Gussie and the other jaded show business figures led audiences to assume it was Franklin's ethics Sondheim condoned. To some Franklin has done nothing wrong. Writing to George S. Kaufman after seeing the original production, movie producer Herman Mankiewicz said, "Here is this wealthy playwright who has repeated success and has earned enormous sums of money, has a mistress as well as a family, an expensive townhouse, a luxurious beach house and a yacht. The problem is: "How did the son of a bitch get into this jam?"(Rich). Many could say the same of Franklin Shepard.

Just as in his other musicals, Sondheim's views in *Merrily We Roll Along* are complex. Nothing is black and white. There are no easy solutions to Franklin and Charley's tug-of-war. The ending doesn't send audiences out of the theater reassured that loyalty, integrity and the fulfillment of one's dreams have won out over loss and betrayal. Franklin has had his way. But he is not without redemption. Lingering regret for the musicals not written is acknowledged as he celebrates his movie. His idealism is intact even as he defends his current situation.

Sondheim's views, presented again through his witty and ironic lyrics, and the sound of cocktail parties, caused theatergoers to overlook Franklin's acknowledgment of his mistake, the tender moments of love and longing and the youthful innocence in *Merrily We Roll Along*. Those who accuse Sondheim of condoning cynicism in *Merrily* have only to think of Franklin's acknowledgment, Charley's adherence to his moral imperatives and look at Franklin, Charley and Mary's youth to see where Sondheim's sympathies lie. Franklin, Charley and Mary's innocence in the second act of *Merrily* gave Sondheim an opportunity to delineate youthful enthusiasm as the trio begin their careers, capture the excitement of Franklin and Charley's first flush of success in "It's a Hit" and define optimism in their stirring anthem to their future:

> It's our time, breathe it in:
> Worlds to change and worlds to win. (13)

A tender moment of love and longing is expressed in "Not a Day Goes By," a song of undying love sung by Beth as she divorces Franklin and later in the musical (earlier in time) by Franklin and Beth, and unnoticed, by Mary:

> Not a day goes by,
> Not a single day
> But you're somewhere a part of my life
> And it looks like you'll stay. (6)

Adhering to their preconceived notions of Sondheim's musicals and *Merrily We Roll Along*, the critical reaction to the revival of the show, presented in New York in the summer of 1994 by the York Theater *Company*, was almost identical to that of the original. Again the critics found the characters unlikable and the show cynical. In the fourteen years since *Merrily* succumbed on Broadway, the musical has undergone extensive revisions in productions from La Jolla, California to Leicester, England and Sondheim and Furth's intentions, their idealism and the question of taking action and the living of lives has come into sharper focus.

George Furth has explored Franklin Shepard's character more fully, making him less a person who thoughtlessly opts for the most expedient means to fame and fortune than one who, wanting to fulfill his original dreams and remain loyal to friends and collaborators, hesitates before each decision to do otherwise. At the same time Charley Kringas has become even more insistent on upholding his moral principles while Gussie has become the villainess who lures Franklin away from the writing of great musicals and his wife. Sympathy now extends to Franklin as well as Charley. Sondheim has strengthened this sympathetic view of Franklin by the replacement of "Rich and Happy," a song about being rich and famous, with "That Frank" which more specifically addresses Franklin's attributes and by the addition of "Growing Up," a contemplation of friends' expectations of one another which questions why friends want old friends to remain the same:

> Why is it old friends
> Don't want old friends to change?
> Every road has a turning,
> That's the way you keep learning. (6)

The musical's point is further reinforced by Sondheim reminding the audiences, after each event in Franklin's life, of dreams and following them:

> How does it start to go,
> Does it slip away slow

So you never even notice
It's happening? (5)

It is in keeping with Sondheim's maturation, despite the critical reaction, that the revised *Merrily We Roll Along* more emphatically emphasizes the question of the living of lives and the struggle to uphold moral imperatives. In the decade and a half since *Merrily* was on Broadway, Sondheim himself has continued to live by the principles of loyalty and integrity, adhering to his creative demands, searching out new collaborations, never before tried ideas and innovative forms for the musical theater. Avoiding didacticism and never advocating simplistic solutions to the complex issues of contemporary morality, he has continued to force theatergoers to explore their own actions and to bring to them new and unexpected musicals while seeking for himself and audiences the better way to live one's life.

❧

Works Cited

Rich, Frank. "Should We Expect Magic to Happen When the Theatre Lights Darken?" *New York Times* 10 December 1981.

Sondheim, Stephen. *A Stephen Sondheim Evening.* RCA Red Seal CBL2-4745.

——. *Company.* Book by George Furth. New York: Random House, 1970.

——. *Merrily We Roll Along.* Book by George Furth. Varèse Sarabande VSD-5548.

——. *Into the Woods.* Book by James Lapine. RCA Victor 6796-1-RC-4.

——. *Passion.* Book by James Lapine. New York: Theatre Communications Group, 1994.

——. *Sunday in the Park with George.* Book by James Lapine. New York: Dodd, Mead, 1986.

——. *Anyone Can Whistle.* Book by Arthur Laurents. New York: Leon Amiel, 1976.

——. *Assassins.* Book by John Weidman. New York: Theatre Communications Group, 1991.

——. *Sweeney Todd, The Demon Barber of Fleet Street.* Book by Hugh Wheeler. New York: Dodd Mead, 1979.

"Let the Pupil Show the Master"
Stephen Sondheim and Oscar Hammerstein II
Andrew Milner

> It's a very ancient saying
> But a true and honest thought
> That when you become a teacher
> By your pupils you are taught
> — Oscar Hammerstein II, "Getting to
> Know You," *The King and I*, 1951

> My life was changed by teachers. The Latin teacher in
> high school, the music teacher in college. The passion of
> those teachers came across. And I think that teaching is
> about frontiers, going through doors. That's the only job
> of teachers.
> — Stephen Sondheim, Southern Methodist
> University, 1994 (Salsini 6)

Twelve July 1995 marked the 100th anniversary of the birth of Oscar Hammerstein II, who is undeniably one of the most seminal figures, if not the most important figure, in modern American musical theater history. Through his collaborations with Jerome Kern and Richard Rodgers, Hammerstein propelled the Broadway stage, heretofore the home to burlesque jokes, leggy chorus girls and irrelevant plots, into a forum for complex characterization and philosophical ideas.

Whereas other Broadway writers had relieved their proverbial audience of tired businessmen with well-crafted fluff, Hammerstein informed his work with emotional and social weight. Other songwriters might have come up with the Hit Parade ballads of a *South Pacific* (1949), but only Hammerstein would have insisted that the musical's libretto acknowledge racism—and not a blatant racism confined to flat, melodramatic villains, but instead a subtler form of prejudice held by two of the play's protagonists. "The villain in *South Pacific* is not the Japanese but man's racism," historian Ken Bloom would note. "The idea of the villain of a musical as a part of each character's persona was revolutionary at the time.... [This idea] is one reason [Hammerstein's] characters are so three-dimensional and his shows so full of humanity" (2764).

Hammerstein's work carried dramatic weight. The shows he wrote with Richard Rodgers from 1943 until 1959 were recorded on cast albums, the first generation of musical theater pieces to be so preserved. The first six Rodgers and Hammerstein musicals were collected in one volume and published in the Random House Modern Library anthology series, alongside the works of such 20th-century writers as Faulkner, Fitzgerald and Joyce.

1995 also marked the approaching 50th anniversary of an event that, while perhaps not pivotal in Hammerstein's life, was the defining moment of his son Jimmy's school friend. In late 1945 15-year-old Stephen Sondheim presented Hammerstein with a musical he and two classmates had written at the Quaker-run George School in Newtown, PA, a Philadelphia suburb near Hammerstein's Doylestown home.

By George was a standard student-written entertainment; the names of the characters were puns on teachers' names, and so forth. But the teenaged Sondheim saw *By George* as the equal to *Oklahoma!* and in that vein sent the script to Hammerstein with the proviso that Hammerstein read the work as if it were by a fellow professional. When Hammerstein called him in the following day Sondheim blithely expected an unqualified rave, even a Broadway production.

"It's the worst thing I've ever read," Hammerstein said firmly to a devastated Sondheim. He quickly added, "I didn't say it wasn't talented. It was terrible, and if you want to know why it's terrible I'll tell you."

Hammerstein proceeded to spend that very afternoon dissecting the play line by line. While he may not have considered *By George* Broadway-caliber, he nonetheless respected Sondheim enough to analyze a prep school musical with a professional eye. In later years Sondheim would frequently call Hammerstein's tutoring "four hours of the most *packed* information. I dare say, at the risk of hyperbole, that I learned more that afternoon than most people learn about songwriting in a lifetime" (Gottfried 15).

By the end of that fateful afternoon, Hammerstein drew up a musical-writing syllabus Sondheim would follow for the next six years. Sondheim would compose four musicals under Hammerstein's tutelage: a musical based on a play Sondheim thought was well-written (*Beggar on Horseback*); a musical based on a play Sondheim did *not* consider well-written (Maxwell Anderson's *High Tor*); a musical based on a non-dramatic work (*Mary Poppins*, which Sondheim wrote almost 15 years before the Disney version) and a musical based on an original idea (*Climb High*, about a young actor trying to establish himself on Broadway). Including a campus satire (*Phinney's Rainbow*), Sondheim had written no fewer than six musical comedies by the time he graduated from Williams at age 20 in 1950.

There is little doubt that Oscar Hammerstein would have played a pivotal role in Stephen Sondheim's development regardless of what career Sondheim would have chosen. Sondheim's parents had divorced when he was 11, and his relationship with his parents, particularly his mother, drove him to seek guidance and approval from outside sources. Sondheim has often said of Hammerstein simply, "He saved my life." But Sondheim's decision to become a lyricist and composer for the Broadway stage only cemented that link, and ensured a professional bond encompassing most of the 20th-century, from Hammerstein's first stage work in 1917 through Sondheim's most recent musicals of the mid-1990s.

"The history of the book musical is the history of Oscar Hammerstein II and Stephen Sondheim," theater historian Thomas S. Hischak declared in his book on Broadway lyricists, *Word Crazy* (1991):

> The careers of these two men...do more than chronologically parallel the growth of the American musical. Both men were instrumental in determining the direction that growth took, and most musicals are influenced by one or the other or both. An American musical theatre without Porter or Hart would be a poorer place; one without Hammerstein and Sondheim would be unimaginable. (119)

The *By George* episode has acquired the status of mythology within musical theater circles, and is today told as an inevitable meeting: one Broadway giant passing the torch to another. But had Sondheim never shown *By George* to Hammerstein, or had Hammerstein spared

Sondheim his loathing of the musical, Sondheim might well have eschewed composing and become, as he wanted to be when he grew up, an English or math professor, his relationship with Hammerstein a mere historical footnote. Sondheim's boldness, Hammerstein's honesty—one reason this story resonates as it does, is that it captures an essential characteristic of each man.[1]

On the surface, no two lyricists would appear more different than Hammerstein and Sondheim; the former wrote of larks learning to pray, while the latter's lyrics include "There's a hole in the world like a great black pit / And it's filled with people who are filled with shit." Compared to Sondheim's erudite references to DeMaupassant and Marx, Hammerstein's lyrics appear simplistic. As Hammerstein told one interviewer, "I'm more at home with people who haven't got a big vocabulary. You find people who are primitive in their education— they're more likely, I think, to say what they mean. They haven't got the subtle tools to cover up their meaning" (qtd. in Mordden 79).

Also, Hammerstein consciously chose not to rely heavily on outside references in lyric writing. "A rhyming dictionary," he wrote in the preface to his collected *Lyrics* (1949) "...should be used as a supplement to one's own ingenuity, and not a substitute for it. *I do not open mine until I have exhausted my own memory and invention of rhymes for a word*" (Hammerstein 1949, 20; emphasis author's). Contrast this with one of the more amusing moments in Sondheim's March 1988 appearance on *60 Minutes*, where he told Diane Sawyer how he came up with the "pinch"/"paunch"/"pension" sequence in "The Miller's Son" from *A Little Night Music*:

> SONDHEIM: All right. Let's go to the thesaurus and look up all the words that begin with "p" and have a "ch" sound—
>
> SAWYER(tartly): Go to the *thesaurus*?
>
> SONDHEIM: I have the most well-thumbed thesaurus and rhyming dictionary. Oh, this whole thing, this mystique about not using reference books is *nonsense*. Why should you have to sit there for five days and try to think of all the words that begin with a "p" that have a "ch" when you've got a nice book that *gives* you all the words?

SAWYER: I guess I'll live...

SONDHEIM: Come on. It never occurred to you before this?

SAWYER: No, I tell you it didn't.

SONDHEIM: My goodness.

SAWYER: I was sure you sat there and they tumbled out.

SONDHEIM: Oh, my goodness. Can you imagine the kind of encyclopedic mind you'd have to have to know all the words— you know rhymes, *trick* rhymes, you have to think up yourself. But to rhyme "day"? Do you know how many rhymes there are for that? How many *dozens* of words? You can't think all them up yourself.... And looking down the list will give you ideas. (*60 Minutes*, 1988)

One quality Sondheim clearly inherited from Hammerstein was "clarity of thought.... It's *what* you say first, and *how* you say it second," Sondheim told Max Wilk. "When I started out writing love songs I would write about stars and trees and dreams and moonlight.... That's fine if you believe it, but I didn't" (Wilk 234). Hammerstein told the young, remarkably competitive Sondheim the following advice: "Don't imitate other people's emotions. Speak your own.... If you write what you believe, you'll be ninety percent ahead of all other songwriters" (Fordin 241).

And Hammerstein certainly passed on to Sondheim a more imaginative view of what the theater could offer. Hammerstein's musicals didn't just have characters fall in love; in each of his first five musicals with Richard Rodgers, at least one of the central characters would be killed off or die. Sondheim would not fear tackling difficult scenes throughout his career. The first-act curtain to *West Side Story* left two corpses on the stage; the hero would die in the final scene; by the close of *Passion* (1994) the heroine has died while her lover has been institutionalized. "There's just one thing I hate and that's rules," Hammerstein once snapped at his brother Reggie. "The theater should have no rules" (Fordin 257).

It is therefore instructive to analyze how Hammerstein and Sondheim wrote two of their most rules-breaking musicals, *Allegro* (1947) and *Merrily We Roll Along* (1981) respectively. Although Sondheim has never acknowledged any relationship between *Allegro* and *Merrily We Roll Along*, and while one does not wish to attribute to Sondheim qualities which might belong to *Merrily*'s original authors (Kaufman and Hart) or its musical librettist (George Furth), it is interesting to compare and contrast how two closely related musical theater writers, who generally wrote uncompromising shows, developed ideas for two musicals which share the similar theme of professional and personal compromise.

Oscar Hammerstein was 52 in 1947. As he readied *Allegro* for its out-of-town premiere, Hammerstein was clearly on a professional roll after 15 years of one unsuccessful show after another. His debut show with Rodgers, *Oklahoma!* (1943), was still running. The pair's next show, *Carousel* (1945), was in many ways their masterpiece. Their first musical film *State Fair* (1945) was a box-office hit. And Hammerstein had two independent triumphs with *Carmen Jones* (1943) and the 1946 revival of *Show Boat*. These solid successes gave Hammerstein the financial and emotional security to try something a little different for his next project. Perhaps the fact that all the above works had been adaptations spurred Hammerstein to attempt an original story.

Taking place from 1905 to 1940, *Allegro* told the story of the first 35 years of the life of Joseph Taylor, Jr., an aspiring doctor from a middle-American small town whose plans to help the sick and support his family are thwarted by ambition and worldly success. These qualities are personified in Jenny, Joe's childhood sweetheart and later wife. She flirts with him in college, sending him veiled letters about her other boyfriends. She is so sweetly vicious in damning the Taylor family's living standards ("I don't think I'd be happy as the wife of a starving doctor") (Hammerstein 1955, 223) that after one very mean-spirited conversation, Joe's mother drops dead.

Joe and Jenny marry and spend their early years eking out a living during the Depression before she seduces him into accepting a position at a tony Chicago hospital. Joe spends his days in paperwork and evenings at high-society cocktail parties, catering to neurotic scions and self-indulgent matrons, to the neglect of his practice. His dipsomaniac college buddy Charlie and tart-tongued nurse Emily—

who quietly carries a torch for him—try to salvage Joe's integrity. Only when Joe learns of Jenny's affair with the head of the hospital does he have an epiphany. His mother appears to him and beckons him to "come home" to his father's practice and small-town ideals. Joe publicly turns down a major promotion and, with Charlie and Emily, returns to his hometown.

In February 1960, just six months before his death, Hammerstein told Canadian broadcaster Tony Thomas what he was attempting to say in *Allegro:*

> There are certain things that go along with [success] that have a tendency to drag a man away from doing the very things that made him successful...and that isn't just true of doctors. It's true of lawyers, it's true of librettists, too. I find right now that I'm called away to sit on boards and committees that seem all right in themselves—and they *are*, otherwise I wouldn't sit on them—I'm pulled apart and spread pretty thin, because I am successful. And it requires a great effort to throw aside everything and tell everyone I'm working on a play, at which time they stop and leave me alone. This sounds as if I am a very weak character, but *everyone* is a weak character when it comes to this temptation. Once a man has done well at something, there is a conspiracy in which he takes part to pull him away from that thing. It's something like a runner who runs very fast and wins a lot of races, and then they pin so many medals on him that when he carries those heavy medals, he can't run so fast anymore. (Thomas 1960)

Allegro had one of the most notorious out-of-town tryouts of its era. In New Haven, audience members were alarmed by an alley fire outside the theater, and actress Lisa Kirk (as nurse Emily) fell into the orchestra pit during her torch song, "The Gentleman Is a Dope." Upon its 10 October 1947 opening at New York's Majestic Theatre, *Allegro* received divergent reviews. Brooks Atkinson of the *Times* called it "a musical play of superior quality...it has made history on Broadway.... Rodgers and Hammerstein have just missed the final splendor of a perfect work of art." And Robert Coleman of the *Daily Mirror* dubbed *Allegro* "Perfect and Great [sic]...[it] should be embraced affectionately by discriminating playgoers. It lends new stature to the American musical stage." But William Hawking of the *World-Telegram* considered the musical "a vast disappointment...it lacks consistency of mood, visual excitement and theatrical stimulation." And John Chapman in the *Daily News* called *Allegro* "an elaborate sermon," set "to an andante beat" (Green, 556-57). Thanks to a then-record advance of $600,000, *Allegro* managed to run nine months despite the mixed response, and even went on a national tour.

Here is one eyewitness to *Allegro's* travails:

> What happened was when I was 17, I was a gofer for Oscar on a show called *Allegro*, and they had written *Oklahoma!* and *Carousel*, these two gigantic hits, and [Oscar] tried a genuinely experimental show, and it flopped. And I have a feeling that I may have gotten slightly wary, 'cause it was a terrible disappointment to him and it was really going out on a limb. So my first experience was watching a man go out on a limb and get chopped off.... Luckily, Lenny [Bernstein] and Jerry [Robbins] and Arthur [Laurents] were fearless (in *West Side Story*), that was quickly healed.... One of the things I learned from Lenny was, "You're going to take a chance, take a big chance, don't take a little chance." (Sondheim 1994)

Stephen Sondheim was 51 in 1981 when his *Merrily We Roll Along* opened, almost the same age Hammerstein was when he wrote *Allegro*. And the Sondheim of 1981 was as dominant over Broadway as Hammerstein had been over the post–World War II New York theater scene. During the 1970s Sondheim and director/producer Harold Prince staged five landmark musicals, each of which were listed by Otis Guernsey as among the 10 best plays of their respective seasons. Their final work of the decade in particular, *Sweeney Todd* (1979), was considered a masterpiece, receiving the strongest critical praise of any of the Sondheim-Prince collaborations. As other Broadway figures such as Jerry Herman, Alan Jay Lerner, Sheldon Harnick and Richard Rodgers himself met with one unsuccessful show after another in the 1970s, no other American musical theater figure was receiving the praise Sondheim was getting, and no one else was perceived as being the one true heir to the Rodgers and Hammerstein legacy.

The Sondheim-Prince collaborations of the 1970s generally centered around middle-aged characters, and their last three works had been period pieces set abroad. By the early 1980s Harold Prince's children were teenagers, and he wanted to produce a contemporary musical about America, cast with young adults. He had loved *Merrily We Roll Along* as a boy himself, and hit upon musicalizing it.

Company playwright George Furth updated the story to the 1960s and '70s, but retained the backwards storyline. *Merrily* centered around Broadway composer turned Hollywood producer Franklin Shepard— or, given the reverse chronology of the play, Hollywood producer turned Broadway composer Franklin Shepard. The 1981 play begins with the middle-aged Shepard giving the commencement address at his high school alma mater, charging the graduates to accept compromise. We then see Shepard in 1979 Hollywood at the premiere party for his first movie, a bomb. Mary Flynn, an old friend turned alcoholic critic, disrupts the affair and tells him off. About to lose his second wife, a vapid actress named Gussie, Frank casts off Mary. We are then presented with Frank's career: His collaboration with lyricist-playwright Charley Kringas ended in 1973 when, on a live TV interview, Charley describes Frank as a money-driven phony ("Franklin Shepard, Inc."). Frank chillingly ends their friendship, considering Charley dead. The next scene takes place in 1968, when Frank, Charley and Mary reaffirm their friendship ("Old Friends"). Each further scene sends us back earlier in time. In 1962 Gussie, wife to an influential producer, seduces Frank, who'd rather write serious shows with Charley, into writing a mindless show for her. We next see Frank, Charley and Beth perform at a Village nightclub in 1960, celebrating the incoming Kennedy administration ("Bobby and Jackie and Jack," a song much in the style of *That Was the Week That Was*). Frank marries his pregnant girlfriend Beth, while Mary quietly pines for Frank. The next scene covers two years as Frank, Mary and Charley try to make it in New York ("Opening Doors"). The climactic scene occurs in 1957 as Frank and Charley meet Mary on a New York rooftop—Sputnik's just been launched, and they optimistically sing of their own ascendancy ("Our Time"). In the final scene, an 18-year-old Frank Shepard introduces a song he's written for his high school graduation ("The Hills of Tomorrow").

Merrily's preview perils in the fall of 1981 made *Allegro's* out-of-town woes look positively pacific. Numerous walkouts during the first previews led to venomous word of mouth, and considerable re-writing of both libretto and score. The sets and costumes were over-hauled. Frank was recast and choreographer Ron Field was replaced by Larry Fuller. But it was not enough. *Merrily* received scathing notices when it opened 16 November 1981, led off by Frank Rich's infamous opening to his *Times* review: "As we should have all probably learned by now, to be a Stephen Sondheim fan is to have one's heart broken at regular intervals." Only Clive Barnes of the *Post* (who, as the *Times* critic in the 1970s had notoriously panned Sondheim's *Company* and *Follies*) gave thumbs up to *Merrily*, which ran just 16 performances, the shortest run of a Sondheim show since 1964's *Anyone Can Whistle*. As with *Whistle*, the *Merrily* cast album was recorded the day after the show closed. The legacy of the 1981 fiasco might have ultimately been the end to Sondheim and Prince's professional partnership; they have not collaborated since.

There are striking similarities between *Allegro* and *Merrily We Roll Along*. Each of these shows was among the most autobiographical of Hammerstein's and Sondheim's careers. Joe Taylor, *Allegro*'s central character, loses his mother as a youth and belatedly learns of his wife's adultery. Hammerstein's mother died in 1910 of complications during an abortion. The 15-year-old Hammerstein grieved intensely but privately, making baseball-related scrapbooks to assuage the pain. And his first wife, Myra Finn (a first cousin to Richard Rodgers), carried on openly with other men during the final part of their 12-year marriage. Hammerstein, already beginning an affair with Dorothy Blanchard, an Australian actress who would become the second Mrs. Hammerstein in 1929, was the last to know of Myra's infidelities. He suffered a nervous breakdown and briefly spent time in a New York sanitarium, gathering the strength to file for divorce and reassess his life.

Likewise, *Merrily* parallels Sondheim's life more overtly than any of his other works. Its time frame of 1957 to 1979 (or, rather, 1979 to 1957) coincides with Sondheim's professional development. The 1957 scene occurs after the launch of Sputnik on 4 October, only eight days after *West Side Story* opened, launching Sondheim's career into orbit. *Merrily*'s second act opening ("It's a Hit!") takes place at the opening of Frank and Charley's *Musical Husbands* in 1964, the same year *Fiddler on the Roof, Funny Girl* and *Hello, Dolly!* premiered. In April of that year, Sondheim's innovative, decidedly anti–Rodgers and Hammersteinesque *Anyone Can Whistle* opened, running just a week to mainly disastrous reviews.

And the "Opening Doors" scene is undoubtedly Sondheim's most directly autobiographical work. Frank and Charley are shown composing lyrics and music and performing for producer Joe Josephson—whose wife, as we have seen, will later leave him for Frank. He cynically interrupts their singing (of a song, "Who Wants to Live in New York?" which will eventually become "Good Thing Going") to declare what countless producers and critics (and not a few listeners) have long accused Sondheim of: "There's not a tune you can hum.... I'll let you know when Stravinsky has a hit, give me some melody...." As Joe shows the duo out he illustrates *his* idea of a "hummmmmm-mmmmmmmable melody" by humming "Some Enchanted Evening." To cap the moment, Joe hums the "You may see a stranger" part incorrectly.

Both shows have a similar central lyric motif—of taking steps and trying different roads. In *Allegro's* first scenes Joe's mother and grandmother reach out to the (unseen) infant Joe as he takes his first steps, as the Greek chorus triumphantly sings "One Foot, Other Foot":

> Now you can go
> Wherever you want
> Wherever you want to go
> One foot out
> And the other foot out
> That's all you need to know! (Hammerstein 1955,
> 194–95)

This motif is reprised twice during the show, used to signify Joe's growing independence. The first time comes as Joe appears on stage for the first time at a college mixer, singing "One Foot, Other Foot" to himself to mark time while dancing (Hammerstein 1955, 205). The second time occurs at the play's climax; as Joe renounces both job and wife, the chorus, as the script cues put it, "listens to Joe 'learn to walk again.'" Joe's long-dead mother and grandmother reappear on stage and reenact their response to baby Joe's walking in Act One, as the adult Joe reaches out to Charley and Emily while the chorus reprises "One Foot, Other Foot."

In *Merrily* the motif, established in the title song by the Greek chorus, is one of roads:

> Pick yourself a road
> Get to know the countryside

> Soon enough you're merrily, merrily
> Practicing dreams
> Dreams that will explode
> Waking up the countryside....

"Merrily We Roll Along" reappears between every scene, with slightly different lyrics (and harmonies, tempos and orchestrations) each time. Before the "Bobby and Jackie and Jack" nightclub scene, the "Merrily" reprise hints at the sudden end to the Camelot years (and, by implication, the breakup of the camaraderie of *Merrily*'s triumvirate): "Some roads the ride goes out of control / Grinds to a halt and ends in a hole / Some roads you stop before you can roll...."

The big, take-home ballads in each show are similarly themed, commenting on love's obsessive nature. In *Allegro* "You Are Never Away" is first sung by the chorus, echoing the undergraduate Joe's obsession with the vacationing Jenny. Joe eventually sings the song himself, to Jenny as an affirmation of his love:

> You are never away
> From your home in my heart
> There is never a day
> When you don't play a part
>
> In a word that I say
> Or a sight that I see
> You are never away
> And I'll never be free.... (Hammerstein 1955, 220)

In *Merrily*, "Not a Day Goes By" is likewise heard twice. It is first sung by Frank's wife, Beth, during their divorce proceedings where she bitterly admits that despite his infidelities

> [Y]ou're still somewhere part of my life
> And you won't go away
> So there's hell to pay
> And until I die
> I'll die day after day after day after day
> After day after day after day after day....

(In the 1981 cast recording, this version of "Not a Day Goes By" was sung instead by Jim Walton, who played Frank; Sally Klein, the actress who played Beth, lacked the voice to sing it well.) Thanks to the backwards structure of the show, the reprise is heard in a scene several years *earlier*, at Frank and Beth's informal wedding. This time Mary, already in love with Frank, sings the bitter lyric while Frank and Beth sing glowingly of the future to the same melody: "But you're some-where a part of my life / And it looks like you'll stay…. I want day after day after day after day…."

Each play centered around a core of three protagonists, two men and a woman: the male hero, the female sidekick/love interest, and the male's comic relief best friend. (*Singin' In the Rain* is a perfect example of this setup.) There is also an omnipresent Greek chorus in both shows, commenting on the action.

Both were also staged with minimal sets. Harold Prince initially wanted *Merrily* to have no sets whatsoever, *à la Our Town*, then concluded a Broadway audience wouldn't pay top dollar for a musical without sufficient glitz. Gymnasium bleachers were then installed (in keeping with the teen-centered theme of the musical) and reconfigured from scene to scene, but *Merrily* was not a set-driven show.

And both plays distort the element of time. Within the first act of *Allegro* Joe Taylor grows from birth to manhood. *Merrily*, of course, reverses the time element completely; Frank, Mary and Charley regress from middle-agers to teenagers over the course of the show.

What, then, is the central difference between the themes of *Allegro* and *Merrily*? It is in how the theme of individual integrity is presented. In *Allegro*, Hammerstein illustrates the virtues of not selling out in a *direct* fashion: Joe Taylor comes to a personal crossroads (take the promotion and stay in the big city with an unfaithful wife, or go back home to Dad's small-town practice?) and, with the support of family and true friends, selects the right path. There is a nearly identical moment in *Merrily*—the first-act ending, set in 1966, after Frank and Beth divorce—when Frank can either seek renewal through serious Broadway composing or sink into a funk. Through Mary and Charley's enthusiasm, he appears to want to return to the theater ("Now You Know") but, as we have seen in the first act, he never gets around to writing those important shows with Charley and escapes to Hollywood. Sondheim makes the same point as Hammerstein did, only indirectly. Frank abandons composing, and we are left to contemplate what might have been.

At the risk of reducing the careers of two creative giants to one paragraph, this is a key difference between Hammerstein and Sondheim: Hammerstein generally made his point positively, while

Sondheim acknowledges the ambiguities and choices not made. In "Some Enchanted Evening" from *South Pacific* (1949), Hammerstein exuberantly writes in rich language of finding perfect love unexpectedly from a stranger. Two decades later in *Company* (1970) Sondheim would write in "Someone Is Waiting" both of idealizing Ms. Right (an amalgam of every positive attribute of each of Robert's married female friends) and of not recognizing true love when one sees it, of realizing only too late what might have been; has Robert waited too long to seize the moment? The song's last lines, "Wait for me / Hurry / Wait for me / Hurry," only adds to the overall ambivalence of the musical.

In "Climb Ev'ry Mountain" (1959), Hammerstein's lyric urges the listener to follow their dream to its reality, to capitalize on the moment. In Sondheim's "The Road You Didn't Take" from 1971's *Follies*, the singer looks back on the compromises and "either-ors" that made up his professional rise, acknowledges the lost opportunities he shunned, and concludes with: "The Ben I'll never be / Who remembers him?"

Another difference between *Allegro* and *Merrily* is that while *Allegro*'s score is among Rodgers and Hammerstein's least famous, *Merrily We Roll Along* has more standards than any Sondheim score, from "Not a Day Goes By" and "Good Thing Going" through the irresistible "Old Friends" and "Our Time." Even those nonplused by *Merrily*'s 1981 production liked most of the score, and it is largely for this reason that *Merrily* has undergone more rewrites and reinterpretations than any other Sondheim show.

In 1985, Sondheim and George Furth produced the first major rewrite of *Merrily* in La Jolla, CA, a production directed by Sondheim's then-new collaborator, James Lapine. The 1985 *Merrily* eliminated the high school graduation scenes bookending the show (at the cost of cutting the soaring "The Hills of Tomorrow" alma mater) Sondheim reworked the Broadway production's "Rich and Happy," a curiously flat opening number into the sharper "That Frank," while Frank received a sympathetic soliloquy, "Growing Up," where he acknowledges both his compromises and his friendships. Most importantly, the 1985 *Merrily* was cast with adults. John Rubenstein (a musician himself) starred as Frank, Chip Zien (who would create the role of The Baker in *Into the Woods*) played Charley and Heather MacRae played Mary. The newer *Merrily* worked that much better when the middle-aged cast gradually acted younger and less mature than it had in 1981, when teenagers had to begin as forty-year-olds, then had to revert to adolescence.

The success of the La Jolla production led to further revisions at Washington, D.C.'s Arena Stage in 1990 and at London's Leicester Haymarket Theatre two years later. At long last, *Merrily* returned to New York in the spring of 1994 at the off-Broadway York Theater (where Jacqueline Kennedy Onassis's sudden death lent an even more poignant air to the "Bobby and Jackie and Jack" cabaret number). The 1994 *Merrily* production received infinitely better and far more sympathetic reviews; Michael Feingold of the *Village Voice* in particular placed the show among Sondheim's best. Thanks to Furth's much-improved book and Sondheim's trenchant score revising, the musical production of *Merrily We Roll Along* became more a part of the Sondheim repertoire.

And perhaps it is appropriate that in reworking a misunderstood musical, Sondheim was truly an heir of Hammerstein. Hammerstein was apparently just as close to *Allegro* as Sondheim was to *Merrily*, and was as eager to rewrite his show. In 1958, shortly after Rodgers and Hammerstein scored a coup with the live television broadcast of their adaptation of *Cinderella*, Hammerstein decided to try rewriting *Allegro* for TV. He apparently intended to substitute offscreen voice-overs for the bulky, intrusive Greek chorus, and try for an optimistic ending by strengthening Joe and Jenny Taylor's marriage.

But by 1959 Hammerstein was busy as *The Sound of Music* was readying for Broadway. And he had been diagnosed with the cancer that would eventually kill him. By the summer of 1960 he had decided to spend his last days at his Doylestown home with family and friends, and he invited them there in July for his 65th, and final, birthday.

By the summer of 1960 Stephen Sondheim was a 30-year-old musical theater success. Twice he had asked Hammerstein's advice on doing "just" lyrics; twice Hammerstein encouraged him to put off composing and contribute lyrics. The results, *West Side Story* and *Gypsy*, speak for themselves. By 1960 he was working on *A Funny Thing Happened on the Way to the Forum*, his first Broadway musical score.

Though it was his birthday being celebrated, Oscar gave every guest a gift—a formal portrait, his last, in which he bravely tried to hide the effects of disease and treatment. It was then that Sondheim realized he wanted further, physical proof that he had known Oscar Hammerstein, "who had tutored and nurtured and argued with and tolerated me for nineteen years." He asked Hammerstein to auto-graph the photograph. Hammerstein quickly wrote something down, smiled a cryptic smile, and walked to dinner. Only later that night would Sondheim read the inscription: "For Steve, my friend and teacher" (Gottfried 60).

☙

Note

1.   Sondheim would carry this legacy of counseling young songwriters in particular throughout his own career. His most notable protégé was Jonathan Larson (1960–96), who won a composing competition judged by Sondheim in the early 1980s. Sondheim urged Larson to eschew his drama degree and write music—there were more starving actors than composers, he told Larson—and oversaw each of Larson's projects, culminating in his final work, *Rent* (1996), a stunning piece successfully combining the Broadway know-how of Rodgers and Hammerstein with a modern pop/rock sound. Larson paid homage to his mentor in the exhilarating list song, "La Vie Bohéme," in which the Alphabet City characters drink a toast to "[c]ompassion, to fash-ion, to passion when it's new / To Sontag, to Sondheim, to anything taboo."

WORKS CITED

60 Minutes. "Sondheim," hosted by Diane Sawyer. CBS television network, 13 March 1988.

Bloom, Ken. *American Song: The Complete Musical Theater Companion.* New York: Facts on File, 1985.

Fordin, Hugh. *Getting to Know Him: A Biography of Oscar Hammerstein II.* New York: Random House, 1977.

Gottfried, Martin. *Sondheim.* New York: Abrams, 1993.

Green, Stanley. *The Rodgers and Hammerstein Fact Book.* New York: Lynn Farnol Group, 1979.

Hammerstein II, Oscar. Interview with Tony Thomas, Canadian Broadcasting Corporation, 3 February 1960.

——. *Lyrics*. New York: Simon and Schuster, 1949.

——. *Six Plays*. New York: Modern Library, 1955.

Hischak, Thomas S. *Word Crazy: Broadway Lyricists from Cohan to Sondheim.* New York: Praeger, 1991.

Mordden, Ethan. *Rodgers and Hammerstein*. New York: Abrams, 1993.

Salsini, Paul. "Sondheim, on Campus, Talks About Opening Doors." *The Sondheim Review* 1 (Winter 1995): 3–6.

Sondheim, Stephen. Talk at the Museum of Television and Radio, New York, 1994 (rebroadcast on National Public Radio's "Fresh Air with Terry Gross," 7 June 1996).

——, and George Furth. *Company*. New York: Random House, 1970.

——. *Merrily We Roll Along*. RCA Red Seal RCD1-5840, 1982.

——, and James Goldman. *Follies in Concert*. RCA Red Seal RCD2-7128, 1985.

Wilk, Max. *They're Playing Our Song*. New York: Atheneum, 1973.

Portraits of the Artist:
Sunday in the Park with George *as "Postmodern" Drama*
Edward T. Bonahue, Jr.

Even a cursory survey of recent Sondheim criticism (both academic and theatrical) reveals the distinct vocabulary commonly used to describe the composer-lyricist's contributions to musical drama. Some commentators, detecting fundamental and consequential innovations, boldly label his work "radical," "revolutionary" and even "avant-garde." Others, making more circumspect and conservative claims, find it "unexpected," "unpredictable" or "experimental." Analyzing the structure of the Sondheim "concept musical," critics find elements of "pastiche," "collage" or other "neoimpressionistic" forms, and point out contrasts with the well-made play or the traditional "book musical." "Sondheim has always said that he never set out to revolutionize an art form," notes Stephen Schiff, "but that is precisely what he did" (76). His innovations are so radical, critics would have us believe, as to constitute a wholesale "departure from the traditional patterns of realist theater" (Gordon 10).

Sunday in the Park with George (1984) in particular has been found to interrogate and disrupt the traditional forms of the musical theater, a conclusion at least partially justified by the work's episodic structure and unusually serious subject matter. Like much of Sondheim's work since *Company* (1970), the structure of *Sunday in the Park* embodies not the simple book musical but a sequence of scenes united as much by concept as plotted action. Spanning a century from 1884 to 1984, including scenes in both Paris and New York, ending with a mystical reunion of figures from the past and present, the action does not build, climax or resolve in the traditional dramatic senses of those terms. Thematically, too, the work explores how abstract ideas like art, the artist and the artistic process are defined. Its serious and sustained exploration of creativity, art institutions and even the semiotics of art has led many critics to embrace it as a far-reaching manifesto, a foundation on which to build the future of musical drama. Frank Rich, for example, noting the play's structural and thematic singularity, goes so far as to announce "a musical theater breakthrough," arguing that Sondheim "has transcended four decades of Broadway history." To him, *Sunday in the Park with George* constitutes "perhaps the first truly modernist work of musical theater" and "a watershed event," requiring a complete historical reassessment of the Broadway musical (53–54).

Despite such overwhelming claims, however, for Sondheim in general and *Sunday in the Park with George* in particular, the aesthetic principles promoted by the play are scarcely "revolutionary" and, actually, largely conventional.[1] This musical, as Sondheim has remarked, is committed to conservative definitions of art, ultimately relying on a very traditional aesthetics involving creative genius, mystical inspiration, skillful execution and, on the whole, the creation of a timeless, transcendent artifact. Apart from its conceptual structure, the work's only "radical" feature is its challenging intellectual depth—a welcome relief during a Broadway era otherwise dominated by melodramatic spectacle. Nevertheless, as Sondheim has declared, "*Sunday in the Park*, though it might strike you or others as radical, is meticulously formed—as formed as the picture…. In philosophy of art, generally, I'm a conservative. My beliefs are conservative, but my work is not" (Gordon 300). But what does such a claim mean? Can a dramatic work embracing conservative cultural values truly lay claim to the label of "radical"? Can its structural innovations alone truly "revolutionize the art form," given its conservative message about art and artistic values? My aim in what follows, then, is to recognize *Sunday in the Park with George* as a serious dramatic exploration of art and aesthetics, while suggesting that previous claims for the radical or novel position of the work have been overstated and rest solely on Sondheim's "concept" structure. The work's definition of art and the artist, however, and thus its position relative to contemporary cultural politics, is traditional and conservative.

Sunday in the Park is centered, of course, around two artist-figures who, despite their differences, communicate most of the play's ideas about art and aesthetics. In the first act, Seurat clearly represents the artist endowed with genuine creative genius, whereas in the second act, George has apparently lost his, only to gain it back again at the end.2 From the outset, Seurat is a self-absorbed eccentric, surrounded by a chorus of comments describing his unique, if peculiar, artistic genius. His mother indicates that her son was markedly different in his youth and even seemed fated to become an artist. The young George "always drifted as a child....always in some other place—seeing something no one else could see. We tried to get through to you, George. Really we did" (118). As a mature artist, neither Seurat nor his work conforms with the established methods of the Paris art world. He is isolated and unrecognized, has few friends and no patrons, and Jules has to spell it out for him: "Go to some parties. That is where you'll meet prospective buyers" (80). As is made clear, however, Seurat is unwilling or unable to play such society games, adhering only to his personal code and refusing to paint, as he says, for the approval of anyone else (81).

This familiar picture of the dedicated and misunderstood artist is not limited only to Seurat; rather, the play sweeps all artists into a single category. Dot affirms that, in general, "artists are bizarre. Fixed. Cold" (29), and she is echoed by the Celestes: "Artists are so crazy" (61). Two of *Sunday in the Park*'s working-class characters, the Boatman and Franz the chauffeur, reflect on the difference between the kind of hard manual work they do—and the kind of virile men they are—and the altogether different obsessions of the artist. Complaining about Seurat's pretentious "observing" and "perceiving" (62), the Boatman helps to expose some of the awe surrounding the idea of the elite artist. "Who are you, with your fancy pad and crayons? You call that work? You smug goddam holier-than-thou shitty little men in your fancy clothes—born with pens and pencils, not pricks!" (65–66). Franz likewise perceives the life of the artist to be one of luxury and self-fulfillment: "I should have been an artist. I was never intended for work" (78). Their accusations are wrong, of course, as is shown by the hours Seurat spends with his canvas, meticulously, even tediously applying individual brushstrokes despite his cramping fingers. Nevertheless, Franz insists that "work is what you do for others," what you do to make a living, while "art is what you do for yourself," and so is reserved only for those with the means, or the unrelenting need, to pursue continuous self-gratification (79). Even Jules, who comes across as only a mediocre artist, is reportedly afflicted with mystical spells, as Yvonne admits: "there are times when he just does not know Louise and I are there" (102).

This definition of the artist as a creative genius—preoccupied only with personal principles, perceived by others as a self-righteous snob, isolated from everyone and everything belonging to the workaday real world—is familiar, but, as several critics have noted, too familiar. It is a cliché, a stereotype of the slighted genius, the visionary ahead of his time. Seurat's self pity at being misunderstood also seems trite: "I had thought she understood. They have never understood" (93). As Benedict Nightingale finds—although with a gratuitous attack-dog tone[3]—the play "too often reduces poor Seurat to that stock mythological beast, the brilliant but misunderstood artist whose unswerving dedication to his muse alienates even his nearest and dearest" (7). If we're trying to comprehend what makes *Sunday in the Park* such a compelling and revolutionary musical drama, then we can safely say it is not the portrait of Seurat. Contemporary drama and film are chock full of such representations of the misunderstood and isolated artist, whether it be Mozart in the popular *Amadeus*, the tortured figure of Van Gogh in *Vincent and Theo*, or even Jim Morrison in *The Doors*, to name just a few.[4]

Nevertheless, if *Sunday in the Park with George* has a hero, it is clearly Seurat. Although he demonstrates many personal faults, the play clearly endorses his artistic genius and principled pursuit of his vision. His dedication to his painting, his innovative technique and the value of his finished works are never placed in doubt. In fact, the oafish ridicule of his contemporaries is pointedly intended to show just what a genius he is. I am not arguing here that Seurat represents Sondheim's ideal of the artist; we are clearly meant to be appalled at his self-indulgence and disregard for others. And yet, as I will argue further on, the play ultimately excuses Seurat's foibles and even approves his treatment of Dot.[5] The play's honorific ending, as we shall see, lionizes Seurat into the heroic stereotype.

But Seurat stands as only half of *Sunday in the Park*'s artistic tandem. The work's other artist, the contemporary George, affords different insights into the idea of the artist, offered from the more familiar context of the twentieth century. In contrast with the self-contained Seurat, so oblivious to matters of patronage and public taste, George seems completely engaged with the conventions of his profession. (Of course, that's part of his problem.) "Our contemporary George is an inventor-sculptor, and this is his latest invention, Chromolume #7. The machine is post-modern in design..." (144).

Participating in a public museum program, collaborating with a composer and an engineer, greeting guests at a reception and generally moving with the "post-modern" times, this George is fully immersed in professional conventions. In a further contrast to the idealistic Seurat, George pragmatically realizes that "machines don't grow on trees" (162) and sees how the "foundation" beneath the modern artist lies not only in an artistic vision but on the financial contacts made through "cocktail conversation" (164):

> Every time I start to feel defensive,
> I remember lasers are expensive.
> What's a little cocktail conversation
> If it's going to get you your foundation,
> Leading to a prominent commission
> And an exhibition in addition? (166)

Strikingly, George ends up giving the same advice to his colleague Alex that his great grandfather received from Jules: "It's all politics, Alex. Maybe if you just lightened up once in a while" (171). But what a radical reversal! Whereas the artist of the first act holds fast to his principles, appearing almost as a Keatsian guardian of Beauty and Truth, his second-act descendent here reveals that success actually depends on "politics," on negotiations of cultural power. As is suggested by the cardboard cut-outs George uses to maintain his presence in as many conversations as possible, the artist is merely performing here, rehearsing a series of roles devoid of any pure or essential quality.

Our greatest insights into George's world come from the "Art Isn't Easy/Putting It Together" number at the center of the second act, Sondheim's often-quoted examination of contemporary artistic production. In this number George opens a rare window onto the inner workings of the modern art world, with the result that modern art is ironically and satirically distinguished from true Art—the capital signifying high art, the Beautiful, the True, and so forth. Specifically, art is here revealed not as a work of genius produced by an isolated and dedicated artist, but rather as a product, perhaps even a commodity, constructed, mediated and funded by a range of social, institutional and financial forces. With great irony and perhaps a dose of cynicism as well, Sondheim reveals in this scene how art, which has traditionally been reckoned the crowning pinnacle of civilization, may spring as much from wealthy patronage and media hype as from artistic inspiration and creative genius.

The chorus of arty types in this number includes several distinct voices, each contributing its own self-interested commentary to the overall satire. Thus, the wealthy art patron Harriet admits, "I don't understand completely" what George's new Chromolume is about (154), although that doesn't deter her from underwriting such work. The museum curators Greenberg and Redmond focus more on riding the latest artistic trend than on acquiring work they find valuable (155). The artists Alex and Betty are dubious of the chromolume's originality, stating that "it's all promotion" (155–57) and suggesting the importance of public notice. Public relations man Lee Randolph continues in this vein, telling George, "There's a lot of opportunity for some nice press here," and George agrees that "a little bit of hype can be effective" in "building up [his] image" (168). George hints that the opinion of Blair, the professional critic, is merely an opinion like anyone else's, without real significance for him. Yet she too plays a role: "You never minded my opinions when they were in your favor.... I have touted your work from the beginning" (174). Patron-age, commissions, canonical status, publicity, reviews (not to mention opinionated critics and their essays!)—these are the compositional elements that really matter to the modern George. He works the room, networking, making connections, scampering from one conversation to the next. At the end of the number, "George frames the successfully completed picture with his hands, as at the end of Act I" (179), dramatically signaling that this is where real artistry lies in his world. The very public cocktail party has replaced the private studio as the artist's place of work.[6] In a world where even museum curators "can't tell good from rotten" (178), art lies not in the "difficult to evaluate" artifact itself (167), which seems ambiguous in terms of both value and meaning, but rather in the artist's ability to navigate successfully the treacherous and ever-changing currents of his or her profession. Neither artist nor artwork, apparently, have any essential meaning or value but rather are constructed by highly local and con-tingent social and ideological forces: the patron, the museum, the media, the critic.

In this scene, then, the play questions whether concepts like "inspiration," "creativity," "genius"—once perceived to be essential ingredients of the artistic process—really matter any longer. To be sure, George attempts to maintain his artistic integrity and appears faithful to the worthiness and significance of his own "vision," "always knowing where to draw the line" (166). He publicly disagrees with Blair, who accuses him of repeating himself, churning out "more and more about less and less" (175). But later, he privately agrees that he is just spinning his artistic wheels, as he admits to Dot: "No. I am not working on anything new" (194). And yet, Blair perceptively notes that the art world wouldn't know the difference, wouldn't even notice that the artist has stagnated, "doing Chromolume after Chromolume" (175). Finally, of course, George acknowledges that he is caught in his own "continuing series," trapped in a system that rewards production of the same type of work over and over, and he agrees with Dennis's wish "to do something different" (189–90). My point is that George is clearly not the same kind of self-inspired, self-sustaining artist as his great-grandfather. Rather, the "drink-by-drink, mink-by-mink" state of the arts (179), which is "taking all [his] concentration," has apparently exacted a toll from the quality and originality of his work (177). If Seurat, warts and all, embodies *Sunday in the Park*'s artistic hero, then George, though more likable and self-effacing, is the lost soul in need of artistic guidance. This George lacks the aesthetic wherewithal and self-sufficiency of his great grandfather. In contrast to the mythologized Seurat, George and his work represent a deflation of the artist and a dark commentary on the sad state of the art world's affairs. Thus, in the end, George must turn to his own roots, both his family roots and the artistic principles that guided Seurat, for inspiration. The struggling young artist looks to the past for guidance and renewal of purpose.

But how comfortable are we with this relationship between the older generation of true artistic ability and the younger generation befuddled by its own trendiness? On one hand, of course, all the characters' cocktail-party schmoozing and networking in the second act carries heavy irony; the play is obviously not exposing the negotiations, frustrations and anxieties of the art world for the audience to admire. But on the other hand, the very presence of this material in the play raises important and persistent questions. For example, is there any way in which the play's final salute to Seurat, the figure of the true artist, is unsatisfactory? Do we accept the play's implicit dismissal of the ambiguous Chromolume #7 and, by extension, of other types of modern art and aesthetic innovation? Indeed, what makes

Seurat's experimentation with color and light the work of a "genius" (138), and George's experimentation with color and light open to question? Is there any room in Sondheim's museum for the modern artist, or are we content to see George and his Chromolumes defer to the paradigms of the past?

Although Sondheim might well disagree, I contend that those truly interested in capturing what makes *Sunday in the Park with George* a "revolutionary" work would do well to begin with these questions. Customarily, serious works in the visual or theatrical arts promote or reproduce their own categorization as Art or Drama, as serious forays of creative imagination, and rarely question the social and political circumstances behind their own genesis. *Sunday in the Park*, then, speaks with uncommon candor about the less-than-ideal circumstances that can underlie any artistic creation. Thus, when "Putting It Together" unmasks the inner mechanisms and shifty negotiations of the art industry, the play potentially offers an aesthetic position contesting the traditional aesthetics associated with Seurat. "Putting It Together" aggressively challenges the traditional claim of art to represent transcendent Beauty and Truth, and instead reveals such ideas as highly subject to negotiation and construction by manifold cultural, financial and ideological forces. In the process, the ideas of art and the artist are opened up, demystified, brought down to a more accessible level of human understanding. Certainly George's open revelations and discussion of compromise and conventionality, carry none of the idealism surrounding Seurat. Moreover—and this question is crucial to a correct understanding of the relation between Seurat and George—are we to believe that the art produced in nineteenth-century Paris was less subject to cultural politics than that of twentieth-century America? Not likely: Act 1's constant discussion of party-going, meeting buyers, exhibiting the work reveals that no artist exists in a vacuum. Art is always contained to some extent by the local social forces in which it is formed.

From this viewpoint, then, the play offers a postmodern revision of traditional notions of art. Although poststructuralists, Marxists, and feminist theorists disagree on a precise definition of "postmodern," all agree that it entails resistance to universal notions that supposedly transcend place and time. For example, under a postmodern aesthetics, "claims to novelty stem not from wholly new imaginative constructs or from assertions of independent thought, but from the rearrangement of the relations within which particulars stand to one another in a constructed order" (McGowan 22); moreover, "artistic autonomy is neither possible nor desirable" (McGowan 25). This position seems appropriate for *Sunday in the Park*'s conventional and compromising second-act George, as well as for Sondheim's ironic commentary on musical theater.

And yet, despite this implied postmodern challenge to traditional aesthetics, I have no doubt that, overall, *Sunday in the Park* as a whole does little to recommend itself as a radical or subversive articulation of postmodern principles. Quite the contrary: in its final scenes the play returns to the traditional assumptions with which it began—the genius of the artist, the ineffable moment of imaginative inspiration, and the timeless value of a true artistic masterpiece. The ending, of course, confronts us with other problems as well: For example, whereas Seurat is applauded for his dedication to the optical laws governing his artistic method, George is advised to keep moving on, to avoid rigid forms; as Dot tells him, "If you can know where you're going, / You've gone.... Just keep moving on" (196). How do we reconcile the play's different attitudes about the artist's adherence to his own principles? Moreover, when Dot affirms that George's earlier critical judgments about her were correct, and that she needed to change herself as her lover advised, the play edges towards condoning Seurat's careless and callous behavior (194, 198).

Despite these tangential issues, however, two components from the conclusion make the play's insistence on traditional principles unmistakably clear: the modern George's final, noumenal encounter with Dot, and the return of characters from the Seurat painting at the end of the play, apparently for the purpose of honoring the true artist. When Dot reenters the action and encounters the modern George at Grande Jatte, there is no doubt this character is the first-act Dot, although plenty of uncertainty about what she represents. This Dot knows about the years she spent in America and her daughter Marie. But she also addresses George as her former lover, as if the second-act artist were his own great-grandfather: "Not that I ever forgot you, George. You gave me so much" (194). When George speaks of the way "his" relationship was with Dot, he uses the first person, speaking in the voice of his famous forebear, as in "I am certain that I did" care about Dot and her life (198).

But what has happened to the modern George? Is he still in this scene? When George and Dot finally sing, "We've always belonged together.... We will always belong together" (198), who is singing? The two Georges here somehow merge, Dot somehow reappears, and the lovers themselves take on a kind of transhistorical property that is emotionally felt rather than logically explained. Certainly *this* is the postmodern Sondheim. What is important is that the play's structure allows for the reintroduction of Dot—*and* the Old Lady, *and* the figures from Seurat's painting—as, perhaps, ghosts from the past, or characters symbolizing George's family history, or figures of George's imagination representing creativity and inspiration, or a combination of these possibilities. The issue is never clarified for us, and it need not be. What matters is that George has somehow been able to "connect" with the past (187) and regain the creativity he has lost. Likewise, when Seurat's recently deceased mother reappears, she addresses George as if he were her son, and she too exists as some source of renewed inspiration. She is at first "disappointed" that her formerly brilliant son sees nothing more in the Grande Jatte scene than assorted colors. But George's second comment, that "the air is rich and full of light," is rewarded with an emphatic "Good" (200), confirming that George has regained some kind of enlightened way of perceiving the world. Finally, all the characters from the Seurat painting reenter, singing to George and Dot, and the worlds of past and present, living and dead, reality and artifice, are unified for a moment in the performance of "Sunday." Structurally, this is Sondheim at his most innovative and challenging. It is difficult to imagine such nebulous characters and action promenading through the end of a play by, say, O'Neill, or Mamet, or Andrew Lloyd Webber. Even for recent playwrights influenced by Absurdism—Pinter, Albee, Stoppard, and so forth—the use of unexplained characters is usually more overtly symbolic, whereas in *Sunday in the Park*, and especially in the case of Dot, these characters figure a whole range of interpretive options.

This means of addressing George's artistic dilemma is creative and innovative, to be sure. But apart from its structural appropriateness, the retreat into the past could hardly be called revolutionary. Despite our glimpse into how art is *really* produced, this emotional finale returns to the first-act stereotypes of the artist—immersed in mystical communion with an artwork, inspired by an escape from reality into a world of artifice. Skeptics may even view such a moment as an escapist fantasy, where the contradictions of George's art world—private self-fulfillment versus public exhibition, self-reliance versus dependence on funding, personal creativity versus professional collaboration—are magically reconciled. The scene leaves certain questions unanswered as well: for instance, now that George has his inspiration back, will he retreat from public programs back to the isolated studio? Will he never again collaborate on another multimedia project or "sculpture"? Will he never again need a commission or financial support? None of these, of course, are likely.

Finally, the reappearance of the characters from Seurat's painting comprises the play's ultimate insistence on the traditional notion of art. As George rediscovers the principles of his famous great-grandfather—"Order, Design, Tension, Composition, Balance, Light, Harmony" (199–201)—the characters from the painting return to the stage and reprise "Sunday." And at the climax of the song, when the musical and dramatic tension of the whole play seem contained in the word "Forever," the stage direction commands, "All bow to George" (201). At this moment, perhaps the most memorable of the play, the artist is reverenced as a God-like figure, worthy of praise and honor for creating something beautiful and important and valuable and timeless. One could assume a less philosophical view of the moment and, taking a hint from the play's metadrama, argue that the characters in the painting are merely thanking George for preserving them in the painting. Yet it is clear from their remarks at the beginning of the second act—"It's hot up here," "This is not my good profile," "I hate this dress," "I am completely out of proportion," and even "I hate these people" (131–32)—that none of them are any too pleased to be preserved in this way. The impact of the moment, then, is that the brilliant work of Seurat, although misunderstood during his life, has finally justified the artist's idiosyncratic genius a century later. This artwork will remain a thing of beauty, "forever."

What kind of statement about art, then, does *Sunday in the Park with George* finally communicate? The musical contains, I think, a peculiar tension, a combination of both structural and thematic elements clearly not postmodern but not wholly traditional either. Structurally, the conclusion resists the impulse to explain how everything works and instead melds together the worlds of actuality and fiction, providing a postmodern blur to traditionally rigid boundaries. At the same time, the ending amounts to a magical transformation that is convincing because it replicates the effect powerful art has on all of us. The work convincingly affirms that there is something *unmediated*, something genuine and pure in the one-on-one encounter between any work of art and its percipient. However, *Sunday in the Park* also suggests that the "ideals" enveloping the art world, mediated as they are by finance, ideology, criticism and institutions, are far less ideal than we'd like to think. The ironic exposé of George's art scene need not be understood as complete satire so much as an opportunity to understand all the contributing forces that impact on how a culture conceives of art. Taken to its logical conclusion, the work may even undercut its own message about the beauty and power of art: in its revelation that success in art, both in nineteenth-century Paris and today, depends on going to parties and meeting the right people, does the play subvert its own suggestion that Seurat's painting will endure as a masterpiece "forever"?

I began by referring to the critical vocabulary that has grown up around Sondheim—"revolutionary," "radical," "avant garde"—but have tried in this essay to complicate those terms without denying their partial validity. I emphasized that claims for the "revolutionary" quality of Sondheim's work rest on its structural innovations and on comparisons with the traditional American book musical. Widening the field for comparison, however, shows that in terms of structure, too, Sondheim's work still fits well within the mainstream. Obviously *Sunday in the Park*, despite its innovative conclusion, does not approach the theatrical experimentation of, say, Spalding Gray, Robert Wilson, or Elizabeth LaCompte and the Wooster Group, and is far from the wide-open performance art of Karen Finlay, Laurie Anderson and others.[7] Much of the experimentation undertaken by such performers, of course, is politically as well as aesthetically iconoclastic, and Sondheim has studiously attempted to avoid engaging with contemporary politics in any way.[8] So if we are to look for a "departure from the traditional patterns of realist theater," I think looking to Sondheim equals looking in the wrong place; philosophically as well as formally, even Tom Stoppard's *Travesties* offers more twists and turns.

The questions this essay poses to *Sunday in the Park*—and to the current critical consensus—are important ones, albeit not those posed by the musical itself. But that Sondheim's work can engage with these questions at all marks it as an accomplishment above and beyond the run-of-the-mill book musical. The argument above is certainly not intended to diminish in any way the achievement of *Sunday in the Park with George*. In fact, quite the opposite: my goal here has been to suggest critical temperance and due seriousness; in our understandable haste to embrace and commend Sondheim's work—in this case, an exciting yet thoughtful drama about artists and their work—we do it a disservice if, in our enthusiasm, we merely gloss it over. Personally, this Pulitzer Prize–winning musical persists in my own memory as one of the most fascinating and entertaining works of the contemporary American theater. But embracing *Sunday in the Park*, and other Sondheim pieces as well, as legitimate dramatic texts deserving analysis from literary and cultural studies requires that they be placed on the same playing field as other important works. We must bring to the serious musical the same kind of careful critical techniques as we do to other drama, we must ask the same difficult questions, and we must be willing to criticize as well as praise. The thoughtfulness and depth of *Sunday in the Park with George* place it not only among the best musical dramas of recent decades, but among the best plays as well.

෬

NOTES

1. In the argument that follows, I am concerned with *Sunday in the Park with George* as a whole and not with isolating Sondheim's individual contribution. As Craig Zadan makes clear in *Sondheim & Co.*, this musical developed amidst extensive collaboration involving not only Sondheim and writer-director James Lapine, but also the actors, especially Mandy Patinkin and Bernadette Peters, who worked through numerous early versions and often contributed suggestions for additions or revisions (Zadan 295–312). Nor am I concerned here with the musical aspects of the work, which are examined closely in Stephen Banfield's *Sondheim's Broadway Musicals*. Instead, my chief concern is to determine how the text(s) of the drama—both lyrics and book— together construct an aesthetic statement, a total "philosophy" of art.

2. Throughout this essay, I use "Seurat" to indicate the artist of Act 1 and "George" to mean his second-act descendent.

3. Anyone who works with Sondheim for long quickly realizes that critics who dislike his work can hardly be accused of pulling their punches. David Van Leer, for example, attacks the conventionality of the play's romance, commenting that "George and Dot represent an artist and his mistress at about the same level of complexity as Curley and Laurie in *Oklahoma!* represent a cowboy and his girl" (126).

4. In fact, the play makes Seurat out to be more of an isolated genius than he actually was. For example, the play reports that "he never sold a painting in his lifetime" (148), but this may not be true; see Herbert, pages 325, 405. Moreover, Seurat was an acknowledged leader of the younger generation of Impressionists and a colleague of Pissarro, Toulouse-Lautrec and Van Gogh. Seurat personally escorted the President of France, Sadi Carnot, through the 1890 exhibition of the Société des Artistes Indépendants along the Champs-Élysées (Herbert 410).

5. On this point, I agree with David Savran, who suggests that the play portrays an archetypal "Artist, with a capital A," whose behavior toward Dot and rejection of emotionality is portrayed as the price of true genius, and thus is too easily condoned (237). See Savran's interview with Sondheim, especially pages 236–37. Sondheim maintains that the play is really more about George specifically than artists in general, despite the play's numerous descriptions of "artists" as a whole. Regarding Seurat, Sondheim concludes, "he's not a man I would want to have dinner with" (237).

6. As several critics have pointed out, the parallel between the two worlds is further revealed in the musical numbers, in that the melody of Act 1's "Finishing the Hat" is repeated in an up-tempo version in Act 2's "Putting it Together."

7. Several excellent works have recently explored possible definitions for a "postmodern theatre." The essays in Brater and Cohn's *Around the Absurd* consider theatrical experimentation along a broader historical trajectory, locating postmodern roots even in the early twentieth century. Johannes Birringer and Nick Kaye, on the other hand, attend almost exclusively to innovations since the 1970s.

8. In his interview with Savran, Sondheim repeatedly disavows that his works have anything to do with politics and resists the suggestion that he might sometimes betray a Brechtian political bent (Savran 234–35). The issue of Sondheim and politics certainly deserves far greater study, especially his works dealing with topics on colonialism (*Pacific Overtures*), class struggle (*Sweeney Todd*), and gender (*Company, Follies, A Little Night Music*).

WORKS CITED

Banfield, Stephen. *Sondheim's Broadway Musicals*. Ann Arbor: U of Michigan P, 1993.

Birringer, Johannes. *Theatre, Theory, Postmodernism*. Bloomington and Indianapolis: Indiana UP, 1991.

Brater, Enoch, and Ruby Cohn, eds. *Around the Absurd: Essays on Modern and Postmodern Drama*. Ann Arbor: U of Michigan P, 1990.

Gordon, Joanne. *Art Isn't Easy: The Achievement of Stephen Sondheim*. Carbondale: Southern Illinois UP, 1990. Rev. ed. *Art Isn't Easy: The Theater of Stephen Sondheim*. New York: Da Capo P, 1992.

Herbert, Robert L., et al. *Georges Seurat, 1859–1891*. New York: Metropolitan Museum of Art, 1991.

Hutcheon, Linda. *The Politics of Postmodernism*. London and New York: Routledge, 1989.

Kaye, Nick. *Postmodernism and Performance*. New York: St. Martin's, 1994.

McGowan, John. *Postmodernism and Its Critics*. Ithaca and London: Cornell UP, 1991.

Nightingale, Benedict. "Important Sondheim, but Less than Successful." *New York Times* 13 May 1984.

Rich, Frank. "A Musical Theater Breakthrough." *New York Times Magazine* 21 October 1984, 52–71.

Rosenberg, Bernard, and Ernest Harburg. *The Broadway Musical: Collaboration in Commerce and Art*. New York: New York UP, 1993.

Savran, David. *In Their Own Words: Contemporary American Playwrights*. New York: Theatre Communications Group, 1988.

Schiff, Stephen. "Deconstructing Sondheim." *New Yorker* 69 (8 March 1993): 76–87.

Sondheim, Stephen, and James Lapine. *Sunday in the Park with George: A Musical*. New York: Dodd, Mead, 1986.

Stoppard, Tom. *Travesties*. New York: Grove, 1975.

van Leer, David. "Putting it Together: Sondheim and the Broadway Musical." *Raritan* 7.2 (1987): 113–28.

Zadan, Craig. *Sondheim & Co.* 2nd ed. New York: Harper & Row, 1986.

Assassins and the Concept Musical
Scott Miller

How Did We Get to Be Here?

In 1970 Stephen Sondheim and George Furth's new musical *Company* burst upon Broadway, a musical unlike most people had ever seen, a concept musical with no linear plot, with a completely passive protagonist, and an equivocal ending. In 1990, *Assassins* was the first New York musical in twenty years to tread fearlessly the same path, a concept musical with even less plot and no protagonist at all. America itself was presented as the antagonist and the ending proposed murder as a viable solution to problems. Why did it take twenty years for *Company*'s fascinating experiment to be repeated and carried forward? What happened in the interim? And will the experiment be continued in the future?

"Concept musical" is a term that has been bandied around for two or three decades with a great deal of casualness. It is a term with as many definitions as there are people using it. Shows as diverse as *Company, Hair,* and *Pacific Overtures* have all been called concept musicals. Most shows labelled as concept musicals essentially fall into four categories: musicals built upon a central concept (usually an important social issue) instead of a linear story; musicals whose central concept is most important but that still employ a linear plot; musical character studies with no linear plot but no unifying concept either; and musicals that do not fit into any other categories.

There have not been very many shows like *Company* and *Assassins* that have completely discarded traditional linear plot in favor of a central, unifying concept, probably because these musicals do not usually do very well financially. They are hard to write because there is no easy, logical framework on which to hang the songs and characters; with shows like *Company*, the songs and scenes could be in practically any order and still make as much sense. These shows are harder for audiences to understand because without a story, the audience must discern for themselves what the show is about, and there is often no traditional emotional payoff at the end since there is no story conflict to resolve.

The first Broadway musical in this category—which I call "pure" concept musicals because they are completely focused on a single concept—was *Love Life* in 1948, with music by Kurt Weill, book and lyrics by Alan Jay Lerner. This was a ground-breaking, surrealistic show that explored one married couple through 150 years of American history, using the marriage and its growing cynicism as a metaphor for the birth and growth of the country. The show was billed as a "vaudeville" (as *Chicago* was in 1975) and used vaudeville-style songs placed outside of the action, breaking the fourth wall, to comment on the action. Weill had developed this device in his work with Bertolt Brecht on *The Threepenny Opera* and other shows. *Love Life* had no linear plot, only interconnected vignettes tracing the non-aging couple and their two children from 1791 to the present. As life in America becomes more complex, so too does the family begin to experience a strain on their relationships. Robert Coleman in the *Daily Mirror* called it, "an exciting study of the rise, demise, and rebirth of standards." Though Coleman loved it, other critics found it depressing, cold, hard to understand, and hostile to its audience (accusations also thrown at *Company* in 1970). It ran only 252 performances.

Both *Company* and *Assassins* also fall into the category of "pure" concept musicals, in which linear storytelling is completely discarded in favor of exploring one central idea—long-term emotional commitment in *Company*, political assassination as the underbelly of the American Dream in *Assassins*. Unfortunately, almost no other New York musicals have been created in this mold, and these three fall so far apart historically (1948, 1970, and 1990) that it may be quite some time before the experiment is repeated. Of the three, only *Company* was a financial success.

The second category of concept musicals includes shows whose central concept is the most important element despite having a traditional linear plot. These shows can be seen as either concept musicals that hedge their bets, or conventional musicals with a gimmick. The first Broadway musical in this category was *Cabaret* in 1966, and it is no accident that its director Harold Prince also directed and helped conceive *Company* four years later. Perhaps *Cabaret* was Prince's practice run at creating a concept musical. It was the first such musical since *Love Life*, but this time the show was a hybrid of traditional book musical and concept musical. The scenes in the Kit Kat Klub seemed to be part of a non-linear, thematically developed "pure" concept musical. In these scenes, performers broke the fourth wall (or more accurately, pulled the audience *inside* the fourth wall), there was very little dialogue, and the songs were commentary songs *about* the action rather than a part of it. But the scenes *outside* the club belonged in a traditional book show. These scenes had naturalistic dialogue, an intact fourth wall, and traditional integrated book songs. Perhaps the commercial failure of *Love Life* prompted the *Cabaret* team to hedge their bets by giving their audience the best of both worlds, although *Love Life's* brief run makes us wonder whether *Cabaret's* creators had even seen it. Only later in Bob Fosse's film version were the integrated book songs cut and the show converted into a "pure" concept musical.

A year later, in 1967, *Hallelujah, Baby!* followed in the footsteps of *Love Life* by telling the story of a young black woman who does not age from the turn of the century to the present. Her life acted as a metaphor for race relations in America, but instead of mere vignettes exploring these themes, her story actually did follow a linear plot and employed integrated book songs. In 1972, Bob Fosse's *Pippin* had a strongly conceptual style—a travelling troupe of commedia dell'arte actors played out a young man's life for him. This conceit of scenes being improvised by the actors under the direction of Leading Player figured prominently in every moment of the show, especially the finale. But despite all this high concept, the show still told a linear if episodic story, and the score included both book songs and commentary songs. In 1975, *Chicago* went a little further by eliminating integrated book songs—every song was performed as a vaudeville number. But *Chicago* did not go as far as *Company*—*Chicago* still had a traditional linear plot. Several of Tommy Tune's shows followed *Pippin's* model, including *Nine, Grand Hotel,* and *The Will Rogers Follies*. These shows all dipped their toes in the waters of experimentation, some further than others, but none really jumped in.

The third category, musical character studies with no linear plot or single unifying concept, first appeared in 1968 when *Hair* debuted. And calling *Hair* a character study might be stretching it. Billed as

"The American Tribal Love-Rock Musical," *Hair* was so lacking in story, structure, and character development, that it was more a thematic revue than a musical. It succeeded largely because it was the first appearance of real rock and roll on Broadway, and because of its infamous nude scene and consistently vulgar language. *A Chorus Line* followed *Hair*'s lead in 1975, with neither a story nor a single central concept, but at least *A Chorus Line* had a dramatic situation and more serious character development. *Working*, in 1978, fell halfway between *Hair* and *A Chorus Line*. It did not have a unifying dramatic situation like *A Chorus Line*, but it had more of a thematic focus than *Hair*.

The last category of concept musicals includes those musicals that do not fit into any other category; we call them concept musicals for lack of a better label. Not surprisingly, most of these genre-busting musicals are Sondheim shows. *Merrily We Roll Along* was a traditional book musical, except the book ran backwards. *Follies* was mostly a character study yet it had a central concept as well as a mini-mal plot. *Pacific Overtures* had a traditional plot but was told through the conventions of Kabuki theatre, dispensing with many Western storytelling devices.

The road from *Love Life* to *Assassins* has been a complicated one, and the concept musical's evolution has taken a very circuitous route. Weill and Lerner (on the shoulders of Brecht) took a giant step in 1948 by discarding every device of linear storytelling, and provided the model for the commentary songs in *Cabaret, Company, Pippin,* and *Assassins*. Eighteen years later, *Cabaret,* which only partially fol-lowed the lead *Love Life* had set, provided the model for the narrator/devil figure in *Pippin*, and the use of limbo in *Follies* and *Assassins*. Two years later, *Hair* set the precedent for the plotless revue-musicals like *A Chorus Line* and *Working*. Two years after that, *Company* fol-lowed closely the model created by *Love Life* but greatly refined it, solved many of its problems, and became a commercial and critical success. The next year, *Follies* followed *Company*'s lead but focused on deeper character development and provided a genuine resolution at the end of the show. The next year, Bob Fosse began his experiments with high concept design and staging with *Pippin*, using a narrator very much like the Emcee in *Cabaret* (and a light curtain, which Hal Prince had invented for *Cabaret*). Three years later, in 1975, *A Chorus Line* improved upon the model set by *Hair* by adding a unifying dra-matic situation that informed all the action onstage, while *Chicago* continued Fosse's experiment with conceptual staging and design. In 1978, *Working* returned to the anti-structure of *Hair* and only lasted twenty-five performances.

It was 1990 before musical theatre returned to the "pure" concept musical with Stephen Sondheim and John Weidman's *Assassins*. Like *Love Life* and *Company*, *Assassins* discarded entirely a linear plot, using commentary songs instead of integrated book songs. Like *Cabaret* and *Pippin*, the show used a narrator/commentator, who not only led us through the action, but also interacted with the other characters and influenced events. Like *A Chorus Line* and *Working*, the show examined a series of characters, most of whom had only one big moment in the spotlight. As in *Follies*, some of the characters in *Assassins* come to revelations about their actions and motivations, some even making major decisions. Like *Chicago*, the show used musical/theatrical styles appropriate to the period of the characters and events. Like *Hair*, *Assassins* was an overtly political show that intentionally crossed customary lines of taste and dealt with subjects that were considered taboo, particularly in a musical. *Assassins* asked whether our society turns people into assassins, whether the American Dream is a lie, whether in fact the assassins are as different from us as we would like to believe. But whereas *Hair* expressed opinions and ideas that were already being discussed in America, *Assassins* asked questions no one had ever asked before. *Assassins* questioned ideas that form basic threads in the fabric of America's image of itself.

It's About Time

Though *Assassins* does not have a chronological plot, Sondheim and Weidman do use time and chronology in interesting ways. The first assassin they explore is John Wilkes Booth, the granddaddy of all assassins, the man who started it all. Though other men had attempted presidential assassination before Booth, it is safe to say that Booth's success and notoriety began the tradition of assassination in America. He is presented first in the show and is treated with great reverence throughout the evening by both the other assassins and by the authors. Booth is given the great orations, and while several of the assassins are presented as lunatics, Booth is treated very sympathetically. The last assassin the show presents is Lee Harvey Oswald, not the last assassin in U.S. history but certainly the one who brought presidential assassination squarely into our modern world. The progression from Booth, through the others, and finally to Oswald does not follow chronology, but it does move basically forward through time; and though the book depository scene takes place in 1963, it is still essentially "the present" for most audiences.

The assassins all interact across the barriers of time as a physical manifestation of their influence on each other. When Booth tells Oswald to kill Kennedy, it is Weidman's way of telling us that Oswald was aware of Booth, his philosophy, his motivations, and the results of his action. Oswald knows that Booth's act gained him a great deal of celebrity, landing his name in history books. Oswald has learned a lot from reading and hearing about Booth, and in *Assassins* Oswald actually learns these things from Booth himself instead of just from stories. Similarly, when Hinckley asks Oswald for his autograph, it is a stylish (and unsettlingly funny) way to dramatize the sense of accomplishment and fame that Oswald represents to Hinckley. In a sense, these assassins all built upon the acts of those who killed (or tried to kill) before them. They established an American tradition. They worked together even though they never actually met each other. In the surrealistic world of *Assassins*, they interact directly. *Assassins* does not pretend to historical accuracy; it presents psychological accuracy instead.

When the assassins all materialize in the book depository scene to persuade Oswald to join them, it is a frightening tableau for us, seeing these killers all together, smiling and happy. The plastic nature of time throughout the show pays off in this scene, as past, present, and future collide in Oswald's brain. He realizes that he can be part of a centuries-old tradition, that he can belong in a way he never could before, that he can be remembered by future generations. He realizes that not only will he be carrying on the work of Booth, Zangara, Czolgosz and the others; he will also be paving the way for future assassins to continue this work. Oswald's desperate need to belong, to be part of a family is exploited by the assassins, and as their voices begin to overlap and blend together in his head (in the vocal music leading up to the gunshot), it becomes too overwhelming to resist. This psychological and historical phenomenon is represented as an actual corporeal experience, making it so much clearer and more immediate to the audience.

Mr. America

Part of this morphing of time is accomplished with characters who represent concepts. The Proprietor, who brings together in his shooting gallery assassins from throughout history, is not just a one-scene character. He is the assassins' motivation and opportunity. He is America, a land where people are told to follow an American Dream that does not really exist, that abandons those who fail, a country where easy access to guns makes killing a simple way to take out an angry man's frustrations. No other industrialized country has a history of assassination like America's because no other country sells its citizens hopes and dreams which cannot be realized, or makes it so easy for an average citizen to get a gun. The Proprietor knows each assassin's failed dream or unrealized goal, and in each case, he offers a handgun as remedy. Just as the Emcee in *Cabaret* represented the decadence and willing ignorance of the German people, so too the Proprietor in *Assassins* represents America throughout its history.

Who's in Charge Here?

The Balladeer represents the American people, eager to oversimplify, happy to see things in black and white. Good is very good and bad is very bad. Americans want to believe that Booth could not have had legitimate complaints against Abraham Lincoln—he was one of our greatest presidents. His face is on the penny and the five dollar bill. Booth's actions, the Balladeer sings, must have been the result of a fading career or jealousy of his brother. In Booth's scene early in Act I, he details his charges against Lincoln, all of which are absolutely true. But our first reaction is to see Booth as the bad guy and Lincoln as the martyred saint, just as the Balladeer presents them. We laugh as the Balladeer ridicules Booth, but as the show progresses and we see more and more of Booth, we start to wonder if he is in fact the pitiful psychopath that the Balladeer described.

The Balladeer's inane theme-park optimism in every scene—as Czolgosz steps up and shoots McKinley, as Guiteau marches up the steps of the gallows—becomes more transparent as the evening wears on and we get to know the assassins. By the time we get to "Another National Anthem," the playing field has been levelled. We start to think more critically about the Balladeer's picture of the American Dream, where the usherette's a rock star. The lyrics the assassins sing begin to resonate for many of us. We know the frustration of not getting everything we want, of hitting a brick wall when we reach for the American Dream. We know that feeling of being on the outside looking in. Perhaps the assassins are right. Maybe there *is* another national anthem, another American Dream, one that is more real, more attainable. For the first time, the assassins find strength not only in their number but also in their truth. The America they are singing about is the *real* America, as opposed to the fairy tale America that the Balladeer sings about. But we have to remember that the Balladeer is the American public, and it is the *people* of America that perpetuate this lie that anyone can have their dream if they just work hard enough. It is not true, but we keep saying it is, in newspapers, on television, in the movies, from parents to children, from teachers to students. It is the carrot we dangle in front of all Americans from birth to death. In America, we say, *anything* is possible.

The Balladeer is a very strange character, functionally speaking. Is he the protagonist? He seems to be a narrator, except that he disappears before the story is over. In some productions, the actor playing the Balladeer also plays Oswald (the show's creators considered this early on, but ultimately decided against it). Casting the show this way, he goes from being the vessel for the stories (as the American public) to being the receptacle for those stories as Oswald. Like the narrators in *Cabaret* and *Pippin*, the Balladeer sings commentary songs from outside the action, but at some point we begin to doubt the reliability of his commentary, and once the assassins rise up against him, he is silenced. In a sense, the assassins take control of the show away from the Balladeer during "Another National Anthem."

But this interpretation becomes problematic when the show contains "Something Just Broke," the song interpolated into the London production just after the book depository scene. If the assassins have taken over the show and have effectively "fired" the Balladeer, then why do they abdicate the stage to these "average Americans"? If the Balladeer, as the representative of the American people, has been driven offstage, why are the American people suddenly being represented again two scenes later? Without this song, the assassins take over the show and discover their power as a group, act on this knowledge by going together to the book depository, and then declare their triumph with the reprise of "Everybody's Got the Right" as the show's finale. With "Something Just Broke" between the last two scenes, the assassins hand control back over to the public briefly before going on to the show's finale. Either way, the assassins are aware of *Assassins* the musical as their vehicle, as their medium to communicate their message to America. In "Another National Anthem," "The Gun Song," and the finale, they are singing to us. These songs are not internal monologues like "Being Alive" in *Company* or "Moments in the Woods" in *Into the Woods*; they are ideological declarations.

A Musical Within a Musical

Sondheim and Weidman further break the rules of traditional musicals in the development of the character of Leon Czolgosz. More so than with any other character in the show, Czolgosz is given exposition, rising action, climax, and resolution. His scenes form a kind of mini-musical within the larger frame. It is strange because it sits somewhat off-center in the middle of the show and is interrupted by other scenes, and because Czolgosz is not the musical's protagonist. He is neither the hero himself nor can he be a representative of the other assassins because they all have such very different motives (and neuroses) for their acts. Yet, his is the most complete picture we see of how our society makes someone into an assassin.

As with Booth, there is a convincing argument to be made that Leon Czolgosz was completely sane. Like Booth, Czolgosz was acting on his passionately held political beliefs when he shot the president. He was not looking for attention or a cure for indigestion; he wanted to change the world and saw assassination as his only recourse. The progress of Czolgosz from exploited worker to assassin is the fullest characterization in the show. In the barroom scene, Czolgosz delivers a chilling monologue to the other assassins about the insufferable working conditions in the factory where he works. He knows the working conditions and slave's wages are outrageous, but he believes there is nothing he can do about it. Two scenes later, he meets socialist activist Emma Goldman. He is inspired by her words and convinced that he must take action. Goldman leaves him with a political tract on worker's rights, encouraging the working class to rise up against their oppressors.

After another intervening scene, Czolgosz begins "The Gun Song," presenting a handgun as the symbol of industrialized oppression. He argues that a gun kills men through the working conditions of its manufacture as surely as with bullets. Though the gun he holds represents everything he hates, he also knows that it can be the instrument of change. As Booth tells him, all he has to do is pull the trigger and he can change the world. After Guiteau and Moore have joined them to sing a frightening barbershop quartet paean to guns, Czolgosz finishes the song with a list of all the men who have died to make his gun—men in the mines, the steel mills, the factories. In their name, he decides, his gun will kill one more man—the president. Czolgosz has transformed before our eyes from exploited worker to political student to political activist. All that is left is to see him carry through on his decision.

Without a break in the music, the scene changes to the 1901 Pan American Exposition and "The Ballad of Czolgosz," in which Czolgosz carries through with his plan to kill President McKinley. The lyric even echoes Emma Goldman's words, "The idea wasn't mine alone, / But mine—" (53, in the published script) to remind us of her part in creating this activist assassin. This four-scene mini-musical about Czolgosz's transformation ends, and we do not see him again until the assassins all come together in "Another National Anthem" late in the show.

Why is Czolgosz chosen as the one assassin to explore so intimately? Perhaps it is because of all the assassins, only he and Booth are in control of their faculties, acting on political convictions instead of delusions. Though Byck's motivation is also political and his allegations against Nixon et al. are legitimate, Byck is clearly unbalanced. Sondheim and Weidman probably felt Booth's character brought too many audience preconceptions with it for people to examine his motives objectively. We understand Czolgosz's motives and some of us may even agree with his politics. His argument in "The Gun Song," that poverty is as insidious a killer as violence, is still true today. Part of the show's central concept is that these assassins are more like us than we choose to believe. In this portrait of Czolgosz we discover that his grievances are real and that indeed there was no other action he could take that would make a difference (although whether or not his action *did* make a difference is another question). We may not go so far as to say he was right in killing McKinley, but we *understand*, and that is sufficiently disturbing to anyone who wants to see issues like these only in black and white.

Comedy Tonight

Another device that Weidman and Sondheim use most effectively is slapstick comedy. We do not expect to laugh out loud at a musical about assassins, especially assassins who are as deeply troubled as some of these people are. Yet, Weidman opens the show with a number of very funny moments in the shooting gallery—the Proprietor yelling "Watch it now! No violence!" (8) to Hinckley and Czolgosz; the Proprietor holding a gun up over Zangara's head, making him jump for it; Sara Jane Moore pointing her gun at various people absent-mindedly. Byck walks into a barroom full of presidential assassins and asks if anyone has seen Dick Nixon. The bartender replies, "We don't get many presidents in here, pal" (24). Moments later, Guiteau orders drinks for everyone then pays with Hinckley's money.

Then, after Zangara's passionate speech about his stomach problems, Booth off-handedly remarks that he should kill the president. Zangara says, "You think that help?" And Booth replies casually, "It couldn't hurt" (26).

Both scenes with Sara Jane Moore and Squeaky Fromme are outrageous in both their humor and their violence. In their second scene, when Moore points her pistol at her nine-year-old son because he is whining too much, we start to laugh at the extremity of her reaction, then stop ourselves as we realize she is threatening to shoot her child. Sondheim once said of *Company* that he wanted people to laugh their heads off during the show, then go home and be unable to sleep. The same is true of *Assassins*: Hinckley and Fromme's childish bickering; Guiteau's clumsy advances toward Moore; the attention-grabbing bystanders in "How I Saved Roosevelt"; Moore and Fromme's target practice at the Kentucky Fried Chicken bucket; Ford helping to pick up the bullets that were meant for him, are all so absurd we cannot help but laugh. It is only after the fact that we realize just what we were laughing at.

Weidman and Sondheim use the comedy to catch us off guard and to make us draw our own conclusions rather than bludgeoning us with the show's themes. They allow us to laugh at these assassins, using a disarmingly comedic method to make disturbing points about our society, while also giving the characters a kind of non-threatening sitcom status that may make it easier for us to relate to them. It helps remind us that these people are like us—sometimes silly, petty, and overly concerned with the trivia of everyday life.

The Chewy Center

Like *Company* and *Love Life*, *Assassins* is a musical that attacks one fairly narrowly defined issue. Everything in the show, every scene, every song points toward that central concept, just as every scene and song in an integrated book musical supports the story line. The premise of the show is that these assassins are all uniquely American and they all have the profound feeling that they have not gotten what they are owed. The show posits that we, as part of the American society, are responsible for making these people—who are just like us in many ways—into assassins with our too-hyped American Dream and our culture of violence. Perhaps the most shocking thing about *Assassins* is the genuinely sympathetic view it takes of these nine central characters. Interestingly, the script and score do not develop the characters of the presidents at all—only two presidents even make an appearance onstage and one has only two lines—so no sympathy is established for them. They are faceless victims, although again the interpolation of "Something Just Broke" changes that dynamic, making Kennedy's death more personal. The show examines closely the lives and personalities of the assassins, and even those who are crazy are still charming in some way. These perennial villains are the heroes of the piece, and the audience (as part of the larger society) is essentially the villain. This is the rare musical that, like *Cabaret*, does not share a basic moral point of view with its audience, and actually attempts to convince the audience to change its moral stance.

In the last song of *Sweeney Todd*, the lyric implies that we are all Sweeney, that we all have revenge in our hearts and can be driven to extreme acts, and further, that we may be responsible as well for a culture in which corruption is allowed to thrive unfettered. Similarly, in *Assassins* the finger of blame is pointed at us. As discussed earlier, the Proprietor, as a carnival barker, a uniquely American icon, convinces these nine men and women they have a right to kill and then sells each of them a gun. It seems almost ridiculous that the transactions are as quick and simple as they are, but buying a gun in America is nearly that easy. Some people might balk at the implication that we encourage murder, but even a cursory look at American pop culture shows that it is true. Films like *Reservoir Dogs*, *Pulp Fiction*, *Natural Born Killers*, and the films of Schwarzenegger, Van Damme, and Stallone, television shows like *America's Most Wanted*, *Cops*, and a host of detective and police dramas all rack up huge body counts every week. Literature from the National Rifle Association and magazines like *Soldier of Fortune* market guns as problem solvers more earnestly than Hollywood. Our urban streets are filled with semi-automatic weapons and gang warfare. Whether pop culture is the cause or reflection of real life violence is another issue, but either way, America loves guns.

At the same time, the poor, the oppressed, the disenfranchised are being ignored more and more. Politicians employ exclusionary tactics aimed at dividing our country even more profoundly into the haves and have nots. There are people today, like Leon Czolgosz, who feel they have virtually no recourse except violence. They feel powerless, hopeless. These are the people who gun down innocent strangers in post offices and fast food restaurants. Only with guns or explosives can they feel any control over their lives. The kids in the streets with guns are not insane; they are desperate, like Sam Byck, Leon Czolgosz, and others. And *Assassins* argues that we are all to blame. Sam Byck's second monologue supports this concept and ties in closely with the theme in *Sweeney Todd* that we allow the world to be as corrupt as it is.

E Pluribus Unum

Byck's second monologue is about lies. The retail industry lies to us about the products they sell. The politicians lie about what they will do if we vote for them. Parents lie to children. And in our apathy, we allow it all to continue. This monologue is an indictment of the American Dream. "It wasn't supposed to be like this. It wasn't but it *is*. And schmucks like you keep telling us it *isn't!*" Byck says (77). He goes on to describe the terror of finding out that everything is a lie, that nothing works the way it is supposed to, that the American Dream itself is a lie. Because voting does not matter (Byck voted for Nixon), because the Common Man cannot really change things through normal channels, Byck comes to the same conclusion as Czolgosz. "We do what we have to do," he says. "We kill the President" (77).

Byck's scene turns to Limbo as the music for "Another National Anthem" begins, and the assassins describe the reasons for their acts. But subtextually they are also telling us how America, and more specifically the American Dream, failed them. Like Willy Loman, the assassins believed the story they were told that in America they can have anything they want if they work hard enough. In "Another National Anthem," the Balladeer tells the assassins that their acts of violence are not the answer, that they have lost because they gave up on the American Dream. He tells them of the mailman who won the lottery, the delivery boy who made it to Wall Street, the usherette who became a rock star. Of course, he does not tell them about the millions of other mailmen and delivery boys and usherettes who never got anything. He tells them that our country's built on dreams, but he does not mention that it is also built on bloodshed, corruption, ruthlessness, greed, and prejudice. Our industrialized nation was built on the backs of exploited working class men like Czolgosz, our government grown fat by flim-flamming the trusting voters like Byck, and our cities' slums historically populated by poor immigrants like Zangara.

These assassins have learned the hard way that the promises of an American Dream are empty. Like many of us, they believe the Constitution guarantees each of us the right to happiness. But it does not. They are under a grave misconception; the Constitution only guarantees us the right to the *pursuit* of happiness. The assassins have learned that the way to real power, real celebrity, real influence is through disrupting America's pristine image of itself. They have discovered the *other* national anthem, the one we keep hidden, the one that tells the truth about America. This national anthem finds its voice as the assassins finally realize that as a group they possess the power to change things, to disrupt business as usual, to stop the game.

The assassins literally chase the Balladeer—the voice of America— off the stage. They are in control of the musical for the first time, precisely because they are working together for the first time. And it is our fault because we (i.e., the Proprietor) introduced them to each other in the beginning. We told them about each other. As a group they have power. They turn to the audience and literally solicit us to join them, to become one of them, to disrupt the American Dream by any means necessary. Their message is unmistakable and it is hard to argue with it. They are right after all—the American Dream is not real for most of us. We will not win the lottery and we will not become president. We work hard every day just to survive. They end the song by asking us to spread the word, to tell others about this other national anthem, to stop believing the lies. Their message becomes curiously like the Balladeer's—not to get discouraged, not to lose hope—but they are selling faith in something totally different. The assassins have taken over the telling of their story. The Balladeer can no longer laugh at them and make fun of their grief. Now, *they* are the ones in charge.

The book depository scene completes this transformation of the assassins from a bunch of misfits into a strong, unified force of history. They have made their argument to us, and structurally, it is important that we have experienced their persuasiveness, so that we can now understand how Oswald can be swayed by it. As a country, as a society, we have created these killers and we have taught them about each other. As we have done with criminals and lunatics throughout our history, we have made celebrities out of them. Every school child knows the name of John Wilkes Booth—even dropouts like Lee Harvey Oswald. As in the barroom, the shooting gallery, and other scenes, John Weidman brings the assassins together physically to represent the effect on Oswald of his knowledge of them. Weidman argues that Oswald's knowledge that other assassins had gone before him, some successfully, some becoming famous, gave him the idea to shoot Kennedy and the courage to do it. In the surreal world of *Assassins*, instead of stories or books influencing Oswald, the assassins themselves materialize to suggest the assassination and provide the moral support to carry it out. Two arguments are most cogent to Oswald—that he will be remembered and that he will finally belong to a group, to a family. Despite the Balladeer's earlier claim that none of the assassins really changed anything, Oswald will put to an end an era of innocence and optimism. We can only guess about how Kennedy would have dealt with Vietnam, counter-culture protests, and all the turmoil of subsequent generations, but it is safe to say Lyndon Johnson was a very different president from Kennedy. Oswald did cause a significant and possibly infinite ripple effect in American politics and American life. In "The Ballad of Booth," the Balladeer sings:

> Hurts a while,
> But soon the country's
> Back where it belongs,
> And that's the truth. (22–23)

But that is not always true. As one might have predicted, many people did not want to see a musical with this message about America and Americans, especially in 1990 during the Persian Gulf War. But maybe the show's timing was not entirely its undoing as many people have suggested. Maybe Americans want to believe in the American Dream, fabrication or not, and *Assassins* will not allow that.

Where Is the American Musical Headed?

Though *Assassins* was not transferred to Broadway, the show ran in London and is now being produced around the world. Like some of Sondheim's other adventurous shows, this one was not a financial success in New York, but it will have a long and healthy life outside of New York. This is partly due to the fact that genuine innovation and experimentation in musical theatre can no longer take place on Broadway where many argue theatre has become more theme park than art form. With ticket prices at seventy-five dollars each and audiences filled with far more tourists (some of whom do not speak English) than theatre enthusiasts, what choice do producers have? Broadway is, after all, a business.

Today's Broadway can generally only support two kinds of musicals—techno-spectacles and "revisals." The techno-spectacles are the musicals that favor glitz over substance, shows that people come to see for the chandelier or the helicopter as much as to hear the music and witness the drama. Some people would suggest that *Phantom of the Opera* and *Sunset Boulevard* are less the works of Andrew Lloyd Webber than they are the works of John Napier, the set designer. In some cases, the special effects and razzle-dazzle are there to cover weaknesses in the material, and in others, merely because producers know that is what audiences now demand for their seventy-five dollars.

The newest kid on the block is the musical "revisal," heavily revised revivals of past successes. Musicals like *The Who's Tommy* and *How To Succeed in Business Without Really Trying* are revived but often rewritten to make them more palatable (in other words, bland) to the new breed of Broadway theatre-goer. In *Tommy*, the bleaker concept album is modified in the stage adaptation and now ends with a happy "Family Values Moment," as Tommy warmly embraces and forgives Uncle Ernie who molested him as a child. In *How To Succeed*, the producers cut "Cinderella Da:ling" because it is no longer politically correct for women to want to quit work and get married. When great musicals of the past are being changed with an eye towards ticket sales instead of plot and character, some theatre writers find themselves feeling hopeless. When a clumsy "revisal" of *Grease* with Brooke

Shields can run longer than Sondheim's darkly fascinating *Passion* or Nicholas Hytner's intelligent and passionate remounting of *Carousel*, how can anyone feel hopeful about the Broadway musical's future?

But there is still hope to be found. Though Broadway is not supporting new experiments in musical theatre, regional theatres around the country are. New musicals are being produced more than ever, but few of them ever make it to Broadway. To consider where musical theatre is headed, it is also important to look at where non-musical theatre is going. Improvisation and scripted works based on improvisation are becoming more and more prevalent. "New vaudeville" performance art and monologuists are finding receptive audiences. Interactive theatre, like the Neo-Futurists' work in Chicago, is pioneering an exciting new kind of theatre experience in which the audience helps create the piece at each performance. All these forms and others can be explored within musical theatre as well. And as we explore these new forms, the end product will most likely be concept musicals, shows that break new boundaries and old rules.

We have to keep asking the questions that *Love Life, Company,* and *Assassins* have asked. Does a musical have to have a linear plot? Are there other ways to tell a story? Why must scenes follow in a logical sequence? Can we not tell a story out of chronological order (as *Pulp Fiction* did)? Do scenes have to end with songs as the Rodgers and Hammerstein school taught us? Must a show provide a clear resolution or answer at the end of the evening, or can it ask more questions? What can we learn about communicating stories, issues, and concepts from TV and movies, music videos, talk radio, modern dance, performance art, and of course, cyberspace? How can we follow the lead of developing technology by making musical theatre truly interactive? Or conversely, can we shed all the trappings of technology and go back to the basics of the empty stage? After all, *The Fantasticks* is still going strong.

In 1927, Jerome Kern and Oscar Hammerstein turned musical theatre upside down by shattering accepted rules in *Show Boat*. In 1943, Rodgers and Hammerstein began a major new trend in serious book musicals with *Oklahoma!* Hal Prince, Michael Bennett, and Bob Fosse all explored exciting new territory and developed new forms within the musical theatre. Stephen Sondheim is still finding new ways to tell stories with music, in collaboration with both James Lapine and John Weidman. And a new generation of musical theatre writers from coast to coast is ready to break more rules and find new ways to take this uniquely American art form and its audiences into the future.

છ

WORK CITED

Sondheim, Stephen, and John Weidman. *Assassins*. New York: Theatre Communications Group, 1991.

PASSION

Not Just Another Simple Love Story
Gary Konas

In June 1994 I happened to see three thematically related Broadway musicals: *Beauty and the Beast*, *The Phantom of the Opera*, and *Passion*. They offer a range of approaches to the Beauty and the Beast fable. As staged by former Disneyland "skip and wave" show director Robert Jess Roth, the stage adaptation of *Beauty* is a leap backward in creativity from the Oscar-nominated film. *Phantom*, by contrast, boasts big-name talents in director Hal Prince and composer Andrew Lloyd Webber, and its continuing SRO popularity is understandable. Stephen Sondheim and James Lapine have the last word, though, by inverting the B&B fairy tale to make it irresistibly real. In *Passion*, the *woman* Fosca is the beast whose love for—and from—the handsome Giorgio are her only hope for release from the curse of ugliness. If not his best musical, *Passion* certainly continues Sondheim's quest for new approaches to the traditional musical form.

Perhaps most innovatively, *Passion* is performed not only without intermission (as was *Follies*), but also without applause points. Song and dialogue flow back and forth,[1] and the musical numbers are never "buttoned" with decisive endings. In the *Playbill* for the Broadway production, no song titles were provided. Titles are given in the cast album notes, but many are merely labels: "First Letter," "Transition," "Soldiers' Gossip," etc.

Equally striking is Sondheim's avoidance of irony, heretofore always one of his sharpest tools. If *Follies* examined a bitter, ironic love quadrangle, *Passion* straightforwardly explores a love triangle in a way that subordinates the characters to the enduring emotion they experience. Just as Sondheim limited himself in *A Little Night Music* to triple meters (3/4, 9/8, 6/8, etc.), in *Passion* he confines himself to straight talk in his lyrics. The lyrical lines are held together by irregular rhyme, repeated words, and, most importantly, recurring musical motifs, instead of the ABAB rhyme traditionally associated with show tunes. As usual, though, this Sondheim score is a puzzle consisting of small, interlocking melodic pieces painted with a palette of harmonic colors.

The original source for *Passion* is the 1869 novel *Fosca* by Iginio Tarchetti. Emulating Tarchetti's work, Sondheim and librettist-director Lapine have nearly fashioned an epistolary musical, with a dozen or so sung letters. Sondheim embellishes the form, however, by having fragments of letters sung by various characters—the writer, the addressee, even outsiders. And while Tarchetti emphasized the women's personalities by naming them Clara and Fosca (Italian for *light* and *dark*, respectively), Sondheim extends the connection by writing light soprano music for the beautiful blonde Clara and dark alto/contralto music for the homely brunette Fosca. (Tarchetti's women, by contrast, share the same age, height, and hair color.) More-over, as always since *Sweeney Todd*, Sondheim builds melodies around a few recurring motifs, colored throughout by shifting harmony, rhythm, and accompaniment figures, helping to reveal the characters' motivations and moods à la Wagner.

Countless American musicals have been built around love at first sight, followed by complications and eventual romantic resolution. *Passion* depends instead upon Georgio's *revulsion* at first sight that turns into love for the physically repulsive Fosca, which supplants his love for the sexually desirable Clara. This is a difficult task to accomplish convincingly in 110 uninterrupted minutes on stage, whereas in Tarchetti's 200-page novel a more gradual change is shown. Although in this essay I will not consider the show's other—and apparently more direct—source, Ettore Scola's film *Passione d'amore*, it is worth noting that film is a medium that permits time passage to be experienced through montage and other compression techniques, whereas stage work tends to be more immediate and real-time.

Passion begins ominously with a military snare drum beat and a stinging brass chord cluster—a distress call that contrasts with the opening scene of Clara and Giorgio embracing naked in bed, singing of their mutual "Happiness." The number begins with an ostinato consisting of a repeated three-note figure (③) that pairs upwardly moving C–E–G notes with a downward $B^{\flat}$–$A^{\flat}$–$E^{\flat}$, respectively, the effect of which is to disguise the F-minor tonality and to comment dissonantly on the three-syllable word "happiness." As we will see, three-note motifs pervade the score. Although the couple is clearly enraptured, some of the lines have a portentous ring—as when they sing about how they met:

GIORGIO: We were both unhappy.
CLARA: Unhappiness can be seductive.
GIORGIO: You pitied me.
BOTH: How quickly pity leads to love. (2)[2]

This anticipates Giorgio's not-so-quickly transformed feelings toward the pitiful yet seductively unhappy Fosca, who will later assert that "Pity is nothing but passive love" (30). Much of the melody is built upon a five-note pattern (⑤), which is usually associated with the attractive couple. While the actual notes vary considerably, the first four are always eighth notes at the end of the measure, which lead to a quarter (or longer value) note, and the lyrics generally have a trochaic pulse ("Júst anóther lóve story / Thát's what théy would cláim"). Underneath this is an accompanying clarinet figure reminiscent of one used in *Follies'* "Too Many Mornings," with its similar mood of grateful union. Clara and Giorgio acknowledge that the world would see theirs as "Another simple love story— / Aren't all of them the same?" (4). This five-minute opening number uses relatively few rhymes, as if to suggest that the lovers are too consumed with passion to bother. Also, the song fades away with a repeated ③, as do several other numbers in the score, causing one to wonder whether this might be a musical reminder of the love triangle being enacted.

After Captain Giorgio Bachetti is transferred in 1863 from Milan to a remote army outpost, he and Clara continue to sing of their love in a series of letters. He miserably reports, "Clara I'm in hell" (15), and he unknowingly foreshadows Fosca's upcoming maneuvering to win his love when he sings, "My days are spent in maneuvers" (16). Giorgio, learning from his commanding officer Colonel Ricci that Ricci's cousin Fosca hungers for reading material, offers to loan her his copy of Rousseau's *Julie*. This novel is an 18th-century update of the Abelard and Héloïse love story, which subtly foreshadows the lovesick—and physically ill—Fosca's demise. Even before he meets her, Fosca makes her presence known through her offstage playing of "elegant Chopinesque piano music" (stage dir. 13) and through her blood-curdling scream.

Giorgio soon meets the sickly, pathetic woman. The nature of her malady is unclear (in Tarchetti's novel Fosca suffers from epilepsy), but she endures widespread chronic pain. The root of the word *Passion*, by the way, means "suffering" (Latin *passio* translated from the Greek *pathos*). The doctor tells Giorgio that "Her body is so weak that it doesn't have the strength to produce a mortal disease" (18), which suggests a painful chronic condition like fibromyalgia. Such discomfort might well cause her to seek physical love, which would generate endorphins to counteract the pain and comfort her.[3] Significantly, one of Giorgio's fellow officers sings an aria from Donizetti's *L'elisir d'amore* (identified as such only in the libretto), because Fosca's love for Giorgio seems to revive her physically, as well as spiritually. He embodies a nepenthe, an elixir to relieve her sorrow. It is also interesting to note that Giorgio admits in a letter to Clara that on the train ride he cried and had to hide his eyes (13), which recalls *L'elisir*'s well-known aria, "Una Furtiva Lagrima." If this all sounds coincidental, recall that Donizetti's comic opera features a soldier who becomes involved in a love triangle after arriving at a small Italian village.

Fosca returns the novel, telling him in "I Read" (preceded by an oboe plaintively reviving the Chopinesque theme) that she does not read to think:

> I read to dream....
> I read to live,
> To get away from life. (22)

This number introduces Fosca's six-note motif (⑥), the most pervasive and haunting one throughout the score. While the specific note relationships vary somewhat, in all cases the first five notes have short, equal values and the sixth is held on the downbeat, and the lyric is always an iambic trimeter ("I dó not réad to léarn"). The low notes and minor mode underscore Fosca's bleak outlook: "I do not hope for what I cannot have! / I do not cling to things I cannot keep!" (23). Not yet, anyway.

The next sequence takes place in the untended garden of a ruined castle. The setting recalls Hamlet's moody outburst: "Fie on't, ah fie! 'tis an unweeded garden / That grows to seed, things rank and gross in nature / Possess it merely" (I.ii.135-37). In the world Fosca inhabits, which overemphasizes physical beauty, men see women like her as rank, gross creatures and therefore neglect them, instead of nurturing them. Fosca's retreat is analogous to the Beast's forest-enshrouded castle and the Phantom's underground lair. Like Belle and Christine Daaé, Giorgio is revolted at first by the sight of his subhuman beast. The lovely Donna Murphy's transformation into the grotesque Fosca was no less a tour-de-force than that of Terrence Mann into Beast or Michael Crawford et al. into the Phantom. Her change, however, relied more on body language, voice, and attitude (not unlike the strategy employed in *The Elephant Man*) than on makeup: she was no wart-covered refugee from *Into the Woods*. Giorgio nevertheless sees her as subhuman, as he reports in a letter to Clara:

> God, the wretchedness
> And the suffering...
> The desperation
> Of that poor unhappy creature— (26)

During much of the rest of the show, physical action advances the plot but is often not tied directly to the score. Consider the following actions: as Fosca begins to love Giorgio uncontrollably, she falls to the ground, clinging to his legs; she unexpectedly grabs his hand under the dining room table, just out of sight of her cousin; she turns a platonic kiss into a passionate one; Ricci challenges Giorgio to a duel over a misinterpreted letter (Ricci is physically wounded in the duel, Giorgio emotionally so); finally, Giorgio spends several months in a sanitarium. Some of these actions indirectly lead to songs, but most of the score explores emotion, relying heavily throughout on sensory imagery. After going for a walk with Fosca, Giorgio muses in a letter to Clara—which she sings, using ⑥—that all he could think of was Clara.

> To feel a woman's touch,
> To touch a woman's hand,
> Reminded me how much
> I long to be with you. (31)

Perhaps. Or maybe all he really longs for is human contact, something the plain Fosca can provide as well as the physically pleasing but absent—and married—Clara. The fact that the lyric is tied to ⑥, Fosca's motif, further undermines Giorgio's certainty. Yet the letter continues in a new vein with "Love Like Ours," with the ⑤ "Happiness" melody, which tries unsuccessfully to assert a "Love that shuts away the world":

> BOTH: Love that floods
>   Every living moment,
>   Love like—
>   (*Giorgio hesitates, then turns back to Fosca*)
> CLARA: —Ours.
> FOSCA: Love like—?
> GIORGIO: (*As Fosca looks quizzically at him*) Like wine.
>   (33–34)

The song fades out ambivalently on a repeated ③.

Fosca recognizes a kindred spirit in this soldier, who is so unlike his crude comrades: "They hear drums, / We hear music, / Be my friend" (36). The melody first depends on ⑥, then ⑤, hinting that Fosca wishes for the sort of loving happiness that Clara enjoys with Giorgio. An upward three-note motif (⧊), which is tonally simpler and slower than the earlier ③, accentuates the tender feeling. A similar fragment appears in accompaniment figures, as well as in melody, and once again the number fades on this triangular motif.

The "Trio," like the opening number, begins with a distress call. It explicitly begins the love triangle that up to now has only been hinted at. While Giorgio and Clara rhapsodize to each other ("God, you are so beautiful" he exclaims [45], a line taken from the novel), Fosca reads Giorgio's stinging letter to her. As if "My heart belongs / To someone else" isn't sufficiently blunt, he closes by writing her that "There is nothing / Between us / Nothing, nothing" (46–49). These words will come back to haunt not Fosca, but Giorgio.

He visits the gravely ill Fosca, who echoes his words to Clara: "God, you are so beautiful" (57). He honors her request that he write her a letter—which she dictates. She has him write "I Wish I Could Forget You," built upon ⑥ and accompanied by yet a third three-note figure (▣)—this one very slow and melancholy. This blue ▣ often fills space between melodic lines that follow ⑥, thus intensifying the already-somber mood. She then has him describe his relationship with Clara, built entirely on ⑥:

> A love as pure as breath,
> As permanent as death,
> Implacable as stone.

> A love that, like a knife,
> Has cut into a life
> I wanted left alone. (61)

This is perhaps Sondheim's most enthralling lyric since *Sunday in the Park*'s "Finishing the Hat," Fosca's portent of doom notwithstanding. Overall, the dictated letter makes it appear that Giorgio, despite his love for Clara, has deep feelings for Fosca too. She ends with a line that will reverberate at the close of the musical: "Your love will live in me" (61). The letter will become an important plot device when Ricci discovers it and concludes that his cousin is being led on by Giorgio.

A group of soldiers, who form an unreliable Greco-Roman chorus, comments on the action periodically through their gossip, providing comic relief. In clever rhyme they trade snide remarks about Fosca:

> TORASSO: Did you hear the scream last night?…
> COOK: So that wasn't dying, we assume.
> BARRI: No, I think she just fell off her broom.
> TORASSO: Or they hung a mirror in the room
> Of la signora! (71–72)

Otherwise, *Passion* is serious business, with little of Sondheim's customary wit to leaven Fosca's quest for Giorgio's soul.

In a "Flashback," we learn of Fosca's former marriage to an Austrian count, who turned out to be a counterfeit, draining her dowry and deserting her when confronted with the truth. Although the wistful Chopinesque theme makes another instrumental appearance, the ⑥ theme adds weight to the sadness: "How could I be so blind?" "I couldn't face the world" (85). After being jilted Fosca is struck by an epiphany: "Beauty is power… / Longing a disease" (84–85).

In a "Sunrise Letter," Clara begins to wonder whether their love can survive Giorgio's absence: "If only you were here / If I could feel your touch / I wouldn't have such fear" (88). These doubts are underscored by Fosca's ⑥ theme. Meanwhile, the hypotenuse Giorgio is occupied by the love triangle's other leg: Fosca has dropped all pretense in her pursuit, and he expresses to her his feeling of being smothered in "Is This What You Call Love?":

> This is not love,
> This is the reverse.
> Like a curse.

Something out of control.
I've begun to fear for my soul. (92)

As if to underscore this fear, a thunderstorm ensues, during which
Fosca collapses, forcing Giorgio to carry her back home. The soldiers
luridly imagine an intimate relationship between the two: the cook
speculates, "You don't suppose—"

RIZZOLLI: Nobody is that brave.
COOK: Wouldn't you like to peek?
TORASSO: Ugh.
                 . . .
BARRI: He'll be major next week. (94–95)

As usual, they end their comic interlude with "I'll say," repeated three
times. The soldiers promptly shift mood, singing Giorgio's "To feel a
woman's touch" in harmony, which blends with the sad ③ accompaniment to produce a more sensual effect than in the earlier garden
sequence rendering.

Heedless of Giorgio's rebuke, Fosca follows Giorgio—who is
physically spent from fending off her advances and desperate to escape—on his sick-leave to Milan, which the eager but married Clara
anticipates amusingly: "A whole forty days— / Well, forty matinees"
(98). When he discovers Fosca on the train he angrily accuses her of
causing his illness. He asks her to forget him, but she replies calmly,

Loving you
Is not a choice,
It's who I am. (100)

This concise, powerful statement is made even more poignant by each
line being joined to a repetition of ◬, which recurs throughout and
is harmonized in various ways. Up to now Fosca's lyrics have usually
been haunted by ⑥, but her elemental declaration merits the simple
$C–E^b–G$ triad, which places equal stress on each syllable to emphasize her resolve. The song ends with "I will live, / And I would die /
For you" (101). For once, there is no fade out on repetitions of ③, as
if to collapse the triangle into a line connecting only Fosca and Giorgio.

Meanwhile, the soldiers' aim is improving:

AUGENTI: He'd better get out quick
            From the Signora.

> BARRI: That's not an easy trick
>   With the Signora. (105)

How true. At the same time, the distance between Giorgio and Clara, as well as her limited availability even when they *are* together, cause them to see their matinee love fade. Giorgio wants to escape Fosca and cement his relationship with Clara by demanding that she leave her husband, even if that would mean losing custody of her son. Clara counters by asking him to wait for her until the boy is older. When she claims that he isn't thinking clearly and is not himself, Giorgio exclaims defensively, "I'm myself!" (109), the vehemence of which betrays his knowledge that he is becoming Fosca, to the point of taking on her physical infirmity.

Unsurprisingly the common ground between Giorgio and Clara disappears. A repetition of the opening distress call, softened by an oboe instead of trumpets, leads into Clara's "Farewell Letter," some of which ironically uses the same ⑤ melody as "Happiness." They realize that theirs was

> GIORGIO (*bitter, quietly*):   Just another love story.
> CLARA: No one is to blame.
>   . . .
> CLARA: I didn't know that love was a complication.
> GIORGIO: I do know that it's not a negotiation. (115–
>   17)

They agree on one crucial point:

> GIORGIO: —That what we have is nothing...
> CLARA: Nothing...
> GIORGIO: Nothing.... (118; ellipses in text)

Influenced by Fosca's power of love, Giorgio sees that it was he, rather than she, who had suffered from the "disease" of longing only for physical beauty.

Having lost Clara, Giorgio realizes, "No One Has Ever Loved Me" like Fosca:

> Love without reason,
> Love without mercy,
> Love without pride or shame.
> Love unconcerned
> With being returned—

No wisdom, no judgment,
No caution, no blame. (122)

To construct the melody for this essential song, Sondheim abandoned the motifs that had represented Fosca alone (⑥), Giorgio and Clara (⑤), and the love triangle (△). Instead the melody is based loosely on the Chopinesque theme—heretofore wordless—as if to return to the moment Giorgio first heard Fosca, before he had prejudged her based on her physical appearance. Fosca now sings of too much happiness (⑤), but hers is tinged by the ③ accompaniment figure, because it comes "when there's so little time" (123). Although Fosca is dying, the final scene skirts sentimentality, even when Giorgio finally confesses, "I love you"—repeated twice more at Fosca's urging and underscored by the "another simple love story" theme played on flute, then on oboe. She pulls him to her bed, where they will—one as-sumes—make love for the only time before she succumbs. If this seems a relatively demure staging, it follows the novel. Tarchetti, ill with tuberculosis and typhus while writing the book with all the passion he could muster, died at age 29 before reaching this climactic scene, and the book was completed by a friend who evidently lacked Tarchetti's ardor.

Giorgio knows this will be their final meeting, for he is scheduled to duel the next morning with Ricci over Fosca's honor. When Giorgio shoots Ricci, he "lets out a high-pitched howl—a cry that is clearly reminiscent of Fosca's—as lights fade to black" (stage dir. 125). The novel is even more explicit on this matter: "Fosca's malady was trans-fused into me. I had obtained the sad inheritance of my guilt, and my love" (Tarchetti 193). Fosca has, through a loving metempsychosis, succeeded in transferring her soul into Giorgio.

Finally experiencing contentment after a lifetime of misery, Fosca sings, "I don't want to leave" (129). She is reassured by the show's final line, repeated eleven times by various individuals and groups of characters: "Your love will live in me," ironically sharing the earlier "I wish I could forget you" theme. The consonance of love/live and the melodic ⑥ strengthen the line, while the almost mantric chant re-minds one of the repeated Sanskrit *shantih* at the end of Eliot's *The Waste Land.* "The peace that passeth understanding" resonates here, as Fosca has already slipped from life, returning from the grave to participate in the chant. This is a quiet but powerful theatrical moment which reminds us of how a lyric and melody can combine to stun an audience into submission.

What can we make of this *Passion* play, which transcends surface pleasures and conscious choices? To answer this question, let us turn to Carl Jung. James Lapine's interest in Jung is well-known; indeed, his play *Twelve Dreams* is based on one of Jung's case studies. Lapine's libretto for *Into the Woods*, moreover, ventures into not only a dark forest, but also the dark subconsciousness of mythology. *Passion* seems similarly influenced by archetypes and symbolism, though less overtly.

Since I have mentioned dreams, let's begin our exploration of the unconscious there. Sondheim's mentor Oscar Hammerstein was fond of writing about dreams. The early R&H musicals are well-known for their dream ballets exploring subconscious desires, while in *South Pacific*, he used the word "dream" over two dozen times in five songs. In *Passion* dreams are less pervasive but are endowed with deep, often dark, meaning. Fosca, who claims early on, "I read to dream," bitterly adds,

> I do not dwell on dreams.
> I know how soon a dream becomes an expectation.
> How can I have expectations?
> Look at me....
> I know how painful dreams can be
> Unless you know
> They're merely dreams. (22–23)

The attractive couple has no such problems with reveries, as Giorgio and Clara sing together, "To dream of you and then...To feel your touch again" (47–48). Later, when Fosca believes she is dying, she asks Giorgio to put his head next to hers as she goes to sleep. "Can we dream together?" she asks. As if some sort of three-way mind melding has taken place, Clara enters at that moment to read us her letter:

> ...I've just arisen from a dream of you, a dream so real I could swear you were there at my side. I am so used to this, having you in my dreams night after night.... Do you dream of me?... Sometimes I think that when you watch a person sleep there's a transparency that lets you see their soul. (58)

Upon her exit, Fosca awakens and says to Giorgio, "It is you. I thought I was dreaming" (59). Although she cannot yet possess Giorgio in reality, the subconscious connection among the three gives her psychic energy to fuel her pursuit.

Most significantly, we later see Giorgio's feverish hallucination enacted on his bed: "a black-caped form writh[es] as the bed spins. The black figure lifts up: it is Fosca atop Giorgio, who struggles beneath" (stage dir. 95). The doctor hears his cries and awakens him:

> GIORGIO: She was dragging me down into the grave
>   with her. She was hugging me. Kissing me
>   with her cold lips. Those thin arms pulling
>   me, drawing me, like icy tentacles.
> DOCTOR: It was only a dream. (97)

But it is more than that. The apparition of Fosca atop Giorgio suggests a succubus drawing the life force from the young man, which Jung identifies as one form of *anima*, "a magical feminine being (Jung, "Archetypes" 309). The *anima* can be seen as the shadow archetype— the dark side of a man's inner life, an appropriate image for the dark Fosca. Indeed, in Tarchetti's novel Fosca even identifies herself as Giorgio's shadow, and "when I have died for you, you won't be able to forget me" (152). Although at this point Giorgio is haunted by a monstrous Fosca, in the end he declares his love to her, which prompts her to ask, "This isn't a dream?" "This isn't a dream," he assures her (123). We thus come full circle in *Passion*, from unwillingness to dream, to illusory dream love, to nightmare, to dream fulfilled.

While dreams normally take place in the dark, *Passion* is filled with allusions to light that go well beyond the significance of Clara's name. Giorgio initially declares in "Happiness," "I love to see you in the light" (7). Later, when Fosca believes she is dying, she repeats this line verbatim to Giorgio but tries to stay out of the light herself: "I feel better in the dark" (57). When she awakens from what she thought was a dream of Giorgio, she asks him to draw the curtain, so she can "see the stars before the daylight takes them away" (59). In the letter she dictates while ill, she has Giorgio write, "I wanted you to vanish from sight, / But now I see you in a different light" (61)—i.e., fondly if not lovingly. Light remains Fosca's enemy until, on the train to Milan, she looks out the window and says, "The moonlight makes even this landscape look lovely. Look. There seem to be faces in those rocks, smiling back at us" (102). Giorgio sees what she means and smiles slightly. She is beginning to win him over, as we soon realize.

Clara writes to tell Giorgio that her husband is going away for a while, which means

> I can visit you at night,
> We'll be lighted by the moon,
> Not a shuttered afternoon....
> And perhaps at last
> We'll share a sunrise.
> Wouldn't that be beautiful?— (107)

We'll never know, because Giorgio cancels his sick leave to Milan, beginning his move away from the bright sunlight of Clara and toward the subdued glow of Fosca.

Like light, flowers play an important symbolic role in *Passion*. They first appear ominously in Fosca's "I Read":

> There is a flower
> Which offers nectar at the top...
> And bitter poison underneath.
> The butterfly that stays too long
> And drinks too deep
> Is doomed to die. (22–23)

This allegory is meant to caution Giorgio against becoming poisoned by the seductive flower Clara. Flowers are next associated with funerals (26), then futility—"As if a flower or a tree could somehow make one happy," Fosca scowls (31). We see the sources of her negativity in the flashback, in which her parents say "A woman is a flower" (77) and the phony Count Ludovic, upon learning that Fosca likes flowers, says he wishes he had brought her a large bouquet (saying so is cheaper than buying it). After being jilted, Fosca bitterly notes, "A woman's like a flower... / A flower's only purpose is to please..." (84; ellipses in text). Back in the present, while continuing to pursue Giorgio, she asks him why violets and daisies are blooming out of season; he replies, "They mistake Autumn's warmth for April" (90). Although he may be warning that she cannot experience a vernal rebirth with him, the symbolism behind the flowers contradicts him, for the daisy signifies eternal life and salvation, as well as tears (Herder 55).

Similarly, the violet has a long symbolic history: "during the Middle Ages, the violet signified modest virtuousness and humility and thus was a symbol of Mary. Because of its color, it is also a symbol of Christ's Passion" (Herder 208). In Fosca we see both a frustrated nurturer and someone passionately committed to sacrificing herself for the one she loves (indeed, one archaic meaning for the word *passion* is *martyrdom*). We may therefore discern a heroic, even quasi-religious, alternate meaning in the musical's title. Later, as Giorgio miserably recovers from his illness and hallucination, Clara is, ironically, singing cheerfully: "I'm filling up the room, / Our little room, / With every flower in bloom" (99). She is unaware that the bloom is off their romance, whereas the seeds of love for Fosca have been planted in the dark earth of Giorgio's subconscious, waiting for a bit of warmth to awaken and sprout them.

Consulting Jung can help us sort out the meaning of these some-times conflicting actions and symbols. In speaking of archetypes—the universal, unconscious regulators of conscious thoughts and action—he says that "dreams behave in exactly the same way as active imagination, only the support of conscious contents is lacking" (Jung, "Psyche" 75). Dreams can therefore depict true desires that are denied by conscious thought. Also, because a dream seems an almost mystical experience, it can generate great emotion:

> Often it drives with unexampled passion and remorseless logic towards its goal and draws the subject under its spell, from which despite the most desperate resistance he is unable, and finally no longer even willing, to break free, because the experience brings with it a depth and fullness of meaning that was unthinkable before.
> (Jung, "Psyche" 76)

Does this not describe Giorgio's struggle perfectly? One could argue, in fact, that no conscious words and actions alone could persuade Giorgio to switch his love from Clara to Fosca so quickly, that only an archetypal pull could effect such a transformation.

Jung also makes a useful distinction between instinct and spirit. He argues that archetypes are mystical and spiritual; conversely, instincts are those ingrained biological imperatives that may seem contrary to the spirit. Nevertheless, as dual psychic processes Jung sees instinct and spirit as forming the endpoints of a psychic con-tinuum, along which each person slides from moment to moment. We can then see Giorgio as being instinctively drawn to the sexually desirable Clara, with *Passion* being a recording of his reluctant, yet ineluctable, move away from her and toward the spiritual Fosca. Jung notes, moreover, that "Violet is the 'mystic' color, and it certainly reflects the indubitably 'mystic' or paradoxical quality of the archetype" (Jung, "Psyche" 81). As I have shown above, Fosca is associated with the violet flower (and, by extension, the color).

Passion includes additional subtleties. As if the Rousseau reference and Donizetti aria sung early in the show were not veiled enough, Torasso comes back later, when Giorgio is seeing his relationship with Clara fall apart, to sing an Italian Christmas carol with the recognizable melody of "God Rest Ye Merry, Gentlemen" (110). Roughly translated, the carol speaks of peace and tranquility upon the earth, brought about by a child born to save the world from the great power of Satan. It is a story of great happiness for the gathered officers, and perhaps it is yet one more whispered reminder from the authors regarding redemption, for that theme certainly comes across: not only does Fosca help Giorgio save himself through discovering his spiritual side, but she, the one associated with eternal life and salvation through the daisies, sacrifices herself, while gaining everlasting life within Giorgio's heart. Even Clara may be redeemed by being denied her instinctive target, for now that Giorgio is no longer a sexual distraction, she will most likely return to her family, where spiritual fulfillment may await. After all, we never learn anything negative about her husband; apparently she simply found Giorgio more desirable.

Even by diving beneath the surface of consciousness, it is difficult to unlock all the mysteries of *Passion*. For example, throughout the show drums, bugles, and singing soldiers remind us of "This military madness…Uniforms, uniforms" (16 and elsewhere, including even the final sequence). Is Sondheim equating military regimentation with men's uniformly inflexible preconceptions about women? And why do the soldiers so often end their interludes with a harmonized, thrice-sung "I'll say!"? The device is reminiscent of the trio of Italian singers in Frank Loesser's *The Most Happy Fella* who appear periodically to harmonize comically. The triple "I'll say" is another instance of *Passion*'s magic number 3, but any further significance is unclear. One might find comfort in Freud's reminder that sometimes a cigar is just a cigar, but knowing Sondheim's penchant for puzzles, such an admonishment is hardly comforting.

How does *Passion* rate among Sondheim's shows? Even stern critics were observed leaving the Plymouth Theatre wiping away a *furtiva lagrima* or two, and some Sondheim fans speak of the show as if it were a life-changing experience for them. Perhaps it is churlish, then, to note that, even though Giorgio discovers in his decision song that he loves Fosca and will always remember her in death, his realization carries no responsibility for future action. Having already lost Clara, he risks little by declaring his love, however heartfelt it may seem, to the doomed Fosca. In *Follies*, by contrast, the four main characters ultimately choose to re-couple with their respective spouses, which has lasting consequences; in *A Little Night Music*, when Fredrik and Desirée finally connect with each other, they must change partners permanently for the sake of their love. Even resisting such comparisons, when Giorgio declares his love to the dying Fosca, we should feel the pang that Chaplin invokes in *City Lights* when the previously blind woman who owes her new eyesight, not to a rich man as she had assumed, but to the smitten Little Tramp, asks, "You?" The tramp nods with a shy, tentative smile and a puppydog gaze. In that moment we feel the mingled rush of love and pity that Giorgio's thrice-repeated "I love you" fails to generate in me, regardless of how much I admire the show's craft and complexity. I believe the swiftness of the turnabout accounts for this problem; the score certainly cannot be faulted.

Giorgio's quick change of heart leads to the question of *Passion*'s long one-act structure. When *Into the Woods* opened, the first-act curtain seemed to provide a satisfying fairytale ending (except for a final, disquieting "I wish"). *Sunday in the Park* seemed similarly complete at the first act curtain—without even a dissenting note (either melodic or lyrical) to draw the audience back after intermission. Both musicals, however, showed in their important second acts what happens after we thought everything had been resolved. In *Passion*, originally intended to be paired with another one-act musical, Sondheim and Lapine felt the story reached completion with Fosca's wish-fulfillment and death, and most composers would be thrilled to do so well. However, *Passion* leaves us with an idealistic ending by Sondheim's standards, one not to be tested by the real world we saw in the two earlier works. Because Fosca dies, Giorgio does not have to nurse his sickly, homely beloved for the following forty years, nor do we see where (or to whom) his newfound spirituality will lead him next, assuming he does not slide back to the instinct side of Jung's continuum. It becomes difficult, therefore, to judge whether Fosca's love has indeed transformed Giorgio in the way we see nonspecific yet satisfying attitude shifts in Robert (*Company*) and modern-day George (Act II of *Sunday in the Park*). Even conceding that this is Fosca's story, "I wish" I could see what happens next to the new Giorgio. (If this were Hollywood instead of Broadway, a sequel would be inevitable.)

Nevertheless, Sondheim, who has in the past sometimes been criticized for emotional detachment, pulls out all his emotional stops in *Passion*, and he is unabashedly proud of the work, which went through an especially trying preview reception. One of the show's greatest strengths for me lies in its subtle pleasures, such as the fact that a ♥ is camouflaged within the mirrored S's of the logo—letters which also represent the composer's initials!

Although Sondheim would justifiably resent the comparison, *Passion* reminds me of Andrew Lloyd Webber's subdued, relatively unsuccessful musical *Aspects of Love* in at least one way: it shows that, as one of Lloyd Webber's songs asserts, "Love Changes Everything."[4] Sondheim's show, like *Aspects*, is never bombastic in an age that seems to require Broadway musicals to be special effects–laden in order to turn a profit. He deserved a better fate, however, than running third to a levitating, spinning beast-Prince and a chandelier crashing on cue eight times a week. *Passion* is about people—no more, no less. Perhaps another simple love story is *too* simple for Broadway in the 1990s.

The aesthetics of *Passion* likely appealed to the same audience that appreciated *Sunday in the Park* ten years earlier. The fact that *Passion* lasted only around 250 performances, compared to 600 for *Sunday*, may be attributed to the fact that the former had no ticket-selling names in the cast, whereas the latter was blessed with Mandy Patinkin and Bernadette Peters; *Sunday* lasted only a few months after they had both departed.

Lapine once said of *Sunday in the Park* that "You have to think. Not a lot, but some." In *Passion*, it's probably best for the audience *not* to think, but to let Sondheim's sounds wash over them, in order to become part of the tone poem being created on stage. Otherwise, analyzing the motifs and lyrical patterns in the score won't help much. If this musical is a beauty for the eye, ear, and heart to appreciate, it's a beast for the rational mind to comprehend...just like love.[5]

 භ

NOTES

1.   The original Broadway cast album, which includes condensed dialogue passages, runs 56 minutes, or half the show's running time.

2.   Page numbers are given in parentheses throughout for *Passion* (New York: Theatre Communications, 1994).

3.   A fibromyalgia sufferer I spoke to confirms this as a likely response.

4.   It must be a coincidence, but the rhapsodic instrumental ending of "Happiness" is eerily reminiscent of Lloyd Webber's "Unexpected Song" from *Song and Dance*.

5.   An earlier, substantially shorter version of this essay originally appeared in *Mockingbird*, V. 1, 1994.

WORKS CITED

Herder, S.D. *Symbol Dictionary*. Trans. Boris Mathews. Wilmette, IL: Chiron, 1986.

Jung, Carl. "Archetypes of the Collective Unconscious." In *The Basic Writings of C. G. Jung*. Ed. Violet S. deLaszlo. New York: Modern Library, 1959.

———. From *On the Nature of the Psyche*. In *The Basic Writings of C. G. Jung* (above).

Sondheim, Stephen, and James Lapine. *Passion*. New York: Theatre Communications, 1994.

Tarchetti, I.U. *Passion* (orig. title *Fosca*). Trans. Lawrence Venuti. San Francisco: Mercury House, 1994.

Revisiting Greece
The Sondheim Chorus
Barbara Means Fraser

Sondheim and Greece may seem a strange marriage of topics, but in fact, the structure of the chorus in many of Stephen Sondheim's musicals resembles the Greek chorus more strongly than a more typical chorus of the American musical. Sondheim's rather unusual restructured chorus is one of the artistically and culturally exciting qualities evident within his musicals. An understanding of where its antecedents might lie will help directors produce his complex work with better insight and will help scholars see how and why choices are being made to create and communicate the art so effectively.

Before the Sondheim musical can be analyzed insightfully, a brief description of Greek culture, community, and chorus is necessary. The Greek chorus is often misunderstood because it grows so directly out of the culture of ancient Greece. Contemporary Americans have difficulty understanding a conception of character so different from their culture. Americans respect and value the individual. They try to distinguish themselves one from another. They separate any special traits that make them different from the crowd, and take pride in special talents that make them different from other Americans. This conception of character, so effectively captured in the cowboy, the private eye, and the spy, is integrated into American actions, thoughts, and values.

The Greek conception of character is the opposite of American sensibilities. Whereas American culture reinforces and identifies with the individual versus the society, the Greek world of 450–400 B.C. defined itself in terms of the individual *and* society; they celebrated the community. One of the central differences is that Greeks were characterized by an ideal called *areté*. *Areté* has been translated from the Greek as virtue or honor, but neither word truly captures the complete sense of *areté*. Certainly *areté* includes honor and virtue, but it goes beyond that to develop a sense of individual wholeness.

The Greeks would readily understand the assumption of *areté* which is a balance of intellectual, spiritual, and physical qualities. Greeks were not encouraged to perfect a specialized skill, but instead strove for balance of excellence in all things. Seeing themselves in relationship to their natural world, in relationship to each other, and in relationship to the community as a whole was an essential part of *areté*. The Greeks had a sense of responsibility to community and to the spiritual world of the gods above and beyond their commitment to family or self. *Areté* shaped the Greeks' perception of self to require a balance and an ability to see oneself in relation to others.

The other significant concept that defined the Greek character is *dike*. *Dike* literally translates to "justice," but like *areté* the concept is more complex. *Dike* in the Greek world was not an individual justice, but justice within *areté*. It required a balancing of all aspects of a situation to find the appropriate justice with regard to individual and community. Therefore, the characterization of a Greek character is dependent on the individual in relation to community.

While the Greeks saw the world in terms of community, Americans see the world in terms of individuals. Just as an American prides herself on her unique qualities, a Greek would take pride in what was shared. In the American theatre, the individual searches for truth about him or herself. In the Greek theatre, the individual defines him or herself in relation to community. Consequently, there is a logical reason for the chorus. The Greek chorus is central to the play, because it represents the community.

The tragedy of *Antigone* involves both Antigone and Creon losing their sense of *areté*. To recognize fully this loss of balance, wholeness, virtue, and honor, the audience must see Antigone and Creon not so much in battle with each other, but more importantly, the audience must see each individual lose touch with the chorus. The Greek audience would identify with the chorus—the community. Antigone and Creon talk to the chorus, argue with the chorus, listen to the chorus, and disregard the advice of the chorus. As Creon and Antigone reject reason which comes from the community, they lose their *areté*. The result is tragic.

This differs radically from a typical American interpretation, which might make Antigone a rebellious young idealist who martyrs herself before Creon, an arrogant bureaucrat, who is punished in the end for his petty pride. Either concept will play, but the second is definitely an American version—not Greek. The American director who works within the confines of a contemporary sensibility has a problem accounting for and incorporating the traditional chorus.

The chorus of Greek plays also serves an important character function. Many Americans become confused when they read or see Greek plays because they do not understand the important role of the chorus or community. When Antigone pleads her case to the chorus, an American audience is likely to empathize with Antigone, but the Greek audience perceives her behavior in terms of how the chorus responds, not on the basis of her argument alone. When she accuses the chorus of abandonment, the Greek audience knows immediately that she has lost her *areté* because the Greek audience has been keenly aware that the chorus is balanced in its view. The Greek chorus is weighing all the evidence and considering carefully in terms of what is best for the community. Members of the chorus have, in fact, supported her in their interactions with Creon, although they have also not turned a blind eye to her selfish indiscretion. American audiences see the conflict between Antigone and Creon and expect one of them to be vilified and the other to be exonerated because of the American emphasis on individualism. *Antigone*, like most Greek plays, does not exemplify American values. The chorus has the last word and the audience is left with despair which results when individuals place personal passion above the community needs. Members of an American audience might easily miss the community focus because of their understandable disregard for the significance of the chorus. The Greek audience understands that the chorus is the most significant "character" in the play.

The Traditional American Musical Chorus

In the traditional American musical accounting for the chorus is less problematic because, even though most musicals have a chorus, the traditional musical theatre chorus is designed to fit an American sensibility. The traditional American musical chorus, or what will be referred to as the traditional chorus, however, is markedly different from the Sondheim chorus.

Whether speaking of *Show Boat, Oklahoma!, Brigadoon, The Music Man, Fiddler on the Roof, The Sound of Music, Mame, The Phantom of the Opera* or most other popular non-Sondheim musicals, a chorus pattern begins to emerge which is different from the function of the chorus in the Sondheim musicals.

As in the difference between Greek and American culture, the major distinction begins with the variation of focus on individual and community. The traditional musical chorus is subordinate to the individualism of the leading characters. Whether in *The Music Man's* River City where Harold Hill uses the chorus as a device to whip up a little "trouble," or in *The Sound of Music's* mansion where the party guests sing a quick good night to the seven individual Von Trapp children—each a soloist, the chorus is functioning to support the individuals. The community/chorus easily defers in importance and focus.

In practically every musical, a world is established as the central character enters into that world. Members of the audience identify with the individual as they share an introduction to the environment with the lead. The chorus then fades into that environment which supports the story of the leading characters. Tommy and Jeff join the audience as they are introduced to the people of Brigadoon who prepare for the Fair. Tevye breaks right through the fourth wall to welcome the audience to Anatevka and explain their cultural rituals and "traditions." The worlds of these plays are established through the chorus as an extension of the scenery, but the audience clearly understands that they are to empathize with the individual.

In many musicals the chorus adds spectacle through song and dance. Whether the wedding celebration in *Fiddler on the Roof,* the party in *Mame*, the Masquerade ball in *Phantom of the Opera*, beautiful costumes, skillfully choreographed dance numbers, and/or energetic melodic song bring the audience to a euphoric state. Often these numbers are designed to entertain above and beyond the central focus of the musical. Even in these "chorus" numbers the chorus is generally back-up for a more individualized character who joins the chorus.

The chorus also functions as a group of extras. Its members are the unknown, unnamed people of a town who, when the central character needs support, appear to become vocal accompaniment. In *Anything Goes* when Reno Sweeney sings "Blow Gabriel Blow," she needs back-up and there it is. When Alfred P. Dolittle needs to "get to the church on time" in *My Fair Lady*, the other nameless drunks at the bar sing and dance right on cue.

This is what the audiences think of as the traditional chorus, and it is very reflective of American values. There is nothing wrong with this—audiences treasure these theatrical moments—but this is not the type of chorus that Stephen Sondheim has constructed in his musicals. Certainly some of these characteristics are also present in some of his musicals, but he develops the chorus's function beyond this simple supportive function. Sondheim's chorus integrates characteristics from the traditional American chorus and the function of a classical Greek chorus.

The Greek chorus has some general characteristics that find their way into the Sondheim musical. In Greece, the audience would assume a strong relationship with the chorus, whereas in America, the audience would assume a strong relationship with the individual hero or heroine. Therefore, to create the type of audience-community relationship that the Greek theatre audience assumes, the musical's chorus must establish this special relationship.

A Greek chorus also keeps the action flowing and guides the action from one section into another through a specifically structured ritual. The American audience is not familiar with the specific rituals of the Greek structure, but often the chorus guides the action forward and establishes conventions unique to the specific musical, which helps the audience to understand the rules of the particular musical.

As the Greek chorus guides, it provides practical information and serves to comment on the action. Since in a Sondheim musical, the audience is not expected to empathize completely with the individuals, and the characters and their motivations are usually complex, commentary by the chorus helps the audience feel at ease with the discomforting circumstances, while still learning from the experience. The chorus establishes a trust factor with the audience. They can rely on the truth conveyed from the chorus, rather than from the individuals. Like in a Greek play, the chorus may serve as an important character.

In seven of Sondheim's musicals: *Company, A Little Night Music, Pacific Overtures, Sweeney Todd, Merrily We Roll Along, Into the Woods* and *Assassins,* patterns emerge that shift the utility of the chorus into new and different directions. A closer look at the Sondheim chorus in these works will reveal that the Sondheim chorus is closer to the Greek model than the American musical's more traditional chorus. In some instances, however, Sondheim creates functions beyond Greece or the traditional musical chorus by integrating chorus concepts from the ancient past and the recent past into a uniquely Sondheim chorus.

COMPANY

An examination of the chorus in *Company* is an interesting place to begin, because in a traditional sense, there is no chorus. Robert is the individual hero, and the other characters in the musical are his married friends, five couples, and his three girl friends. However, this group of characters functions as a chorus when they are not playing their named roles.

Just as the Greek chorus is responsible for opening the show and establishing the world of the play, so do Robert's friends establish the environment of this musical with a surprise birthday party. They make it clear through the first musical number, "Company" that the play is about relationships and Robert's journey, which his friends interpret as his quest to find a wife. Their world is chaotic and frantic, but his friends always have time for Robert.

Once this world has been established, the *coryphaeus* or leader of the chorus appears as Robert's friend, Joanne, who communicates directly with the audience about the characters and action of the play. Once Joanne has made her connection with the audience and sings the first two verses of "Little Things We Do Together," the rest of the couples enter as a chorus and join her in the last verse. The song is a general commentary on marriage and relationships—the theme of the musical. The chorus of married couples explains:

> It's not talk of God and the decade ahead that
> Allow you to get through the worst.
> It's "I do" and "You don't" and "Nobody said that"
> And "Who brought the subject up first?" (Sondheim
> and Furth, Act I, Scene ii)

Immediately the audience becomes aware that this is not a typical musical comedy where marriage is the happy ending for which the hero and heroine strive. Sondheim's chorus is guiding them along, but the audience may be wary of the path.

Later in the first act, one of the chorus singers comments on the life of single people in the city, and then the audience sees Robert with each of his girl friends. Robert's relationships with these women reflect the words expressed in "Another Hundred People":

> It's a city of strangers—
> Some come to work, some to play—
>   ...
> And every day
> The ones who stay
> Can find each other in the crowded streets and the
> guarded parks,
>   ...
> And they meet at parties through the friends of friends
> who they never know.
> Will you pick me up or do I meet you there or shall we
> let it go? (Sondheim and Furth, Act I, Scene v)

Like the Greek chorus, the company of characters comments on each other and action of the play, and like the Greek chorus, that commentary is central to the action of the play. Marta, the character who sings "Another Hundred People" leaves her role as commentator to become Robert's third girl friend. She speaks frankly to him, and he is fascinated, at least for a time. The three girl friends who comment on his behavior share scenes with him. They are important characters in Robert's life. Joanne, who first communicates to the audience in "The Little Things We Do Together," and the other couples who follow her in song, are his friends. They are all important members of the community at large. But in the Sondheim musical, like in the Greek play, they are also important in their community roles. These people cajole Robert. They haunt him. They are the voices inside his head that finally force him to question his life.

Company includes all of the Greek chorus elements, and then leaps even further into the Greek philosophy of *areté*. As the play concludes, it does not resolve if viewed in terms of Robert, the individual hero. However, the married couples, who comprise the chorus, have rediscovered their bonds of love partly through their interactions with Robert. As Robert sings "Being Alive," questioning his direction and his choices and whether he can commit, the couples give advice, stating their feelings about love and commitment:

> HARRY: You've got so many reasons for not being with
>   someone, but Robert, you haven't got one

good reason for being alone.

...

PETER: Hey, buddy, don't be afraid it won't be perfect. ...
The only thing to be afraid of really is that it
won't *be*. (Sondheim and Furth, Act II, Scene
iv)

The play concludes. Robert is alone still searching, but the couples
have each other, and through their constant advising of Robert, they
have reaffirmed their commitment to their own marital relationships.
They know that relationships are hard work, but worth the pain and
struggle. In this sense, the chorus becomes the focus of the musical.
The finale and curtain call reinforces friendship and the relationships
people share:

That's what it's really about, isn't it?
That's what it's really about, really about?

...

Company!... Life is Company! Love is Company!
Company! (Sondheim and Furth, Finale)

Robert, the individual, is not settled, secure, or satisfied, but the community celebrates life and love. Even if the American audience is not
ready to re-identify with the community, Sondheim, Furth, and Prince
have shifted the focus to the chorus. The result is that Robert seems
to appear even lonelier in his quest.

A LITTLE NIGHT MUSIC

After the unresolved conclusion and thematic complexity of
Company, with *A Little Night Music*, Sondheim returned to the more
traditional American musical structure. Yet, Sondheim is never
slavishly confined to any strict form.

The first noticeable difference appears in the form of a musical
quintet, the *Liebeslieder* group. The show opens with the five singers
warming up at the piano. The script lists them as Mr. Lindquist, Mrs.
Nordstrom, Mrs. Anderssen, Mr. Erlanson, and Mrs. Segstrom, but
they are never referred to by name. They dance, move about the stage
with grace, and woo the audience with their wit and charm.

In the early stages of collaboration, Sondheim saw *A Little Night
Music* as a "fantasy-ridden musical" (Zadan 182). Originally he conceived Madame Armfeldt with a Prospero-like magical power. Madame

Armfeldt would shuffle a deck of cards, and the characters would create their relationship partners during a weekend in the country. As if she was not satisfied with the outcome, Madame Armfeldt would then reshuffle the deck and let the characters begin their weekend of love and intrigue over again. According to Sondheim, "Hugh Wheeler finally gave up on it [the concept]. He just couldn't make it work to his satisfaction" (Zadan 182). In her book *Art Isn't Easy*, Joanne Gordon contends, "There are remnants of these original ideas evident in the final version [of *A Little Night Music*]" (124). Certainly, Sondheim's use of the *Liebeslieder* captures some of the fantasy elements of his original conception.

The quintet is never integrated with the individual members of the story; it remains aloof. However, the quintet establishes a relationship with the audience immediately. The five open and close the play, and as each of the two acts open, they break the fourth wall by singing directly to the audience and establishing the tone and sophistication of the world of this musical. They explain the particular conventions of the natural environment. Much as the Greek chorus would speak of the rivers, the sun, and the mountains, the quintet explains to the audience:

> MRS. ANDERSSEN: The sun sits low,
> Diffusing its usual glow.
> ...
> ALL: Perpetual sunset
> Is rather an unset-
> Tling thing. (Sondheim and
> Wheeler, Act II, Entr'acte)

More is communicated through the quintet than natural setting, however. The perpetual sunset creates a subtle mysterious mood that keeps the couples a bit off-balance in their judgment and behavior. This exemplifies the style and character layered onto the musical through these unusual choral figures.

Once the story begins in earnest, the quintet seems to fade into the background like a traditional chorus of the American theatre, but rather quickly it reemerges in the Sondheim form to comment on the action, moving the story into its next segment and continuing the magical quality of Sondheim's original vision. The chorus helps Desirée pack and unpack as she tours through "the provinces," focusing on the irony of Desirée's romantic illusions. While moving scenery, the five wittily judge her surroundings, breaking the romantic image of the theatre tour. Desirée writes to her daughter about her "glamorous life," but the quintet expresses a different view. They recall packing and unpacking, tacky hotels with "ice in the basin," "cracks in the plaster," and "mice in the hallway" (Sondheim and Wheeler, Act I, Scene i). Their presence communicates style and grace which creates an illusion through another fantasy frame. They comment on the ugliness of Desirée's life on the road, yet they are never sullied by it. Instead, they waltz in and waltz out without even a moment's attachment to the experience. As the *Liebesleider* group continually moves in and out of the story and in and around the characters, it transfixes the audience with beauty, elegance, grace and charm, mesmerizng them in a world apart from the problems of Desirée and Fredrik.

When Fredrik and Anne attend the theatre to see Fredrik's old flame, the quintet comments again, this time to express Fredrik's reverie. The *Liebeslieder* sings and waltzes, capturing a fond memory of romance. This montage is not a literal memory for Fredrik and Desirée, but it lays a foundation of their rich shared history. His silly marriage to child bride Anne pales in contrast. The chorus functions to inform and guide audience reaction.

Along with its commentary, the chorus moves the action forward in literal and physical ways. The physical movement begins in "A Glamorous Life" when the quintet helps Desirée pack and unpack, but the number "A Weekend in the Country" is an even more complex and spectacular example of this kind of physical action. Sondheim creates a beautiful musical number sung in counterpoint, as each character responds according to his or her own feelings. The quintet helps move the people, furniture, and scenery as the stage transforms into the country home of Madame Armfeldt, Desirée's mother. The choral group blends into the stylized theatrical transition without becoming part of the central characters' world. After arriving, the five also serve to set the elegant table while tensions mount in the room. These invisible yet present characters give the audience permission to peek into this foreign world of scandal, intrigue, and sexual promiscuity.

The guidance and magic remain, but the commentary becomes even more predominant in the second act. The quintet provides a running commentary, cleverly taking phrases from the central character's first act songs and layering them over the action within the second act to focus on the ironies. As Anne, Fredrik's young wife, and Henrik, Fredrik's son are running off together, the quintet comments with a phrase from one of Anne's earlier songs in which she refers to Fredrik:

> MRS. SEGSTROM: Think of how much I adore you,
> Think of how much you love me.
> If I were perfect for you,
> Wouldn't you tire of me
> Soon…? (Sondheim and Wheeler,
> Act II, Scene viii)

It seems that Anne's concern about Fredrik should have been Fredrik's concern about Anne.

As Fredrik and Charlotte sit and share their grief over losing their supposed "true loves," both of whom are obviously mismatches, the chorus comments with an earlier lyric from one of Fredrik's songs about his mismatch, Anne:

> MR. ERLANSON: She lightens my sadness,
> She livens my days,
> She bursts with a kind of madness
> My well-ordered ways.
> My happiest mistake,
> The ache of my life…. (Sondheim and
> Wheeler, Act II, Scene viii)

This lyric should reassure the audience that Charlotte's marriage was a mistake, and that this rendezvous is also a mistake.

When Carl-Magnus and Charlotte are reuniting, the chorus comments with a phrase from Charlotte's earlier song about marriage, "Every Day a Little Death,"

> MRS. ANDERSSEN: Men are stupid, men are vain,
> Love's disgusting, love's insane,
> A humiliating business…
> MRS. SEGSTROM: Oh, how true! (Sondheim and
> Wheeler, Act II, Scene viii)

The chorus sings Charlotte's words back to her, suggesting that Carl-Magnus is still stupid and vain—and perhaps her choice to be with him is a humiliating business. The chorus stays above the foolish antics of the lovers, yet it manages to help guide the audience into accepting the broken marriage and divorce of Anne and Fredrik to facilitate a happy ending for all.

This beautiful and elegant play closes, as it opens, with the quintet at the piano. Their style and sophistication has kept them and the audience distanced enough to enjoy without too much empathy with the characters. Creating a happy ending by guiding the audience into an acceptance of divorce was not typical fare of the American musical in 1973. The beauty and grace of the quintet tend to hide the tawdry, little indiscretions that lurk throughout this lovely comedy of manners.

PACIFIC OVERTURES

Pacific Overtures explores Kabuki traditions, but also remains true to the Greek choral conventions. The musical opens with an amiable reciter who functions much like the leader of the chorus in the Greek plays. One of the functions of the chorus, providing the specific background information of the myth, is clear in the first interaction the reciter has with the audience, as he explains the history of Japan:

> Nippon. The Floating Kingdom. An island empire which for centuries has lived in perfect peace, undisturbed by intruders from across the sea. There was a time when foreigners were welcome here, but they took advantage of our friendship. (Sondheim and Weidman, Act I, Scene i)

As he tells the story, other members of the chorus perform in kabuki-style dance. This ritualized theatrical expression is new and different for an American audience. The reciter's role establishes a relationship with the audience as he welcomes its members to the secrets and mysteries of the world of this musical.

Once this new world is established, the reciter goes back and forth between character and chorus, but the audience knows to trust and believe him because when he moves into the chorus role, he breaks the fourth wall and speaks directly to the people. The audience is never left alone or led astray. The reciter nurtures carefully and provides this interesting convention within an ironic context. While the audience feels welcome to visit Japan and learn its customs, the action of the musical involves trying to prevent any Westerners from setting foot on Japanese soil, and then experiencing the slow rape of a culture after Western arrival. This musical structure uses the chorus for practical reasons as well. In *Pacific Overtures* the reciter establishes a sense of flow and direction while the scenery is changing. Although most choruses guide the action and set conventions, in *Pacific Overtures* the scene-change time is used to reestablish the relationship between chorus and audience and to communicate necessary information which moves the action forward.

The chorus figure helps the American audience feel the pain accompanying the transformation of ancient to modern Japan. In the beginning the characters are gracious and respectful. As the Western invasion occurs the characters change. Kayama, who was a simple peasant aware of his place, is raised to a position of authority through his efforts to send Commodore Perry away. By the second act, Kayama has become more important, but has lost his sense of self. This change is exemplified in "A Bowler Hat."

As the song begins Kayama wears his Japanese clothing and grieves for his wife who sacrificed herself according to samurai custom. The song progresses and he wears the alien gifts bestowed on him from the outsiders: a bowler hat, pocket watch, monocle, spectacles, and a cutaway. The song is structured to move action forward and to show the character transition in a short amount of stage time. Kayama exemplified the loyal Japanese subject happy to live a simple life, and the audience watches him transcend his simple dignity and succumb to the temptation of Western graft. Before the song ends, he finds a new wife and has left his new wife with the same casual commitment he has to the silly gifts. This progression receives constant commentary by the reciter to show the slow but drastic value shift happening to the Japanese culture. The satire in "A Bowler Hat," revealed through choral commentary, shows the deterioration of Japanese cultural values as they give way to Western Custom.

The cultural values clash as Westerners impose their desires on traditionalists in "Pretty Lady." Three British sailors mistake the innocent daughter of a samurai for a geisha girl. When the young lady screams for help, her father slays two of the men. Conflict arises as the Western and traditional factions perceive the situation differently.

Sondheim's collaborator John Weidman writes eloquently to clarify the triumph of Westernization through the Emperor, who is played by the same actor as the reciter. The Emperor decides:

In the name of progress we will turn our backs on ancient
ways. We will cast aside our feudal forms, eliminate all
obstacles which hinder our development.

We will organize an army and a navy, equipped with
the most modern weapons. And when the time is right,
we will send forth expeditions to visit with our less enlightened neighbors. We will open up Formosa, Korea,
Manchuria, and China. We will do for the rest of Asia
what America has done for us! (Sondheim and Weidman,
Act I, Scene i)

The most powerful moment comes at the end of the piece through
Sondheim's lyrics and music in "Next." *Pacific Overtures* closes with
the chorus expressing its pride at successfully beating the Western
nations at their own game. The chorus extols:

Who's the stronger, who's the faster?
Let the pupil show the master
Next!
Next! (Sondheim and Weidman, Act II, Scene vii)

The audience feels a full range of conflicting emotions. It has empa-
thized with the simple graceful people. The "heroes" are presenting
an Americanized version of themselves. Japan has been invaded, westernized, and culturally raped. Because the audience has watched a
slow change from a tranquil, beautiful, graceful people into a corrupt, greedy, harsh bureaucracy, it feels the betrayal leveled against
the chorus-community with whom it has identified. When members
of the chorus appear to express excitement at their own survival, the
audience shares an empowering energy, but cannot help but question
Western imperialism.

SWEENEY TODD

Sweeney Todd does not follow the path established in *Pacific Overtures,* which begins innocently and moves the audience to a place of
despair. *Sweeney Todd* begins in a world of despair. The relationship
between audience and chorus is established as the audience is "wel-
comed" into this harsh reality.

Before the audience meets the title character, it encounters the
chorus who begins by explaining directly to them that the protagonist is not a typical hero:

> Attend the tale of Sweeney Todd.
> His skin was pale and his eye was odd.
> He shaved the faces of gentlemen
> Who never thereafter were heard of again. (Sondheim
> and Wheeler, Act I, Prologue)

The chorus is providing enough history to create the parameters and to help the audience understand that they are entering the world of Victorian melodrama.

As the narrative progresses, the audience meets an emotionally disturbed murderous barber and a bizarre but charming business-woman who makes pies out of corpses. However, the audience also learns that these two are victims themselves and were led to their crimes by a corrupt society characterized by a bullying beadle and a rapist judge. The audience needs guidance from the chorus who shares an emotional reaction to the horror. For example, a beggar woman forms a bond of understanding with the audience as she warns the choral world that mysterious and dangerous events are happening in Mrs. Lovett's pie shop. As Sweeney Todd and Mrs. Lovett engage in murder and cannibalism, the half-crazed beggar woman pleads:

> Smoke! Smoke!
> Sign of the devil! Sign of the devil!
> City on fire! (Sondheim and Wheeler, Act II, Scene vi)

The audience knows about Mrs. Lovett's despicable deeds, but assurance from a chorus figure, the beggar woman, allows the audience emotional perspective.

As in most Sondheim musicals, this chorus functions on a practical level to move scenery, but it also constantly addresses the audience directly. Some chorus members become Sweeney's shaving victims and find themselves cooked and ground into Mrs. Lovett's pies, but within a few minutes the actors reappear as chorus figures to help move furniture or comment on the action. The chorus's invincibility enhances the theatricality.

As the play closes and the stage is littered with bodies, the chorus enters to comment and to supply the community reaction. Finally, each of the bloody and dead characters rises and joins the chorus in their final lament:

> WOMEN: Sweeney wishes the world away,
> Sweeney's weeping for yesterday,

> Hugging the blade, waiting the years,
> Hearing the music that nobody hears.
>   …

MEN: No one can help, nothing can hide you—
       Isn't that Sweeney there beside you?
       (Sondheim and Wheeler, Epilogue)

The chorus comments on the evils of society but also personal accountability. The victims of this play remained victims because they were unable to release the angers of the past. They insisted on revenge, which could not lead anyone to happiness. Much like a Greek chorus in the final moments of a Sophoclean tragedy, this chorus speaks to the audience to offer perspective on the mistakes of the central characters.

MERRILY WE ROLL ALONG (THE ORIGINAL VERSION)

Merrily We Roll Along requires a different type of chorus than *Sweeney Todd*. By comparison the world of this musical is quite accessible, and its vision of reality is similar to that in *Company*, Sondheim's earlier collaboration with George Furth.

The Chorus's most important purpose in all versions of *Merrily We Roll Along* is to help the audience realize that the play is moving in reverse order and then to help it make sense of this inversion. The Greek chorus also keeps the action flowing and guides the action from one section into another, but the Greek audience was alert to the established conventions that appeared in all of the tragedies. Each Sondheim chorus seems to function to guide the audience through the new and different conventions of its specific musical. The chorus of *Merrily We Roll Along*, for example, does not provide exposition in the same fashion as the other Sondheim musicals because of its unique inverted chronology.

Although cut from the 1994 revision, the original version of *Merrily We Roll Along* opens with members of the chorus singing an idealistic and hopeful song that Frank wrote in his youth with his friend Charley. Soon, rich and famous Frank is introduced, and the chorus characters unanimously dislike him. When the chorus breaks out of this initial scene, it establishes its relationship with the audience. The choral group is very clear about questioning what happened to make this earlier idealistic man such a cynic. Then, the chorus takes the audience back through Frank's life, watching the key incidents that slowly changed him, guiding the audience within the structure of the play, and verbally setting the dates while also continuing the questioning as Frank's relationships change.

The chorus points to the important issues that Frank has been ignoring. Frank had big dreams that included his friends, Mary and Charley. The audience watches him compromise his ideals and sacrifice his friends to meet his selfish momentary desires. The chorus stops the action and comments:

> Tend your dream...
> Dreams take time...
>   ...
>
> How does it start to go?
> How does it slip away slow...
> ...So you never even notice
> It's happening?[1]

The chorus also functions as background characters to project the essence of the environmental changes within Frank's journey. In "Rich and Happy" (or "That Frank" from the newer version) the chorus members become Frank's groupie parasites, eating his food, drinking his liquor, and gossiping behind his back. When Frank comes near, they become sycophants: gushing and praising his every move.

The chorus leads the audience from a cynical rich and famous Frank back to a nice, warm, sincere, loyal and idealistic Frank. The audience watches the transitions and the warnings. This transition has happened within a reversed narrative so the audience has not witnessed opportunistic and insensitive Frank since the opening scene. As the play comes to a close, Frank, Charley, and Mary seem so sincere, romantic, and hopeful that the contrast to the contemporary cynical Frank is crushing.

> Feel the flow,
> Hear what's happening:
> We're what's happening.
>   ...
> It's our time, breathe it in:
> Worlds to change and worlds to win.
>   ...
> Our dreams coming true,

> Me and you, pal,
> Me and you! (Sondheim and Furth, Act II, Scene iv)

The chorus sings this song with Charley, Mary, and Frank. The separation is over. The chorus has led the audience to this moment and left the audience to draw its own conclusions. The final moment of the original version is the same as the introductory moment, but a generation later. Again, it is a high school graduation where dreams of hope are high.

> Behold! Begin!
> There are worlds to win!
> May we come to trust
> The dreams we must
> Fulfill! (Sondheim and Furth, Act II, Scene v)

Frank wrote this song and felt this hope. The members of the audience are left with a sense of euphoria—for a moment. As the messages and feeling of the whole play filter through their emotions, they are startled into the solemn actuality. If Frank, Charley, and Mary had such a visionary beginning, what does that suggest about their lives?

INTO THE WOODS

Sondheim's musical *Into the Woods* seems to take a departure from these formal elements of the Greek chorus. The musical contains a narrator, who might seem to act as a Greek chorus figure since he comments on the action and presents the necessary expositional information, but he does not really enter the story as a character. The narrator does speak directly to the audience, but remains aloof so that later when the characters decide to sacrifice him, the audience does not suffer a serious loss. (In the Broadway production, the actor Tom Aldredge played both the narrator and the mysterious man, but this does not change the function of the narrator since the characters are separate and could just as easily have been played by two different actors.)

The narrator functions to objectify the stories, but instead of introducing a community chorus as the other musicals do, *Into the Woods* focuses on individuals. In some respects it is like a Greek play because the audience knows the basic myths. With one exception, these are individuals with whom the audience already has a longstanding relationship. The individuals are Cinderella, Jack of "Jack and the Beanstalk," Little Red Riding Hood, and Rapunzel. The exceptions are a baker and his wife, created by Lapine and Sondheim, but the baker is a long-lost brother to Rapunzel.

Ultimately one of the significant themes of *Into the Woods* involves turning these individuals into a community willing to sacrifice selfish needs to help one another solve their mutual problem and to support one another emotionally and personally. As the play progresses, the individuals become the chorus.

Cinderella, who sheds her gowns, returns to her rags and goes back "Into the Woods" to help slay the giant's wife, instead learns of her Prince's philandering. Shattered, she joins the Baker who is coping with his own grief at losing his wife who was crushed by the giant. Cinderella and the Baker put aside their own grief to console the younger Jack and Little Red Riding Hood who have lost their mothers. After a time of blaming and releasing their frustrations, they realize they only have each other and can only make it as a group, a chorus, a community. The Baker and Cinderella explain:

> BOTH: People make mistakes,
> Holding to their own,
> Thinking they're alone.
> . . .
> CINDERELLA: Just remember:
>
> BAKER: Just remember:
>
> BOTH: Someone is on your side.

Little Red Riding Hood and Jack respond:

> *Our* side.

Baker and Cinderella reinforce:

> *Our* side.
> . . .
> Things will come out right now.
> We can make it so.
> Someone is on your side— (Sondheim
> and Lapine, Act II, Scene ix)

Sondheim has blended the structural usage of Greek chorus and community into the overall themes of *Into the Woods*. The musical does
not exactly contain a chorus—it becomes a chorus and reinforces the
human need for community.

ASSASSINS

Following *Into the Woods* which leaves the audience with hope,
albeit within a holocaust, Sondheim collaborated with John Weidman
on a unique and startling subject for the American musical—the men
and women who attempted or succeeded at assassinating American
Presidents. Like all of Sondheim's musicals, *Assassins* is a departure
from his previous work, but it also contains some similar structural
elements and the chorus again follows a Greek format in some ways
but also breaks from both classical and American musical tradition to
facilitate the special needs of this unique musical creation.

This musical begins without any immediately recognizable choral characters with whom the audience can identify. The stage is full
of unhappy individuals and one man seems to have control of the
scene, but most Americans would not be drawn to him. He is an
unsavory American icon—a carnival barker at a shooting gallery who
is wooing passersby to try "to shoot a President" (Sondheim and
Weidman, Scene i). With a series of appeals he encourages the desperate:

> No job? Cupboard bare?
> One room, no one there?
> Hey, pal, don't despair—
> You wanna shoot a President?
>   (Sondheim and Weidman, Scene i)

This opening is intentionally disturbing. Sondheim and Weidman
create an unattractive and menacing world. *Sweeney Todd's* environment was unpleasant, but the chorus was there to sustain some em-
pathic connection with the audience.

The Carnival barker, who would not make most of us feel welcome and safe, is simply an American businessman selling his game.
The game is not physically harmful, but the concept behind it is rather
frightening. When a person feels despair, rather than working through
the issues behind his or her pain, the barker suggests that such a need
deserves an instant fix:

> Everybody's
> Got the right
> To be happy.
> Don't stay mad,
> Life's not as bad
> As it seems.
> If you keep your
> Goal in sight,
> You can climb to
> Any height.
> Everybody's
> Got the right
> To their dreams.... (Sondheim and Weidman, Scene i)

For this American proprietor, the dream for sale is to kill a President. One might argue that a chorus is introduced—the misfits, the disenfranchised, the marginalized Americans who become the group of assassins, but they are really the central figures of the story. Similar in structure to *Company*, the chorus and soloists are one.

By the second scene, the real choral figure, in the form of the Balladeer, is introduced to give the audience some relief and direction. He is a simple, honest, American working man with a banjo who comes on stage immediately after the first assassination and begins developing a relationship with the audience.

The Balladeer questions and tries to understand, then stops to listen as he is interrupted by an argument between Booth and his accomplice. Finally the Balladeer questions Booth, who tries to justify the assassination and pleads with the Balladeer to tell his story. Rather than telling Booth's story, the Balladeer serves to comment on the action as all Greek chorus figures do. The Balladeer takes Booth to task:

> How could you do it, Johnny,
> Calling it a cause?
> You left a legacy
> Of butchery
> And treason we
> Took eagerly,
> And thought you'd get applause.
>
> But traitors just get jeers and boos,
> Not visits to their graves.... (Sondheim and Weidman,
> Scene ii)

Since this is the first assassination, the Balladeer takes the time to establish the play's vision of reality. Sondheim and Weidman are not condoning or mocking this serious national tragedy. They are presenting an urgently serious issue through a traditionally entertaining genre. Identification with this chorus figure is essential to guide the audience through the malaise ahead.

As the play progresses, the audience meets many of the men and women to whom the Balladeer alluded as he guides:

> Listen to the stories.
> Hear it in the songs.
> Angry men
> Don't write the rules,
> And guns don't right the wrongs. (Sondheim and
> Weidman, Scene ii)

Leon Czolgosz and Charles Guiteau appear to be normal Americans. Czolgosz is trying his best until he discovers the system is not fair to all:

> Czolgosz
> Working man,
> Born in the middle of Michigan,
>   ...
> Saw of a sudden
> How things were run,
>   ...
> Some men have everything
> And some have none.... (Sondheim and Weidman,
> Scene viii)

The Balladeer tries to show the audience that Czolgosz was a simple man who believed that equality was available to everyone who was willing to work hard to achieve it, but when experience showed him a rigged system, he lost his hope and extracted a price from all Americans. The Balladeer, who condemned all the assassins earlier, is alerting Americans to the growing dissatisfaction that also needs attention.

The Balladeer also communicates with the audience as he observes the final words of Charles Guiteau. Guiteau is a devoted Christian who believes he has acted on behalf of the Lord:

> I am going to the Lordy,
> I am so glad!
> I have unified my party,
> I have saved my country.
> I shall be remembered!
>
> I am going to the Lordy.... (Sondheim and Weidman,
> Scene xii)

The Balladeer clarifies these words with Guiteau who was an optimistic, positive thinking, yet misguided man. Whereas Czolgosz was a embittered cynic who felt angry and cheated, Guiteau was a bright light who lost a grip on reality. These men would probably not be picked out of a crowd as dangerous assassins, but with easy access to guns they did a lot of damage.

Later in "Another National Anthem," the assassins present their complaints, disappointments and excuses, and they try to justify their actions, but the Balladeer challenges their premises.

> And it didn't mean a nickel,
> You just shed a little blood,
> And a lot of people shed a lot of tears.
> Yes, you made a little moment
> And you stirred a little mud—
>
> But it didn't fix the stomach
> And you've drunk your final Bud,
> And it didn't help the workers
> And it didn't heal the country
> And it didn't make them listen
>
> And they never said, "We're sorry".... (Sondheim and
> Weidman, Scene xv)

The Balladeer, who has been a trustworthy voice of Americans, begins to sound like a shallow politician spewing campaign rhetoric:

> I just heard
> On the news
> Where the mailman won the lottery.
>   ...
> You can choose
> What to be,
> From a mailman to a President.
> There are prizes all around you,

> If you're wise enough to see:
> The delivery boy's on Wall Street,
> And the usherette's a rock star.... (Sondheim and
> Weidman, Scene xv)

The assassins have lost hope. They represent an American faction
that has grown tired of the lies. They know the odds of winning the
lottery or becoming a rock star. As the Balladeer encourages them to
make their own success through luck or chance, they gather together
and force him off the stage. Just as the audience lost the Narrator in
Into the Woods, the Balladeer has similarly vanished, but this time the
audience is left with a gang of the dangerous and desperate.

After this community of assassins is resurrected in its meeting
with Lee Harvey Oswald, he joins them and they break the fourth
wall to address the audience:

> BOOTH: Everybody's
>   Got the right
>   To be happy.
>   ...
>
> BOOTH AND CZOLGOSZ:
>   Everybody's
>   Got the right
>   To their dreams.
>   ...
>
> ALL: Free country—!
>
> HINCKLEY: Means that you've got the choice:
>   ...
>
> ALL: Free Country—!
>
> CZOLGOSZ: Means that you get a voice.
>   ...
>
> ALL: Means the right to expect
>   That you'll have an effect,
>   That you're gonna connect....
>   (Sondheim and Weidman, Scene xvii)

Their intonation reveals bitter sarcasm as they express their shared
anger and frustration at a failed American Dream. The song ends
with each assassin pointing and firing his or her gun at the audience.
The impact is intense. The Balladeer, who, at the beginning of the
play, saw the issues and the people in perspective is gone. All the

audience has left is a group of dangerous disenfranchised people with guns. The play is a wakeup call. The chorus—the representation of our community—is ready to attack. This musical's use of the chorus may be the most powerful of all Sondheim musicals. He twists and distorts the chorus. The audience begins in confusion without a connection to the chorus, but then they are allowed to relax when the Balladeer arrives to function as their guide. When their reassuring figure, the Balladeer, cannot reach the assassins because he has been co-opted by the American myth, the assassins remove him. The audience is left alone in a very dangerous world. The impact is even more terrifying because the audience feels abandoned.

Conclusion

The Sondheim chorus is most effective as a representation of audience values. Whether it is warning the audience to beware of Sweeney Todd, to learn from Frank's mistakes and hang onto their dreams, or whether they are expressing the shared sorrow at the victimization of an entire nation, the chorus represents the feelings, values and attitudes of the audience. The audience may feel depressed by the turn of events in the story. A happy ending should not be expected. Like the catharsis of Greek tragedy, the stirring of a full range of emotions and a shared learning experience is far more dramatically satisfying. The audience can take solace in its empathetic bonding with the chorus.

The plays in this chapter—*Company, A Little Night Music, Pacific Overtures, Sweeney Todd, Merrily We Roll Along, Into the Woods,* and *Assassins*—were selected for several reasons. This collection offers a range of Sondheim musicals which include a number of collaborators and a range in chronology from his earlier to later work, and these seven musicals portray significant differences in their choruses, yet offer clear examples to establish the Sondheim chorus.

The selection of these specific plays does not imply that examples could not be found in the other Sondheim musicals. *Anyone Can Whistle, Sunday in the Park with George,* and *Passion* have choruses that are consistent with the thesis, but the selected musicals provide clearer examples. *Follies* includes less chorus. The younger/older character convention provides opportunity for the commenting practices of the Sondheim and Greek chorus, but the effects are exemplified better in *Company* and *Assassins*. *West Side Story, Gypsy,* and *Do I Hear a Waltz?* were excluded from the analysis because Sondheim was primarily the lyricist, and although he may have contributed to compositional decisions in some situations, the major compositional credit belongs to Leonard Bernstein, Jule Styne, and Richard Rodgers. *A Funny Thing Happened on the Way to the Forum* has its roots in Classical Roman comedy which serves to reinforce Sondheim's fascination and experience with historical theatrical structure, but Roman and Greek culture were significantly different, and *Forum* is naturally more reflective of Roman than Greek cultural elements. *Frogs*, based on the Aristophanes play, so obviously has its roots in Greece that it would hardly prove anything. All of Sondheim's musicals could be analyzed in terms of this thesis, but specific selections provide ample material for exploration.

Sondheim has cultivated the chorus of the American Musical Theatre. Just as he has pioneered changes in thematic content by challenging American values and myth and changes in musical sophistication by moving beyond the AABA form, his modifications in the functioning of the chorus have contributed to the refinement and maturity of the American Musical Theatre.

෴

NOTE

1. Stephen Sondheim and George Furth, *Merrily We Roll Along* (New York: Music Theatre International, 1982) Act One, Scene One. This musical opened on Broadway on November 16, 1981 to a short run. It was slightly revised for productions in San Diego, Seattle, and London, and in 1994 further changes were added for the York Theatre Company's production, in New York. The analysis will largely be based on the original Broadway production.

WORKS CITED

Ehrenberg, Victor. *The Greek State*. New York: Norton, 1964.

Gordon, Joanne. *Art Isn't Easy: The Achievement of Stephen Sondheim*. Carbondale: Southern Illinois UP, 1990.

Hauser, Arnold. *The Social History of Art*, Vol. 1. New York: Vintage, 1951.

Kitto, H.D.F. *The Greek*. Baltimore: Penguin, 1951.

Sondheim, Stephen, and George Furth. *Company*. New York: Dodd, Mead, 1970.

——. *Merrily We Roll Along*. New York: Music Theatre International, 1982.

——, and Hugh Wheeler. *A Little Night Music*. New York: Applause, 1991.

——. *Sweeney Todd*. New York: Dodd, Mead, 1978.

——, and James Lapine. *Into the Woods*. New York: Theatre Communications, 1987.

——, and John Weidman. *Assassins*. New York: Theatre Communications, 1991.

——. *Pacific Overtures*. New York: Dodd, Mead, 1977.

Watson, Jack, and Grant McKernie. *A Cultural History of the Theatre*. New York: Longman, 1993.

Zadan, Craig. *Sondheim & Co.* Second ed. New York: Harper and Row, 1986.

Contributors

EDWARD T. BONAHUE, JR., has taught at the University of North Carolina and the University of Florida, and his work has appeared in *Studies in English Literature, Studies in Philology, Renaissance Papers*, and *South Atlantic Review*. He is at work on a book about history and social class in early modern London.

DOUGLAS BRAVERMAN, a playwright and lyricist, has had his comedy, *Snowman*, produced Off Broadway, and he is the librettist of two popular children's operas, *Cheering Up A Princess* and *Aesop's Fables*, which have been presented throughout the United States. He is currently completing his first novel—a murder mystery—entitled *Who Killed Bobby Berwick?*

DAVID CRAIG is recognized as the foremost instructor of performing techniques in the musical theater. He began his teaching in 1948 and now conducts classes in Los Angeles, New York, and in universities throughout the country. In 1952 Ira Gershwin and George Kaufman appointed him vocal arranger and music coordinator for the first major Broadway revival of *Of Thee I Sing*. In 1955 he co-wrote the revue Phoenix '55 and on Broadway in 1958, performed a similar function for *Copper and Brass*. Craig has served on the faculty of Carnegie Mellon University, North Carolina School of the Arts, and UCLA.

His books—*On Singing Onstage, On Performing: A Handbook For Actors, Dancers and Singers, A Performer Prepares*, and, in a revised edition, *On Musical Theater Stages* (to be published in 1997)—are considered definitive volumes on the subject of performing on the musical theater stage. His wife was the celebrated comedienne Nancy Walker.

MARI CRONIN is a literary agent in New York. She has written theater reviews and feature articles for various publications, a theater history column for *TheaterWeek* and is currently working on an authorized book about Stephen Sondheim.

JAMES FISHER, professor of theater and chair of the theater department at Wabash College (Crawfordsville, Indiana), has authored three books, *The Theater of Yesterday and Tomorrow: Commedia dell'arte on the Modern Stage* (Edwin Mellen, 1992), and *Al Jolson* and *Spencer Tracy,* both published by Greenwood Press, 1994, and he is working on another on Eddie Cantor, to be published in early 1997. He has held several research fellowships in the U.S. and England and has published numerous articles and reviews in varied periodicals. He currently edits book reviews for the *Journal of Dramatic Theory and Criticism* and edits *The Puppetry Yearbook.* Fisher has also directed and acted in well over 140 theatre productions.

LEONARD FLEISCHER holds a Ph.D. in dramatic literature from New York University, and has taught at Brooklyn College, Long Island University, New Jersey Institute of Technology, and the University of Akron. He has lectured on American musical theatre at the University of North Carolina (Chapel Hill) and the New School (New York). For twelve years he headed Exxon Corporation's philanthropic giving in the arts. In addition, he served a three-year term on the Tony Awards nominating committee, and has been a member of the Board of Directors of the Young Playwrights Festival and the Drama League.

BARBARA MEANS FRASER is an associate professor of theatre at Santa Clara University in California. She contributes articles to *The Sondheim Review.* Fraser is a playwright and a director as well as a Sondheim scholar. She earned her Ph.D. from the University of Oregon.

JOANNE GORDON is a professor of theatre arts at California State University, Long Beach. The author of *Art Isn't Easy: The Theatre of Stephen Sondheim* (1990), she contributed an essay to the Casebooks on Modern Dramatists collection on August Wilson. She is also an accomplished professional director and the recipient of numerous awards in directing.

LAURA HANSON is the associate costume shop manager in the design department at New York University's Tisch School of the Arts. She is a Phi Beta Kappa graduate of St. Louis University, where she also earned a master's degree in theatre arts. In addition to her practical experience in theatre, opera, and dance, Laura researches and writes on theatre history, particularly that of musical theatre, and is currently at work on her doctoral dissertation on the musicals of Stephen Sondheim.

LOIS KIVESTO, a doctoral candidate in educational theatre at New York University, is currently working on her dissertation entitled "The Theatre Work of James Lapine: Playwright, Librettist, Director." A native of Toronto, Lois teaches high school instrumental music, mathematics, and drama there. She has recently served as research/ educational consultant on the Canadian Stage Company's Canadian professional premieres of Sondheim and Lapine's *Into the Woods* and *Passion*.

GARY KONAS received his Ph.D. in English from the University of California at Davis, where he studied with Professor Ruby Cohn. He holds degrees in mathematics, wine chemistry, and creative writing as well. He is the editor of *Neil Simon: A Casebook* (Garland, 1997). Presently he is under contract with Southern Illinois University Press for a book on Pulitzer Prize–winning musicals. Musical theater is his primary field of interest.

SCOTT MILLER has been directing musicals for eighteen years and has written book, music, and lyrics for eight musicals. His book *From Assassins to West Side Story: The Director's Guide to Musical Theatre* has just been published, as well as two of his musicals, *Breaking Out in Harmony* and *Attempting the Absurd*. He writes for national theatre magazines, and has composed music for television and radio. The original cast album of his musical *In the Blood* has been released nationwide on CD. Scott is a graduate of Harvard University and a member of the Dramatists Guild of America. He is the artistic director of New Line Theatre, an alternative musical theatre company in St. Louis.

ANDREW MILNER has written for *The Cooperstown Review, The Dictionary of Literary Biography* and *Spy*, and contributed to Turner Publishing's acclaimed *Our Times* reference book/CD-ROM. He is a graduate of Syracuse University, where he was a founding member of the "Null and Void" comedy troupe. He is now content editor at InterMedia Interactive Software in Philadelphia, where he creates crosswords for *TV Guide*'s web site, and he is also a critic for the Philadelphia *City Paper*.

JOHN OLSON is an advertising agency executive, theater fan, and free-lance writer in Milwaukee, Wisconsin. He has written articles for *The Sondheim Review*, including "Parallel Minds Who Meet," an analysis of the Sondheim-Furth collaborations *Company* and *Merrily We Roll Along,* which appeared in the Fall 1995 issue. His article, "The Mysteries—A Form and a Pattern," discusses Sondheim's murder mysteries *The Last of Sheila* (co-written with Anthony Perkins) and *Getting Away with Murder* (co-written with George Furth). The latter article appeared in the Summer 1996 issue of *The Sondheim Review.*

JUDITH SCHLESINGER is a writer and musician with a Ph.D. in psychology from New York University. She is the author of *Music and Madness,* a guide to the psychological impact of music on individuals and society, and is working on a new book about the myths of creativity and mental illness. A psychotherapist and humor columnist for *Topia Magazine,* Judith teaches psychology at Pace University and lives with her husband Bill in Dobbs Ferry, New York.

Index